The Incarcerated Woman

Rehabilitative Programming in Women's Prisons

❖

SUSAN F. SHARP, Ph.D.

University of Oklahoma
Editor

ROSLYN MURASKIN, Ph.D.

Long Island University
Series Editor

Prentice
Hall

Upper Saddle River, New Jersey 07458

Library of Congress Cataloging-in-Publication Data

The incarcerated woman : rehabilitative programming in women's prisons / Susan F. Sharp, editor.
  p. cm.
 Includes bibliographical references.
 ISBN 0-13-094067-4
   1. Women's prisoners—Services for—United States.   2. Female offenders—Rehabilitation—
United States.   3. Reformatories for women—United States.   I. Sharp, Susan F.

  HV9304 .I47 2002
  365'.43'0973—dc21   2002016997

Publisher: Jeff Johnston
Executive Editor: Kim Davies
Assistant Editor: Sarah Holle
Production Editor: Hilary Farquhar, Stratford Publishing Services
Production Liaison: Barbara Marttine Cappuccio
Director of Production and Manufacturing: Bruce Johnson
Managing Editor: Mary Carnis
Manufacturing Buyer: Cathleen Petersen
Creative Director: Cheryl Asherman
Cover Design Coordinator: Miguel Ortiz
Marketing Manager: Jessica Pfaff
Cover Design: Marianne Frasco
Cover Image: Scott Picunko/SIS/Images.com
Formatting and Interior Design: Stratford Publishing Services
Printing and Binding: Phoenix Book Tech Park

Pearson Education LTD, *London*
Pearson Education Australia PTY, Limited, *Sydney*
Pearson Education Singapore, Pte. Ltd.
Pearson Education North Asia Ltd., *Hong Kong*
Pearson Education Canada, Ltd., *Toronto*
Pearson Educación de Mexico, S.A. de C.V.
Pearson Education—Japan, *Tokyo*
Pearson Education Malaysia, Pte. Ltd.

10 9 8 7 6 5 4 3 2 1
ISBN 0-13-094067-4

Contents

❖

Preface

❖

Welcome to our *Women's Series*. This is the first of many volumes on particular topics that deal with women and issues of criminal justice. Women have had to struggle to be considered equals since the inception of our country, and gender-based disparity has certainly been very apparent in the field of criminal justice. Women were not supposed to get arrested. Women were not supposed to work in the field. Women belonged in the home, preserving the sanctity of family and life as it was "meant to be." But all that changed over the many decades of our country.

Women are and have been getting into trouble since our nation was founded. Women are getting arrested and women are working in the field of criminal justice. And yet in the twenty-first century women are still looking to be treated as equals. Gender-based disparities have been under investigation for a long time now, and it is only recently that we find such unequal treatment being acknowledged as unacceptable.

For years now, female offenders, crime victims, and criminal justice professionals have been neglected. It has always been assumed that if a female "dares" to participate in the criminal justice system, be it as offender, victim, or professional, she should receive the same treatment as her male counterpart. Over the last decades, we have recognized that greater emphasis and concern has to be focused on women. Programs for women have always suffered, because criminal justice and women were not similar terms. Women have always had to struggle for acceptance not only as professionals, but as individuals who do commit crimes, and are in fact victims of crimes. Gender inequality has always been deeply rooted in the workplace, having been based on societal expectations. Women have always had to face many drawbacks and obstacles in what has been noted as male-dominated fields. For women to be considered to work in the professions of criminal justice was almost unthinkable. Early female police officers were thought to be capable only of watching over women who committed unthinkable crimes, or of directing traffic. The idea of women working in the field of corrections was totally unacceptable until the 1970s.

There was a common perception that the criminal behavior of women and the delinquent actions of young girls were not serious problems. Women, if they did commit crimes, were thought to commit only the simplest and most minor of offenses. Historically, they constituted a very small proportion of the prison population. These facts masked a trend that currently attracts our attention: the dramatic rise in the number of prison and jail inmates, even though crime rates are down. However, when we look at women who commit crimes, we find that their rate of offending is increasing faster than those of their male counterparts, and therefore, so is the need for women criminal justice professionals. Today, women are being arrested at a faster rate than men. There is also the discussion of whether gender should be given special consideration, rather than simply treating female offenders exactly the same as their male counterparts.

Attention needs to be focused on women to understand their status as both offender and victim. We need to recognize women as professionals in the criminal justice system. As an example, violence against women—including domestic violence or intimate violence, sexual assaults, sexual harassment, and stalking—have been in the limelight of late and therefore recognized as having some significance for those who study criminal justice.

Admittedly, there have been limitations on the data collected because crimes against women and data on women as offenders have been underreported. Today, there are probably about 200,000 women offenders in prison; what put them there? Incarcerated women seem to be disproportionately women of color, from low-income backgrounds, and individuals who face violence on an everyday basis. There are those women who commit crimes to survive—who are they? What have we done to help them, or better yet, to prevent such situations from occurring? Is there a correlation between women who are victimized and those who offend?

This women's series, as developed, will focus on many of the topics that formerly have not been considered pertinent to the study of criminal justice. Without studying what happens to women, how women gain entry into working as professionals in the criminal justice system, we do not give the complete picture of criminal justice in the United States in the twenty-first century.

We welcome you to our first book, *The Incarcerated Woman: Rehabilitative Programming in Women's Prisons,* compiled by our guest editor, Susan Sharp. Significant progress has been made, but not enough. Women's unequal treatment constitutes a massive violation of human rights. We are here to direct your attention to the problems and issues and underscore what the costs of inequality are, what has kept it in place in the past, and what we need to do to move forward.

Roslyn Muraskin, Ph.D.
Series Editor
Long Island University

Acknowledgments

❖

The idea for this book began several years ago, upon my arrival at the University of Oklahoma. My faculty mentor, Susan Marcus-Mendoza (see Chapter 8), encouraged me to respond with her to a call for proposals. We made a proposal and received funding for research on the effects of incarceration on families of offenders. Because "family" means different things to men and women prisoners, we structured the research to explore gender differences in the effects of incarceration. Thus began a winding journey that has led to this book. To give credit where it is due, I want to express my appreciation to Susan Marcus-Mendoza for her guidance, to Dan Lawrence of the Oklahoma Department of Corrections, who facilitated our research, and to the women who participated in our original study. Through learning their histories, I became more aware of the needs of women prisoners, as well as the dearth of appropriate treatment available to them. I would like to thank the following reviewers: Barbara Belbot, University of Houston, Houston, Texas; George Evans, William Harper College, Palatine, Illinois; Carolyn Brown-Dennis, Fayetteville Community College, Fayetteville, North Carolina; James Jengelski, Shippensburg University, Shippensburg, Pennsylvania; and Janet Hagemann, San Jose State University, San Jose, California. Finally, I would like to thank Roz Muraskin for allowing me to do this project, and Kim Davies and Sarah Holle of Prentice Hall for their support and guidance.

About the Contributors

❖

Volume Editor:

Susan F. Sharp, Ph.D., is an assistant professor of sociology at the University of Oklahoma. Her areas of interest encompass gender and the criminal justice system, gender and deviance, and the effects of criminal justice policies on families. Prior to obtaining her doctorate, she worked as a substance abuse counselor, primarily with offender populations. Recent research includes work published in *Women & Criminal Justice, The Prison Journal, Deviant Behavior, Journal of the Oklahoma Criminal Justice Research Consortium, Journal of Youth & Adolescence,* and *Journal of Contemporary Ethnography.* She is active in the Division on Women and Crime of the American Society of Criminology, serving as newsletter editor since 1999.

Contributors:

Tammy L. Anderson, Ph.D., is an assistant professor in the Department of Sociology and Criminal Justice and an ethnographer for the Center for Drug and Alcohol Studies at the University of Delaware. She has published extensively in the area of drug abuse, focusing on gender and race differences, the contributing role of abuse, HIV transmission, and social policy change. Currently, she is directing a longitudinal ethnographic study of the environmental risks for relapse and recidivism among male and female graduates of in-prison drug-treatment programs. Dr. Anderson is the incoming chair (2001–2002) for the division on Drinking and Drugs of the Society for the Study of Social Problems and is also a council member for the Alcohol and Drugs section of the American Sociological Association. She has been active in these organizations and in the American Society of Criminology for ten years.

Joanne Belknap, Ph.D., is an associate professor of sociology at the University of Colorado in Boulder. She received a Ph.D. in Criminal Justice and Criminology from Michigan State University in 1986. She is currently an associate professor in both sociology and women's studies at the University of Colorado. Dr. Belknap has published numerous scholarly works, most of which investigate violence against women, and female offenders. She has served on state advisory boards for female offenders and women in prison, on former U.S. Attorney General Janet Reno's Violence Against Women committee, and gave expert testimony to the Warren Christopher Commission investigating the Rodney King police-brutality incident in Los Angeles. She is currently working on research projects assessing the court processing of woman battering cases and on delinquent girls. The second edition of her book *The Invisible Woman: Gender, Crime, and Justice* was published in 2001. Dr. Belknap is the recipient of the 1997 national award "Distinguished Scholar of the Division on Women and Crime" of the American Society of Criminology and won the student-nominated University of Colorado Teaching Award in 2001 (for classes of 75 to 149 students).

Dennis R. Brewster, M.A., is a doctoral student in sociology at the University of Oklahoma. He completed a double major in sociology and psychology from Southwestern Oklahoma State University in 1996 and received a Master of Arts degree from the University of Oklahoma in 1999. Future research plans include work on the effects of long-term (more than ten years) incarceration on both male and female offenders. Brewster has spent time volunteering in correctional facilities as co-sponsor of correctional programs involving inmates and also worked for the Oklahoma Department of Corrections in both the Western Regional Office and at the Oklahoma Criminal Justice Resource Center.

Meda Chesney-Lind, Ph.D., is professor of women's studies at the University of Hawaii at Manoa. She has served as vice president of the American Society of Criminology and president of the Western Society of Criminology. Nationally recognized for her work on women and crime, her books include *Girls, Delinquency and Juvenile Justice,* which was awarded the American Society of Criminology's Michael J. Hindelang Award for the "outstanding contribution to criminology, 1992" and *The Female Offender: Girls, Women and Crime,* published in 1997 by Sage. Her most recent book, an edited collection entitled *Female Gangs in America,* has just been published by Lakeview Press. In 2001, she received the Bruce Smith, Sr., Award "for outstanding contributions to Criminal Justice" by the Academy of Criminal Justice Sciences, and she was named a fellow of the American Society of Criminology in 1996. She has also received the Distinguished Scholar Award from the Women and Crime Division of the American Society of Criminology, the Major Achievement Award from the Division of Critical Criminology, and the Herbert Block Award for service to the society and the profession from the American Society of Criminology. Finally, she received the Donald Cressey Award from the National Council on Crime and Delinquency in 1997 for "her outstanding academic contribution to the field of criminology." Locally, she has been awarded the University of Hawaii Board of Regent's Medal for "Excellence in Research." Chesney-Lind is an outspoken advocate for girls and women, particularly those who find their way into the criminal justice system. Her work on the problem of sexism in the treatment of girls in the juvenile justice system was partially responsible for the recent national attention devoted to services to girls in that system. More recently, she has worked hard to call attention to the soaring rate of women's imprisonment and the need to vigorously seek alternatives to women's incarceration.

Diane M. Daane, Ph.D., is an associate professor of criminal justice at the University of South Carolina—Spartanburg, where she teaches courses on corrections, victimology, and women and crime. She has worked in both male and female prisons, a halfway house for felony offenders, and as a public defender. She earned a J.D. from the University of Missouri—Kansas City, and a M.S. in Criminal Justice Administration from Central Missouri State University. Her primary research interests include sexual assault, family violence, and women in prison.

Lori B. Girshick, Ph.D., is a sociologist and community activist. She teaches sociology and women's studies at Warren Wilson College in Asheville, North Carolina. She is the author of *No Safe Haven: Stories of Women in Prison* (1999, Northeastern University Press), and *Soledad Women: Wives of Prisoners Speak Out* (1996, Praeger). She has worked with battered women for 11 years, and facilitates a support group for battered women in prison and a support group for battered lesbians. She wishes to thank Evanne, Tracy, Caretha, and Tammy for their insights into programming for women in prison. Lori can be reached at lgirshick@mindspring.com.

Margaret S. Kelley, Ph.D., is an assistant professor of sociology at the University of Oklahoma. She received her doctoral degree in sociology from New York University in 1999. Her dissertation, *A Social Ecology of Methadone Maintenance Treatment: Organizational Compliance and Involvement of Injection Drug Users,* utilized both qualitative and quantitative longitudinal data collected from drug users in the San Francisco Bay area. In it, she examined drug use and HIV/AIDS high-risk behaviors across clinic organizational types, hypothesizing that clinic structure and style influence treatment outcomes. Her areas of interest include drug users, methadone maintenance and other drug treatment, women and crime, and mixed methodologies.

Susan T. Marcus-Mendoza, Ph.D., is an associate professor of human relations and women's studies and the chair of the Department of Human Relations at the University of Oklahoma. She is also a licensed psychologist. Previously, Dr. Marcus-Mendoza was the chief psychologist at a federal prison camp for women.

Pamela J. Schram, Ph.D., is an assistant professor in the Department of Criminal Justice at California State University, San Bernardino. She received her Ph.D. from Michigan State University in 1996. Her research interests include women in the criminal justice system, with an emphasis on women in prison, general issues pertaining to corrections, as well as juveniles in the justice system.

Angela D. West, Ph.D., is an assistant professor of justice administration at the University of Louisville. Her teaching interests include corrections, research methods, statistics, and theory. Her research involves program and policy evaluation at all levels of the justice process, race and gender-related issues, and issues pertaining to correctional release, homelessness, and recidivism.

Erin Wright, M.A., graduated from Providence College in 1998 with a degree in humanities and foci in African American studies and women's studies. In 2000 she received a master's degree in human relations, with a focus in women's studies. She currently resides in New Hampshire with her husband.

Barbara H. Zaitzow, Ph.D., is an associate professor in the department of political science and criminal justice at Appalachian State University. She has a B.A. in sociology from San Diego State University and an M.S. and Ph.D. in sociology from Virginia Polytechnic Institute and State University. She continues her research in both men's and women's prisons in North Carolina and was co-investigator on a national grant-sponsored study of gangs in prisons. Zaitzow has been involved in local, state, and national advocacy work for prisoners and organizations seeking alternatives to imprisonment. She is currently on the editorial board of the *Journal of Contemporary Criminal Justice* and reviews manuscripts for a variety of journals and book publishers. A member of several national and regional sociological and criminal justice organizations, her primary research areas of interest include female criminality, corrections, and alternatives to incarceration.

Overview

Roslyn Muraskin, Ph.D.

❖

When I was researching and writing my dissertation in the late 1980s, little did I think that the same or similar problems would remain a subject under consideration today. The question posed by my dissertation was, could an instrument be developed that objectively measures treatment in correctional institutions and determines the extent of disparate treatment? Laws were developed to create categories in which some individuals may be treated unequally, and historically, federal and state governments frequently treated disparate groups differently. From the research conducted by Susan Sharp and her contributors, it appears that this statement still holds true today.

In dealing with the questions of equal protection and due process, an analysis is needed of the reasonableness of the regulation. My dissertation established a procedure for systematically measuring conditions in correctional institutions' housing units to assess the actual treatment of inmates.

Since the decision in *Hart v. Sarver* (1970), where the court declared an entire prison to be in violation of the Eighth Amendment and imposed detailed remedial plans, the judiciary has taken an active role in the administration of correctional facilities. Some of the cases discussed in this book challenged the inequity of treatment between male and female prisoners. Ostensibly, the needs of male and female prisoners appear to be the same. They are not. Although some inmate interests are similar, others are separate, and distinct. In many institutions, criteria developed for males were automatically applied to females, with no consideration or modification for gender differences. Research discussed here demonstrates that females typically experience more medical and health problems before incarceration than male inmates and continue to do so in prison. Classification officials have noted over the years that female offenders are in need of parenting skills, child welfare, pregnancy and prenatal care, home stability, and an understanding of the circumstances of their crime. This still holds true today in the twenty-first century. Historically, assignments to program and treatment resources in the correctional facilities have been based more on what *is* available than on what *should* be available. Those individuals and administrators responsible for making correctional policies, over the years, have had little understanding of the nature and extent of the needs of all inmates. In many cases administrators and individuals in the correctional facilities have been held responsible, as evidenced by the litigation that has occurred and is still taking place.

A review of the literature, legal cases, and assessment issues dealing with disparity of treatment reveals that each takes note that females continue to represent a small minority in both prisons and jails, but the proportion of women committing crimes and being incarcerated today is higher than that of the men who commit crimes. The effects of incarceration are in many but not all respects similar for males and females. Each suffers the trauma of being separated from family and friends. When either males or females become imprisoned they experience a loss of identity as well as a devaluation of their status. Regardless of the inmate's sex, prison life coerces conformity to an environment alien to the individual where one's every movement is dictated each and every minute. However, as evidenced in this work, the female may suffer more.

Because most challenges to prison conditions have neglected the special needs of female prisoners, it is useful to focus our study on the denial of female prisoner rights. In the past, female correctional facilities have not received funding comparable to male correctional facilities. Education and vocational training programs for the female have been seriously underfunded. "Benign neglect [has] . . . created a situation of unequal treatment in many states" (Hunter, 1984, p. 133). Correctional administrators, for example, have insisted that the small numbers of females within their facilities made it too expensive to fund such necessary programs. The courts, however, have always ruled that cost is not an acceptable defense. Women have always deferred to policies that were designed for the male offender. Research has always identified the woman as deferring to males when it comes to the economic, social, and political spheres of life. Women have historically been forced into the status of being less than equal. And in today's world, we are still faced with the same kind of prejudice and disparate treatment.

When inmates similarly situated find themselves being treated differently, there exists a violation of equal protection. "The prisoners' rights movement [was] a direct outgrowth of the civil rights and civil liberties movement, when lawyers and civil rights–civil liberties organizations began to use the courts as a means to challenge legal barriers to equality and redress grievances" (Aron, 1981, p. 190). This was stated in the 1980s; how different is it today?

Constitutionally, no obligation exists for the government to provide any benefits beyond basic requirements. However, this does not excuse insidious discrimination among potential recipients. The tenets of case law have always held that benefits afforded to some cannot be denied to others solely based on a person's race and sex.

In the case of *Reed v. Reed,* the central question was the "degree of state interest which can justify disparate treatment among offenders." The ruling established that the "classification must be reasonable, not arbitrary, and must bear a fair and substantial relation to the object of the legislation or object." Courts, traditionally, have found sex classifications to be irrational because they appear to have been enacted solely for the convenience of the correctional administrators, which is not an acceptable legal justification for disparity of treatment.

The legal uprisings against intolerable conditions in correctional facilities and prisoners' rights litigation were initiated by male attorneys and male prisoners. In the early stages of this litigation female inmates did not turn to the courts nor did officials at female institutions fear lawsuits, condemnation by the public, or inmate riots. With so few females incarcerated, there was little females felt they could do. All that has changed. Female prisoners continue to sue and demand parity with male prisoners. They demand certain programs and demand certain benefits. The Fourteenth Amendment, in particular its equal protection and due process clauses, has been the legal basis for challenging disparate treatment of inmates. The Fourth Amendment has been the source for issues of violation of privacy, while the Eighth Amendment has been used for cases involving cruel and unusual punishment.

Differential sentencing—where women are sentenced to indeterminate terms whereas men receive determinate sentences—of similarly situated men and women convicted of identical offenses has been found to violate the equal protection clause. Sentencing women to state prison on charges for which men were held in county jails has been held to be in violation of the Fourteenth Amendment. If male prisoners are placed under the authority of the State Board of Parole, then so too should women, rather than the U.S. Board of Parole. There is to be no substantial difference in male and female prisoners' opportunities to participate in work programs.

All prisoners are entitled to an uncensored press, to have their persons free from unreasonable searches and seizures, to be free from cruel and unusual punishment, to be allowed due process and equal protection of the law regarding disciplinary procedures and rehabilitative opportunities. All this was decided decades ago; what has happened since?

Full strip search policies are not allowed for women if men are not strip-searched (except cases in which there is reason to believe that a weapon or contraband is present). To do so would violate the Fourth Amendment. State officials have an affirmative obligation to ensure that all inmates have access to law libraries. The paucity of women in certain facilities is no excuse. Women inmates cannot be transferred routinely to other states to serve out their sentences if such a policy is not in effect for men, or it violates the women's equal protection and due process. If on intake, men are classified according to maximum, medium, or minimum security, so too shall women, who have the same right to minimum security facilities as do men prisoners.

In areas such as work programs, vocational programs, education, training and community programs, there must be parity of treatment for males and females according to the courts, unless there is a substantial reason for making such a distinction. Case law has held that there can be no discriminatory selection for any kind of work programs based on race, religion, or sex—any arbitrary or capricious selection for participation is prohibited by the courts.

The medical needs of all prisoners have to be met; this includes prenatal care, treatment for sex-related illnesses, and AIDS. There cannot be a continued deliberate indifference to the medical needs of female inmates. This was established case law in the 1980s and should be evident today. All prisoners, including women, must be given a system of educational, vocational, and work programs. The courts have ruled continuously that women prisoners must be provided program opportunities on a parity with men. Institutional size is not a justification but an excuse for the kind of treatment afforded women prisoners. This was decided in *Glover v. Johnson,* and this principle still holds true today.

Prior to these landmark cases, the female prisoner was essentially a forgotten offender. This was true when I wrote my dissertation in the 1980s, and it is a fact that has come back to haunt us. Testimony by a teacher in the *Glover* case indicated that whereas males were allowed to take advanced shop courses, females were taught at a junior high level, because the attitude of those in charge was "keep it simple, these are only women." This mindset should not be tolerated today.

Litigation has provided an opportunity for inmates to have a role in altering conditions of their confinement, but a judicial opinion requiring comprehensive change does not necessarily bring about change. Viewed from a nonlegal perspective, litigation is but a catalyst for change rather than an automatic mechanism for ending wrongs found.

Hopefully, we have left the days when a double standard persisted traditionally in both the law and treatment of inmates:

> Overlooking, letting go, excusing, unwillingness to report and to hold, being easy on women are part of the differential handling of the adult female in the law enforcement process from original complaints to admission to prison. The differential law enforcement handling seems to be built into our basic attitudes toward women. The operation of such attention can be called euphemistically the *chivalry factor.* (Reckless, 1967)

Theories have abounded concerning the causes of criminality by female offenders. Certainly the chivalry theory does not appear to be favored today. Once the female offender enters the correctional facility, she does not necessarily benefit from the benevolence of the criminal justice system. The theories of female crime continue to emphasize the natural differences between males and females, but fail to explain why females commit the crimes they do. Years ago, we were told that "discrimination and sexism are serious and pervasive problems in statutes, law enforcement, courts and correctional agencies. All society is being harmed by a serious overkill in the processing of females and by the inhuman conditions which continue to prevail in correctional agencies" (Sarri, 1979, p. 194). Can this be true in the twenty-first century? It is clear that female prisoners have been treated differently, and at times worse than male prisoners over the years. Should this not be stopped? Females suffer even more than males because they are normally housed in facilities that lack privacy, are faced with insensitive visiting rules (most states have only one, at most two facilities for females) thereby making it difficult for children to visit them, and to maintain a relationship with families.

In the 1970s, it was recommended by the Advisory Commission for the Correctional Facilities that the criminal justice system reexamine policies, procedures, and programs to lend more relevance to how the system served the problems and needs of female inmates. The commission had the following recommendations:

- Facilities for women offenders should be considered an integral part of the overall correctional system.
- Each state should determine differences in the needs between male and female offenders and implement differential programming.
- Appropriate vocational training programs should be implemented.

- Classification systems should be investigated to determine their applicability to the female offender.
- Adequate diversionary methods for female offenders should be implemented.
- State correctional agencies with such small numbers of women inmates as to make adequate facilities and programming uneconomical should make every effort to find alternatives to imprisonment for them. (Flynn, 1971, p. 113)

This was 1971; now what? Much of the neglect in assessing disparate treatment is attributed to writers believing that the experiences in prison for both men and women are the same, and are not areas calling for special investigation. Studies have been done on relationships between inmates and their children as well as the biases in the delivery of health care given to female inmates. The community programs then and now show that there is evidence of a lack of sensitivity while there continues to exist differential treatment afforded to the female prisoner.

It was Jessica Mitford (1973) who stated that "the entire criminal justice system for all offenders in the United States could not be characterized as a just or humane system, but in the case of the female offender its ineffectiveness and inhumanity are even more apparent."

Women convicted of crimes historically have been regarded as moral offenders, whereas men are believed to be asserting their masculinity. The disparate treatment of male and female prisoners is no more than the result of stereotypic thinking. We supposedly have come a long way, but we are faced today with an unequal system of criminal justice, and a lack of understanding of what is needed to bring the female offender back into the community. The research and findings gathered in this book indicate that women may still be the forgotten offenders, but this should not be allowed to continue. The woman offender should be treated fairly not simply because she is *a woman,* but because she is a member of the human race, and as such deserves decent treatment.

REFERENCES

ARON, N. (1981). Legal issues pertaining to female offenders. In *Representing prisoners.* New York: Practicing Law Institute.

FLYNN, E. (1971). The special problems of female offenders. In *National Conference on Corrections.* Williamsburg: Virginia Division of Justice and Crime Prevention.

Glover v. Johnson, 478 F. Supp. 1075 (1979).

Hart v. Sarver, 309 U.S. F. Supp. 362 (E.D., Ark. 1970).

HUNTER, S. (1984, Spring/Summer). Issues and challenges facing women's prisons in the 1980s. *The Prison Journal, 64* (1), 129–135.

MITFORD, J. (1973). *Kind and unusual punishment.* New York: Alfred A. Knopf.

RECKLESS, W. (1967). *The crime problem.* New York: Appleton–Century–Crofts.

Reed v. Reed, 404 U.S. 71 (1971).

SARRI, R. (1979). Crime and the female offender. In E. S. Gomberg and V. Frank (Eds.), *Gender and disordered behavior-sex differences in psychopathology.* New York: Brunner/Mazel.

PART I

The Problem: Rising Female Incarceration Rates

In Chapter 1, Meda Chesney-Lind sets the stage for this book by documenting the changes in women's imprisonment over the past two decades. During the 1970s, many states did not even have women's prisons, instead housing the few women prisoners in men's facilities or in other states. Then, in the 1980s, the United States began incarcerating increasingly larger numbers of women. Indeed, the increase in women's incarceration rates began outpacing men's. Chesney-Lind goes on to explain the primary causes of this trend. She examines the role that public policies have had on women, particularly women of color. Drug enforcement policies designed to stop large-scale distribution have instead netted large numbers of women charged with drug possession. This, Chesney-Lind informs us, is "equity with a vengeance."

The large number of women prisoners leads to new problems, particularly when they are treated like men prisoners. Part of the problem is that we do not treat men prisoners well, either. This issue is made worse by the differences between men and women prisoners. Women prisoners have special and unique needs that current criminal justice policies are ill equipped to handle. Chesney-Lind suggests an alternative way to treat women who commit crimes. She stresses the importance of placing women's needs in the center when devising criminal justice programs for them. Even alternatives to sentencing must be viewed differently for women offenders. Finally, the importance of dealing with the issues of these women prior to incarceration is addressed.

1

Reinventing Women's Corrections

Challenges for Contemporary Feminist Criminologists and Practitioners

Meda Chesney-Lind, Ph.D.

❖

Girl and women offenders have been largely invisible or "forgotten" by a criminology that emerged out of the Industrial Revolution to complement, explain, and occasionally critique state efforts to control and discipline unruly and dangerous men. Male criminality was regarded as an understandable, if not normal, response to the injuries of class (and far less frequently, race). In the classic texts on delinquency and crime, however, girls and women literally "disappeared" from data sets, discussions of crime patterns, and plans for the structure of jails and prisons. Very often, little or no thought was given to the female offender until she appeared at the door of an institution (Rafter, 1990). It was as if crime and punishment existed in a world in which gender equaled male, and women were correctional afterthoughts, at best.

The relative paucity of scholarship on "unruly" women (Faith, 1993) has permitted two troubling trends to develop, particularly in the United States and Canada. First, the lack of solid scholarship has permitted the occasional discovery of "bad" women during periods when their presence would serve patriarchal interests. In the 1970s, the media touted female offenders as by-products of the then emerging social movement of feminism, which was seeking legal and social equality for women (Chesney-Lind, 1986). In more recent years, renewed public debate about female aggression and violence, particularly among girls, has again assigned blame to the women's movement (see Chesney-Lind, 1993; DeKeseredy, 2000).

More important, the lack of research about women and crime has meant virtually no available information about women offenders, an oversight that developed into a policy crisis as the number of women sentenced to jail and prison began to increase dramatically in the last two decades of the twentieth century. This chapter reviews those incarceration trends in some detail, and then considers some of the programmatic challenges that these increases pose for the emerging field of what might be called women's corrections.

TRENDS IN WOMEN'S IMPRISONMENT IN THE UNITED STATES

For most of this century, we imprisoned about five to ten thousand women (Calahan, 1986). In 1980, there were just over 12,000 women in U.S. state and federal prisons. By 1999, there were 90,668. In two decades, the number of women being held in the nation's prisons increased eightfold, and the women's imprisonment boom was born. It is important to note that the increase in women's imprisonment is not simply a mirror image of what is happening to the numbers in male corrections. First, women's share of total imprisonment has actually increased—more than doubling in the past three decades. At the turn of the twentieth century, women made up 4% of those imprisoned; by 1970, this had dropped to 3%, and women accounted for only 3.9% of those in prison in 1980; but by 1999, women accounted for 6.7% of those in prison (Beck & Karberg, 2001, p. 5).

The rate of growth of women's imprisonment has also outpaced that of men; since 1990, the annual rate of growth of female prisoners has averaged 8.1%, higher than the 6.2% average increase in male prisoners. As a result, in the last decade (1990–2000), the number of women in prison increased by 110%, compared to a 77% increase in the male prison population (Beck & Karberg, 2001, p. 5).

Similar patterns are seen in adult jails: Women constituted 7% of the jail population in the mid-1980s, but today they account for 11.4%. Likewise, the rate of female increase since 1990 has been 6.6% for women compared to 4% for men (Calahan, 1986; Beck & Karberg, 2001, p. 5).

Finally, the rate of women's imprisonment is also at a historic high, increasing from a low of 6 sentenced female inmates per 100,000 women in the United States in 1925 to 66 per 100,000 in 2000. In 2001, Texas led the nation with 12,714 women in prison, followed by California (11,432), Florida (4,019), and New York (3,423) (Beck & Karberg, 2001, p. 5).

As a result of these increases, the number of women incarcerated in prisons and jails in the United States is now approximately 10 times more than the number of women incarcerated in Western Europe. This despite the fact that Western Europe and the United States are roughly equivalent in terms of population (Amnesty International, 1999, p. 15).

Although the United States leads the world in women's incarceration, we are, sadly, not alone in our mania to imprison. Women's cell space in Canada has tripled since 1992 (Faith, 1999, p. 111); in Great Britain, the number of women in prison jumped 19% between 1996 and 1997 (Carlen, 1999, p. 122); and in New Zealand, the same two-year period showed a 20% increase (Morris & Kingi, 1999, p. 141). Essentially, it appears that around the world, there is an increased willingness to incarcerate women.

What has caused this shift in how we respond to women's crime? What unique challenges are now presented by the remarkable numbers of women inmates? And what could we do better or differently, as we struggle to create a woman-centered response to the current state of our nation's penal system?

BUILDING CELLS: INVENTING WOMEN'S CORRECTIONS

Throughout most of our nation's history, women in prison have been correctional afterthoughts. Ignored because of their small numbers, female inmates tended to complain
about their treatment, not riot, making it even easier for institutions to overlook their unique
needs. Perhaps as a consequence, the United States never developed a correctional system
for women to replace the reformatory system that fell into disuse shortly before World War
II. In fact, by the mid-1970s, only about half the states and territories had separate prisons
for women, and many jurisdictions housed women inmates in male facilities or transferred
them to women's facilities in other states (Singer, 1973).

The correctional establishment, long used to forgetting about women, was taken by
almost complete surprise when the numbers of women sentenced to prison began to expand
in the 1980s. Initially, women inmates were housed about anywhere (remodeled hospitals,
abandoned training schools, and converted motels), as jurisdictions struggled to cope with
the dramatic increase in women's imprisonment.

More recently, however, states have turned to opening new units and facilities to
respond to the soaring numbers of women inmates. Data collected by Nicole Rafter docu-
ment this clearly. Between 1930 and 1950, the United States opened only about two to
three facilities for women a decade, but over 34 were opened in the 1980s alone (Rafter,
1990). By 1990, the nation had 71 female-only facilities; five years later, that number had
jumped to 104—an increase of 46.5% (Chesney-Lind, 1998).

This remarkable statistic should not be seen simply as a reflection of what was happening in male incarceration; in many states there was simply *no* system at all for women
when the numbers started going up. For this reason—good or bad—the nation embarked on
the invention or, more precisely, the reinvention of women's corrections in the United
States. The last such experiment occurred during the Progressive Era, when women
reformers, many affected by the first wave of feminism, began to boldly enter the previously men-only field of corrections and create women's reformatories. A natural outgrowth
of earlier involvement of feminists in prison reform, the reformatory movement enthusias-
tically embraced female imprisonment in institutions that were designed to "save" fallen
girls and women (see Brenzel, 1983; Rafter, 1990).

Box 1.1

TRENDS IN THE IMPRISONMENT OF WOMEN IN THE U.S.

- Between 1980 and 1999, the number of women in U.S. state and federal prisons
  increased from 12,000 to over 90,000.
- The percentage of women prisoners increased from 3.9% in 1980 to 6.7% in 1999.
- The number of women incarcerated in the U.S. is approximately ten times the
  number of women incarcerated in all of Western Europe.
- The number of female-only correctional facilities increased 46.5% between 1990
  and 1995.

The current revolution in women's corrections has been thrust upon correctional administrators, including many gifted women working in the mostly male environment of modern corrections. The challenge that these administrators face on a daily basis was the subject of a national symposium that gathered both academics and correctional administrators from over half the states and jurisdictions to discuss the soaring number of women in prison, and the need to design services for this unique population and seek alternatives to their incarceration in male-modeled facilities (Office of Justice Programs, 2000). This group of women working in corrections, then, might be cast fairly in the role of "reluctant" incarcerators, as so many of them express the opinion that most of the women in U.S. prisons today do not necessarily need to be there (Office of Justice Programs, 2000). These women, like their earlier counterparts in the reformatory movement, have a strong belief in the value of gender-specific or gender-responsive programming. As Bona Miller, then warden of the Pocatello (ID) Women's Correctional Center, wrote in her essay, "Different, Not More Difficult," "working effectively with women offenders requires an in-depth understanding of their specific characteristics and needs, as well as a broader comprehension of the major social and economic challenges facing women today" (Miller, 1998, p. 144).

In sum, the United States has embarked on a challenging course, one that other nations are also facing. How do we craft a system (not simply prisons) that responds to the issues presented by women offenders? Moreover, how do we avoid responses to women's crime that treat them as though they were men, in the name of equality? We will examine shifts in women's offending as well as detailing a few issues that have surfaced around their treatment in the criminal justice system, with a special focus on their treatment in prison.

COLLATERAL DAMAGE: ADULT FEMALE OFFENDERS AND THE UNITED STATES'S IMPRISONMENT MANIA

How should the criminal justice system, and more specifically, corrections, respond to the increasing numbers of women in their system? Should these women be treated as if they were men? Certainly, that has been the response of many in criminal justice—who often justify such treatment as a form of equality. Setting aside the legal aspects of this dispute, will treating women offenders as if they were men result in effective responses to their criminal behavior? Research on women's pathways into crime clearly disputes this, and suggests that gender matters in the forces that propel women into criminal behavior. For this reason, gender must be considered when crafting effective responses to a female offender's problems.

For example, a national survey of imprisoned women in the United States found that they have far higher rates of physical and sexual abuse than their male counterparts. Forty-three percent of the women surveyed "reported they had been abused at least once" before their current admission to prison; the comparable figure for men was 12.2% (Snell & Morton, 1994, p. 5).

For about a third of all women in prison (31.7%), the abuse started when they were girls, but continued as adults. A key gender difference emerges here: A number of young men who are in prison (10.7%) also report abuse as boys, but this situation does not continue to adulthood. One in four women reported that their abuse started as adults, compared to only 3% of male offenders. Fully 33.5% of the women surveyed reported physical abuse, and a slightly higher number (33.9%) had been sexually abused either as girls or young women, compared to relatively small percentages of men (10% of boys and 5.3% of adult men in prison) (Snell & Morton, 1994, p. 5).

Girls are, it turns out, much more likely than boys to be the victims of child sexual abuse, with some experts estimating a roughly 70% to 30% split (Finkelhor & Baron, 1986). Not surprisingly, the evidence also suggests a link between child sexual abuse and girls' delinquency—particularly running away from home (see Chesney-Lind & Shelden, 1998). Studies of adult women in prison clearly indicate the role that girlhood victimization has played in their lives, suggesting that society's failure to adequately address girls' serious problems—and worse, even criminalizing girls' survival strategies, such as running away from home—is inextricably linked not only to girls' delinquency but also to later criminal behavior in adult women.

WOMEN'S LIVES AND WOMEN'S CRIME

A look at the offenses for which women are incarcerated further puts to rest the notion of hyperviolent, nontraditional women criminals. "Nearly half of all women in prison are currently serving a sentence for a nonviolent offense and have been convicted in the past of only nonviolent offenses" (Beck, 2000, p. 10). By 1998, about half of all women in the nation's prisons were serving time either for drug or property offenses (Beck, 2000, p. 10).

Even when women do commit violent offenses, gender plays an important role. Research indicates that of women convicted of murder or manslaughter, many had killed husbands or boyfriends who repeatedly and violently abused them. In New York, for example, of the women committed to the state's prisons for homicide in 1986, 49% had been the victims of abuse at some point in their lives and 59% of the women who killed someone close to them were being abused at the time of the offense. For half of the women committed for homicide, it was their first and only offense (Huling, 1991).

But what of less dramatic and far more common offenses among women? Kim English (1993) approached the issue of women's crime by analyzing detailed self-report surveys she administered to a sample of 128 female and 872 male inmates in Colorado. Her research provides clear information on the way in which women's place in male society colors and shapes their crimes.

She found, for example, that women were far more likely than men to be involved in forgery (it was the most common crime for women and fifth out of eight for men). Follow-up research on a subsample of "high crime"-rate female respondents revealed that many had worked in retail establishments and therefore "knew how much time they had" between stealing the checks or credit cards and having the theft reported. The women said that they would target strip malls, where credit cards and bank checks could be stolen easily and used in nearby retail establishments. The women reported that their high frequency of theft was motivated by a "big haul," which meant a purse with several hundred dollars in it as well as cards and checks. English concludes that "women's overrepresentation in low-paying, low status jobs" increases their involvement in these property crimes (1993, p. 370).

English's findings about two other offenses, where gender differences were not apparent in participation rates, are worth exploring here. She found no difference in the participation rates of women and men in drug sales and assault. However, when examining the frequency data, English found that women in prison reported significantly more drug sales than men, but not because they were engaged in big-time drug selling. Instead, the high number of women's drug sales can be attributed to the fact that they "concentrated in the small trades (i.e. transactions of less than $10)." Because they made so little money, English found that 20% of the active women dealers reported twenty or more drug deals per day (1993, p. 372).

A reverse of the same pattern was found when she examined women's participation in assault. Here, slightly more (27.8%) women than men (23.4%) reported committing an assault in the previous year. However, most of these women reported only one assault during the study period (65.4%), compared to only about a third of the men (37.5%).

In sum, English found that both women's and men's crime reflect the role that "economic disadvantage" plays in their criminal careers. Beyond this, gender has a profound influence in shaping women's and men's response to poverty. Specifically, women's criminal careers reflect "gender differences in legitimate and illegitimate opportunity structures, in personal networks, and in family obligations" (1993, pp. 3, 74).

WAR ON DRUGS AS A WAR ON WOMEN

Is the dramatic increase in women's imprisonment a response to a women's crime problem spiraling out of control? Certainly, research on the backgrounds of those in prison gives little indication of this, nor do studies of contemporary women offenders' crime patterns. These continue to demonstrate a history of victimization and participation in crimes of economic marginalization, not serious, nontraditional offenses (see Bloom, Chesney-Lind, & Owen, 1994). In addition, arrest data do not suggest major changes in women's criminal behavior. As an example, the total number of arrests of adult women, which might be seen as a measure of women's criminal activity, increased by only 14.5% between 1990–1999 whereas the number of women in prison increased by 105.8% (Federal Bureau of Investigation, 2000, p. 217; Beck, 2000, p. 6).

And, despite media portrayals of hyperviolent women offenders, the proportion of women doing time in state prisons for violent offenses has been declining steadily from about half (48.9%) in 1979 to just over a quarter (28.5%) in 1998 (Bureau of Justice Statistics, 1988; Beck, 2000, p. 10).

What does explain the increase? A recent study by the Bureau of Justice Statistics indicates that growth in the number of violent offenders was the major factor for male prison growth, but for the female prison population "drug offenders were the largest source of growth" (Beck, 2000, p. 10). One explanation, then, is that the "war on drugs" has become a largely unannounced war on women. A decade and a half ago (1979), 1 in 10 women in U.S. prisons was doing time for drugs. In 1998, it was 1 in 3 (33.9%) (Beck, 2000, p. 10). Finally, although the intent of "get tough" policies was to rid society of drug dealers and so-called kingpins, many of the women swept up in the war on drugs are minor offenders. An analysis by Human Rights Watch of women incarcerated under New York's draconian Rockefeller drug laws revealed that nearly half (44%) had never been in prison before and 17% had never been arrested before (Fellner, 1997, p. 13).

POLICIES THAT INCREASE WOMEN'S IMPRISONMENT

Many observers suspect that the increase in women's imprisonment can be explained by the array of policy changes within the criminal justice system, rather than a change in the seriousness of women's crime. Certainly the demographics of women in prison indicate the passage of increased penalties (mandatory sentences) for drug offenses has been a major factor. Also important has been the implementation of a variety of sentencing "reform" initiatives that, although devoted to reducing class and race disparities in male sentencing, paid no attention to gender.[1]

Likely the most powerful factor in the increase in women's imprisonment has been mandatory sentences for drug offenses, which all states have in some form. Estimates are that these policies increased the likelihood of being imprisoned for a drug offense by 447% between 1980 and 1992 (Mauer, 1999, p. 2). Initially, mandatory sentences appear to be gender blind, but in practice, many criminologists suspect that women are at a considerable disadvantage in plea negotiations that are permitted by our legal system. Essentially, one of the few ways that a mandatory sentence can be altered is if the defendant can provide authorities with information that might be useful in the prosecution of other drug offenders. Because, as noted earlier, women tend to be working at the lowest levels of the drug hierarchy, they are often unable to negotiate plea reductions successfully. Such was the case for Kemba Smith, who, in one high-profile example, was initially sentenced to 24 years in a federal penitentiary for a drug offense; she was later pardoned by President Bill Clinton (Copeland, 2000).

Data on the offense characteristics of women in federal institutions further confirms the role played by policy shifts in response to drug convictions. In 1989, 44.5% of the women incarcerated in federal institutions were being held for drug offenses. Only two years later, this figure was up to 68%.[2] Currently, it stands (as noted earlier) at 72%. Essentially, 20 years ago, nearly two thirds of the women convicted of federal felonies were granted probation, but increasingly, the mandatory sentences attached to drug crimes mean that women accused of even relatively minor drug offenses "do the time" (see Mauer, Potler, & Wolf, 1999).

The scant evidence we have certainly suggests that sentencing reform also played a role in the soaring increase of women in federal prisons. In 1988, before full implementation of sentencing guidelines, women made up 6.5% of those in federal institutions; in 1999, women accounted for 8.6% of those in federal prisons (Beck, 2000, pp. 3, 6).

As a result of these pressures, the federal prison system now holds 9,186 women, and the number of women incarcerated in federal facilities continues to increase at an even faster pace than that found in state prisons. Additionally, women make up an even larger proportion of those incarcerated in federal prisons (7.4%) compared to 6.3% in state prisons (Beck & Karberg, 2001, p. 5).

Other less obvious but related policy changes have also played their part in sending more women to prison. Take new technologies for determining drug use (e.g., urinalysis). Many women are being returned to prison for technical parole violations because they fail to pass random drug tests. Of the six thousand women incarcerated in California in 1993, approximately one third (32%) were imprisoned due to parole violations. In Hawaii, 55% of the new admissions to the Women's Prison during a 2-month period in 1991 were being returned to prison for parole violations (mostly drug-related). Finally, in Oregon, during a 1-year period (October 1992–September 1993), only 16% of female admissions to Oregon institutions were incarcerated for new convictions; the rest were for probation and parole violations (see Chesney-Lind, 1997, for a full discussion of these issues).

The impact of gender-blind sentencing, then, coupled with what might be seen as an increased policing of women's behavior while on probation or parole (which could be seen as an extension of the historic paternalistic interest in women's deportment) have both played major, though largely hidden, roles in the growth of women's imprisonment.

THE EMERGENCE OF VENGEFUL EQUITY

What has happened in the last few decades, then, signals a major and dramatic change in the country's response to women's offending. Without much fanfare and almost no public discussion or debate, the male model of incarceration has been increasingly accessed as a response to the soaring number of women inmates.

Some might argue that this pattern is simply a product of a lack of reflection or imagination on the part of those charged with administering the nation's prison systems. They are, after all, used to running prisons built around the model of male inmates, and as one correctional officer put it to the author at a national meeting, "An inmate is an inmate is an inmate." However, an additional theme is emerging in modern correctional response to women inmates: vengeful equity. This is the dark side of the equity or parity model of justice—one that emphasizes treating women offenders as though they were men, particularly when the outcome is punitive, in the name of equal justice.

Perhaps the starkest expression of this impulse has been the creation of chain gangs for women. Although these have surfaced in several states, the most publicized example is found in Arizona. Here, a sheriff pronounced himself an "equal opportunity incarcerator" and encouraged women "now locked up with three or four others in dank, cramped disciplinary cells" to "volunteer" for a 15-woman chain gang. Defending his controversial move, he commented, "If women can fight for their country, and bless them for that, if they can walk a beat, if they can protect the people and arrest violators of the law, then they should have no problem with picking up trash in 120 degrees" (Kim, 1996). Other examples of vengeful equity are women's boot camps, and the argument that women should be subjected to capital punishment at the same rate as men.

Box 1.2

VENGEFUL EQUITY

- The male model of incarceration is being used to respond to the soaring number of women in prison.
- Arizona has created chain gangs for women.
- Treating women and men the same is the dark side of the equity or parity model of justice.

As extreme as these examples seem, legal readings by correctional administrators and others that make any attention to legitimate gender differences "illegal" (which results in treating women as if they were men with reference to cross-gender supervision, strip searches, etc.) while ignoring how gender influences every aspect of women's imprisonment, is a sinister theme. Recently, this approach has been identified by Human Rights Watch as a major contributing factor to the sexual abuse of women inmates (Human Rights Watch, 1996).

What is needed, instead of vengeful equity, is a system crafted to be conservative, careful, and gender-responsive—a woman-centered correctional system, if you will, that derives its modes of supervision at all stages of the correctional process from a thoughtful weighing of the problems and needs of girl and woman offenders. Ever mindful of public safety, this system must first imagine what corrections would look like if women offenders (not their male counterparts) were at the center. Given what we already know about women offenders, one can quickly see that such a system can attempt things that the male system cannot. We know women are largely minor offenders, that they have unique needs, and that most can be safely returned to the communities where they lived. This is the challenge of inventing women's corrections, one embraced by the authors of the many essays in this book.

CONCLUSION

All good feminist research is challenged to investigate aspects of women's oppression while "seeking at the same time to be part of the struggle against it" (Kelly, 1990). Clearly, this mandate is much needed in the area of women's crime and imprisonment. Women in conflict with the law have become the hidden victims of our nation's imprisonment binge, and as a consequence, women's share of the nation's prison population, measured in either absolute or relative terms, has never been higher. All of this has occurred without serious planning, consideration, or debate. Even more alarming, it appears that the incarceration binge is beginning to spread to the juvenile justice system as well, and it is clear that the United States approach to female defiance is being emulated, in some form or another, by other countries.

With reference to girls' and women's crime, we face a clear choice. We can continue to spend our tax dollars on the costly incarceration of women guilty of petty drug and property crimes, or we can seek other, more creative solutions to the problems of drug-dependent women. Given their demographic profiles, it is clear that the decarceration of many women currently in prison would not jeopardize public safety. Further, the money saved could be reinvested in programs designed to meet women's needs, which would enrich not only their lives but the lives of many other women who are at risk for criminal involvement.

Clearly, any in-community or alternative sentencing programs should be crafted with women's needs at their center rather than on the periphery. As an example, many traditional forms of in-community sentences involve home detention—clearly unworkable for women with abusive boyfriends or husbands, but also problematic for women who are drug dependent and/or unemployed. Restitution is also not a viable choice for women offenders for many of the same reasons.

Women's programs must, first and foremost, give participants strategies to deal with their profound substance-abuse problems; they must also be gender sensitive. Program designers must understand that most women take drugs as a form of self-medication (rather than for adventure or challenge as men often do); they must also be sensitive to women's unique circumstances (by providing services such as child care and transportation). Community programs must also deal with women's immediate need for safe housing and stable employment, an undertaking made more difficult by the passage of the Felony Drug Provision of the Welfare Reform Act, which bars women with drug convictions from receiving services. Clearly, any national strategy for dealing with the problems of women in prison must include a call to repeal this mean-spirited initiative, as well as advocating for the creation of women-centered programs to accompany any efforts to shift women from prison back to their communities.

By moving dollars from women's imprisonment to women's services, including correctional services, in the community, we will not only help women—we also help their children. In the process, we can help break the cycle of poverty, desperation, crime, and imprisonment, rather than perpetuate it.

DISCUSSION QUESTIONS

1. What has happened to the female incarceration rate since the mid-1980s? How does this compare to changes in the male incarceration rate?

2. What has caused the immense increase in the number of women prisoners? Why does Chesney-Lind say that many women working in corrections are "reluctant" incarcerators?

3. How do women's lives relate to women's crime?

4. What does the author mean by "equity with a vengeance"?

WEBNOTES

Go to the site for Prison Activists—women in prison (http://prisonactivist.org/women/women-in-prison.html). Read the article. How do the statistics given compare to women prisoners overall in the U.S.? What does the article say are 11 things you should know about women in prison?

Then read Amnesty International's report on the impact of the War on Drugs on incarceration of women (http://www.amnestyusa.org/rightsforall/women/report/women-102.html). Be prepared to discuss this report in class.

NOTES

1. Raeder notes, for example, that judges are constrained by these federal guidelines from considering family responsibilities, particularly pregnancy and motherhood, which in the past may have kept women out of prison. Yet the impact of these "neutral" guidelines is to eliminate from consideration the unique situation of mothers, especially single mothers, unless their situation

can be proved "extraordinary." Nearly 90% of fathers in prison report that their wives are taking care of their children; by contrast only 22% of mothers in prison could count on the fathers of their children to care for them during their imprisonment (Raeder, 1993, p. 69). This means that many women in prison, the majority of whom are mothers, face the potential, if not actual, loss of their children. This is not a penalty that men in prison experience.

2. The comparable male figure was 58% in 1993, up from 39.6% in 1989.

REFERENCES

AMNESTY INTERNATIONAL. (1999). *Not part of my sentence: Violations of the human rights of women in custody.* Washington, DC: Amnesty International.

BECK, A. (2000). *Prisoners in 1999.* Washington, DC: U.S. Department of Justice, Bureau of Justice Statistics.

BECK, A., & KARBERG, J. C. (2001). *Prison and jail inmates at midyear 2000.* Washington, DC: U.S. Department of Justice, Bureau of Justice Statistics.

BLOOM, B., CHESNEY-LIND, M., & OWEN, B. (1994). *Women in prison in California: Hidden victims of the war on drugs.* San Francisco: Center on Juvenile and Criminal Justice.

BRENZEL, B. (1983). *Daughters of the state.* Cambridge: Massachusetts Institute of Technology Press.

BUREAU OF JUSTICE STATISTICS. (1988). *Profile of state prison inmates, 1986.* Washington, DC: U.S. Department of Justice, Bureau of Justice Statistics.

CALAHAN, M. (1986). *Historical corrections statistics in the United States, 1850–1984.* Washington, DC: U.S. Department of Justice, Bureau of Justice Statistics.

CARLEN, P. (1999). Women's imprisonment in England. In S. Cook & S. Davies (Eds.), *Harsh punishment: International experiences of women's imprisonment.* Boston: Northeastern University Press.

CHESNEY-LIND, M. (1986). Women and crime: The female offender. *Signs, 12,* 8–96.

———. (1993). Girls, gangs and violence: Reinventing the liberated female crook. *Humanity and Society, 17,* 321–344.

———. (1997). *The female offender: Girls, women, and crime.* Thousand Oaks, CA: Sage.

———. (1998, December). The forgotten offender: Women in prison. *Corrections Today, 66*–73.

CHESNEY-LIND, M., & SHELDEN, R. G. (1998). *Girls, delinquency and juvenile justice.* Belmont, CA: Wadsworth.

COPELAND, L. (2000, February 13). Kemba Smith's hard time. *Washington Post,* p. FO1.

DEKESEREDY, W. (2000) *Women, crime and the Canadian criminal justice system.* Cincinnati, OH: Anderson.

ENGLISH, K. (1993). Self-reported crimes rates of women prisoners. *Journal of Quantitative Criminology, 9,* 357–382.

FAITH, K. (1993). *Unruly women: The politics of confinement and resistance.* Vancouver, BC: Press Gang.

———. (1999). Transformative justice versus re-entrenched correctionalism. In S. Cook & S. Davies (Eds.), *Harsh punishment: International experiences of women's imprisonment.* Boston: Northeastern University Press.

FEDERAL BUREAU OF INVESTIGATION. (2000). *Crime in the United States: 1999 Uniform Crime Reports.* Washington, DC: U.S. Department of Justice.

FELLNER, J. (1997). *Cruel and unusual: Disproportionate sentences for New York drug offenders.* New York: Human Rights Watch.

FINKELHOR, D., & BARON, L. (1986). Risk factors for child sexual abuse. *Journal of Interpersonal Violence, 1,* 43–71.

HULING, T. (1991, March 4). *Breaking the silence.* New York: Correctional Association of New York.

HUMAN RIGHTS WATCH. (1996). *All too familiar: Sexual abuse of women in U.S. state prisons.* New York: Human Rights Watch.

KELLY, L. (1990). Journeying in reverse. In L. Gelsthorpe & A. Morris (Eds.), *Feminist perspectives in criminology.* Milton Keynes, UK: Open University Press.

KIM, E. (1996, August 16). Sheriff says he'll have chain gangs for women. *Tuscaloosa News,* p. 1A.

MAUER, M. (1999). *Drug policy and the criminal justice system.* Washington, DC: The Sentencing Project.

MAUER, M., POTLER, C., & WOLF, R. (1999). *Gender and justice: Women, drugs and sentencing policy.* Washington, DC: The Sentencing Project.

MILLER, B. (1998, December). Different, not more difficult. *Corrections Today,* 142–144.

MORRIS, A., & KINGI, V. (1999). Addressing women's needs or empty rhetoric? In S. Cook & S. Davies (Eds.), *Harsh punishment: International experiences of women's imprisonment.* Boston: Northeastern University Press.

OFFICE OF JUSTICE PROGRAMS. (2000). *National symposium on women offenders.* Conference proceedings. Washington, DC, December 13–15, 1999.

RAEDER, M. (1993). Gender and sentencing: Single moms, battered women and other sex-based anomalies in the gender-free world of the Federal Sentencing Guidelines. *Pepperdine Law Review, Vol. 20,* No. 3, 905–990.

RAFTER, N. H. (1990). *Partial justice: Women, prisons and social control.* New Brunswick, NJ: Transaction Books.

SINGER, L. R. (1973). Women and the correctional process. *American Criminal Law Review, 11,* 295–308.

SNELL, T. L., & MORTON, D. C. (1994). *Women in prison.* Washington, DC: U.S. Department of Justice, Bureau of Justice Statistics, Special Report.

PART II

Educational and Vocational Training

Educational and vocational training are important aspects of prison programming. Ideally, the prisoner has the opportunity to become more employable upon release. However, the two chapters in this section suggest that simply providing educational and vocational programs does not guarantee that women prisoners receive appropriate training, nor does it guarantee that they will benefit from the training received.

Many women enter prison without a high school diploma and with no marketable skills. At the same time, the majority are the sole source of income for themselves and their minor children. Thus, it is essential that correctional systems better prepare these women for life outside of prison.

However, that is the ideal, not the reality, as we see in Pamela Schram's incisive examination of how social control is tied to historical perceptions of "appropriate womanhood." She poses the question, "Are stereotypes a form of social control over offenders?" Using this as a launching point, Schram explores the history of female stereotyping in American culture at large, then throughout the history of women's prisons, then examines the cultural ideal of womanhood and its impact on early women's reformatories. Schram delineates the historical attempts to reform the female offender into a "true woman"—that is, one who meets white middle-class standards of womanhood.

Finally, Schram examines the ways in which sex stereotyping has worked against parity for women prisoners in vocational programming. She addresses important issues in women's programs, including the smaller numbers of women's prisons and the different needs of women prisoners, the role of work assignments, and the need for positive female role models. The chapter traces the history of efforts to improve educational and vocational programs in women's prisons. An overview of relevant legal cases is provided. Schram points out that seeking parity may not be the best solution. Rather, the differing needs of male and female inmates must be taken into account.

In the following chapter, Dennis Brewster examines the relationship between prison education and recidivism in Oklahoma during the early 1990s. He argues that many women come to prison without a high school diploma or marketable job skills. During incarceration, female inmates therefore may have the opportunity to improve their chances of success in staying out of prison by completing a General Equivalency Diploma (GED) program or vocational training. Thus, he examines postrelease outcomes, comparing "completers" with "noncompleters" in both types of programs. His findings are disturbing.

Using the population of all inmates released from the Oklahoma Department of Corrections between January 1, 1991, and December 31, 1994, Brewster first examines recidivism rates among those who entered prison without a high school diploma or GED certificate. He explores the effect that completing a GED program while incarcerated has on the outcomes. As would be expected, his findings indicate that completion of the GED program increases the length of time that the women remain out of prison. However, when he turns to the entire population of releasees and examines the effect of vocational–technical (Vo–Tech) programs on recidivism, his findings are much less optimistic. Among women who were released between 1991 and 1994 in Oklahoma, it appears that those who completed a vocational program were likely to return to prison sooner than those who did not complete a program. Furthermore, Brewster points out that this replicates earlier studies by the Oklahoma Department of Corrections. In other words, Vo–Tech programs have a detrimental effect on a woman's chances of staying out of prison.

There are several possible explanations for this finding. It may be that a selectivity factor is at work—those who enter the program are already more at risk of recidivism before completing the training. Or, there may be factors related to the Vo–Tech training itself that are creating the problem. The data used do not provide information about which specific vocational program each inmate undertook. It may be that the quicker return to prison is linked to specific programs that do not provide the inmate with marketable skills. This in turn, Brewster suggests, may lead to unrealistic expectations for the women.

Brewster concludes that the research raises more questions than it answers, and stresses the need for a comprehensive study of the different programs. He singles out the low rates of completion for both the GED and Vo–Tech programs as a starting point for future research to determine why so few women participate in these programs. Finally, he emphasizes the importance of understanding women's programming in a more holistic framework. He asks whether the training provided in the prison fits with the role of single mother and its inherent needs.

2

Stereotypes and Vocational Programming for Women Prisoners

Pamela J. Schram, Ph.D.

❖

Within Western cultures, women have been stereotyped into dichotomized images of "good" or "bad," and as having limitations or negative traits because of their gender. Some criminologists argue that these cultural stereotypes have been reflected in and perpetuated by the criminal justice system, which, in their view, functions as an instrument of social control (Belknap, 2001; Feinman, 1980; Klein, 1995; Rafter, 1990). If the criminal justice system is an agent of social control, and stereotypes have permeated the criminal justice system, then to what extent are stereotypes a form of social control over female inmates?

This chapter examines how these cultural stereotypes can influence a woman offender's experience in the criminal justice system. Specifically, the discussion focuses on one aspect of the prison experience—vocational programs offered to women prisoners. The first section briefly explores how stereotypes function as a form of social control. Using this conceptual framework, we consider how cultural stereotypes of women have permeated the criminal justice system. The next section then specifically examines current vocational programming for female inmates, followed by a brief discussion of the various legal challenges these programs have faced.

STEREOTYPES AS A FORM OF SOCIAL CONTROL

The literature has proposed various conceptualizations of the construct "social control." In most instances, they are created by identifying the means in which social control is implemented (e.g., Amir & Biniamin, 1991; Cohen, 1983; Etzioni, 1961; Gagne, 1992;

Green, Hebron, & Woodward, 1987; Lengermann & Wallace, 1985). According to Smart and Smart (1978),

> The social control of women assumes many forms, it may be internal or external, implicit or explicit, private or public, ideological or repressive. Now although it *may* no longer be appropriate to talk of 'the problem that has no name' when referring to the discontents of women, the Women's Movement having provided a voice and a language with which women may articulate their manifest grievances, there remains the problem of showing the existence of specific *covert* forms of oppression and control, and of revealing that their location lies in the public sphere rather than in the individual psychologies or personal lives of oppressed women. (p. 2)

Social control theories have their critics. Cohen (1983) argued that the construct of social control has become a "Mickey Mouse" concept, implemented to explain a wide range of social processes. Chunn and Gavigan (1988) seriously questioned the conceptual and analytical adequacy of the social control construct, concluding that it has a limited utility "for developing an historically and theoretically informed understanding of the complex and the contradictory relationship of women to the state and law" (p. 120). Rather than abandoning the concept of social control, one needs to reconceptualize and reevaluate it within the context of women and the criminal justice system. An initial step in this process is to ask, "What are the extent and forms of social control that women experience in the criminal justice system?" One may further ask, "If stereotypes can be found in the criminal justice system, *and,* if the criminal justice system is a mechanism of social control, are stereotypes a form of social control over female offenders?"

Cultural Stereotypes of Women

From antiquity to the present, cultures have categorized women into "either-or" roles (Pomeroy, 1975). One such pervasive conceptualization is the Madonna/whore duality, grounded on two contrasting perceptions of so-called normal female nature, and especially sexuality. The Madonna image personifies women as faithful and submissive wives as well as nurturing mothers. The whore image portrays women as temptresses of men's sexuality and self-control (Feinman, 1980; Rafter, 1990). This dichotomy, however, has been described from a white, upper-middle-class woman's perspective. Young (1986) argued that the categorizations for African American women have not been designated as either

---

Box 2.1

MADONNA OR WHORE: DO WOMEN OF ALL RACES FALL INTO THIS DICHOTOMY?

Perceptions of females frequently fall into a "good/bad" dichotomy such as Madonna/ whore. However, evidence suggests that for African American women, there is no "good" category, only a choice of negative ones.

"good" or "bad." According to Young (1986), there is no "good" category for African American women, who are generally designated "as an Amazon, a 'sinister Sapphire,' a mammy, and a seductress. Unlike characterizations of her white female counterpart, which are either good or bad, all the categorizations of the black female are bad" (p. 322).

Another related and pervasive conceptualization is the notion of femininity and its associations with traits such as gentleness, sensitivity, nurturance, and passivity. Comparatively, masculinity connotes intelligence, aggressiveness, independence, and competitiveness (Dugger, 1991). These conceptualizations become problematic when such traits are assumed to be inherent to an individual's sex, or are considered as "biological fact" rather than definitions associated with gender (Brownmiller, 1984; Edwards, 1989). Furthermore, it is confusing when people use the terms sex and gender imprecisely and interchangeably, or assume that everyone understands the definitions and the distinction between the two (Lorber & Farrell, 1991). West and Zimmerman (1991) defined gender roles as behavior and role enactment within a social situation. Gender is not a set of characteristics or a variable or a role; rather, gender is a product of social "doings." Those who do not recognize the distinction make

> the assumption that doing gender merely involves making use of discrete, well-defined bundles of behavior that can simply be plugged into interactional situations to produce recognizable enactments of masculinity and femininity. The man "does" being masculine by, for example, taking the woman's arm to guide her across a street, and she "does" being feminine by consenting to be guided and not initiating such behavior with a man. (West & Zimmerman, 1991, p. 22)

Gender roles are not based on biological differences between males and females; rather, they are socially constructed differences between men and women.

The Connection Between Stereotyping of Women in Prison and the Prison Experience

As discussed previously, when reconceptualizing social control one may ask, "What are the extent and forms of social control that women experience in the criminal justice system?" Heidensohn (1985) argued that there are various forms of social control, both informal and institutional, that define as well as limit the behavior of women:

> Of all the subtler constraints on the way women act and are supposed to act, few are more complex than the working of social policies. . . . Social policies are not usually regarded as instruments whose prime purpose of the definition and enforcement of prescriptions about gender roles, especially women, but a growing body of analyses shows that such prescriptions underpin, or are an effective part of certain policies. (p. 191)

Continuing with the above-mentioned question, one may ask, "If stereotypes can be found in the criminal justice system, *and,* if the criminal justice system is a mechanism of social control, are stereotypes a form of social control over female offenders?" The following section addresses this question by initially focusing on the historical experiences of women in prison. Next, the discussion explores how women prisoners continue to experience social control through stereotypes within the context of vocational programming.

HISTORICAL OVERVIEW OF WOMEN IN PRISON

Historically, many correctional practices were attempts to rehabilitate the female offender into an idealized concept of a "true woman." This need to rehabilitate or change a woman offender was based on the premise that she lacked the proper internalization of society's definition of a "true woman." If a woman did not "internalize" these qualities, then she was deviant and needed to change or be changed.

Several writers contend that historically, women in prison have been affected by stereotypes regarding femininity (Dobash, Dobash, & Gutteridge, 1986; Feinman, 1983; Fox, 1984; Mann, 1984; Pollock-Byrne, 1990; Rafter, 1990; Zupan, 1992). Most female offenders had violated society's moral standards, especially sexuality, rather than standards of law-abiding behavior. Feinman (1983) asserted that during the urbanization and industrial period of the United States, the "Cult of True Womanhood" extolled the four virtues of femininity: piety, purity, submissiveness, and domesticity (Carlen, 1982; Smith, 1990; Welter, 1973).

A woman deemed as "bad" usually had at least one of the following characteristics: she was indecisive and lacked "moral fortitude"; she was promiscuous; or she was irresponsible because not only was she loosening her own morals and values, but those of her mate and offspring as well (Hahn, 1980). Women involved in criminal activity were *worse* than men because they not only sinned, but they also loosened the moral constraints on men. Because women were born pure, female offenders were more depraved than male offenders. This justified the severe treatment of female criminals (Freedman, 1981). In the nineteenth century, however, prison reformers began to perceive female offenders as being "misguided" rather than evil—the archetypal "fallen women" (Pollock-Byrne, 1990; Rafter, 1990):

> Late nineteenth-century beliefs about the nature of women in general helped demote the female criminal from the status of a mature, if wicked, woman to that of an impressionable girl. As social class distinctions hardened within nineteenth-century society, middle-class women became "ladies," delicate and vulnerable creatures. No one expected factory girls or domestic servants to display all the attributes of the lady, but in discussions of "women's nature," traits associated with the lady were generalized to all women. Even the female offender was now depicted as frail and helpless, more a vulnerable child than a hard-hearted enchantress. (Rafter, 1990, pp. 49–50)

The history of women in prison illustrates how such philosophies regarding true womanhood influenced the treatment of female offenders.

In 1873, the Indiana Reformatory Institution for Women and Girls, the first all-female institution, was established (Rafter, 1990). The reformers advocated three goals that would result from the establishment of separate institutions for female inmates:

> First, sexual abuse and exploitation of female prisoners would be prevented. Second, the female staff would set a moral example of "true womanhood" for the female offenders to emulate. Finally, these staff would provide sympathetic counseling to their charges. (Zupan, 1992, pp. 297–298)

The primary ideological motivation for separate institutions, as well as separate treatment, was a policy heavily influenced by gender stereotypes:

> While the reformers obtained separate prisons for women under women administrators and staff, and improved treatment for incarcerated women, they reinforced and perpetuated stereotypical sex roles for women. Women's corrections would be matriarchy where "good" staff women, acting as mothers, would teach the inmate-children to be proper women in a simulated homelike environment in the prison. (Feinman, 1983, p. 19)

Female inmates were not considered "potential breadwinners." Rather, the primary goal of the reformers' movement was to mold these women into "good housewives," capable of establishing and maintaining a successful family life (Dobash, Dobash, & Gutteridge, 1986, p. 64).

Are these historical trends in any way reflected in the contemporary treatment of female prisoners? Some criminologists assert that the lack of understanding and negative stereotypes regarding women offenders are still prevalent today and continue to influence the treatment of women in prison (e.g., Belknap, 2001; Pollock-Byrne, 1990).

TODAY'S WOMEN PRISONERS

Vocational Programming for Women Prisoners

Pollock-Byrne (1990) outlined various types of programming for female inmates including maintenance of the institution, educational, vocational, rehabilitative, and medical care. In reference to vocational programs, Pollock-Byrne maintained that

> [o]rdinarily, women's institutions do not have the same number or kind of vocational programs as are offered at institutions for men. For years, the only vocational programs available were those that prepared women for domestic service, clerical work, or cosmetology. Although nothing is wrong with such programs, and they continue to exist at a number of institutions, many women have no interest in these fields or will need more lucrative employment upon release to support themselves and their children adequately. (p. 91)

Owen (1998) argued that it is essential to understand a woman's life prior to incarceration—her pathways to imprisonment—to appreciate her experiences while in prison. One facet of this is a woman's economic marginalization. Approximately 44% of women incarcerated in state prisons have not received a high school diploma. Female prisoners have had more difficult economic circumstances compared to male prisoners. Approximately 4 in 10 women were employed full-time prior to their arrest, compared to almost 6 in 10 men. Nearly 37% of female prisoners had incomes of less than $600 per month prior to their arrest, and almost 30% of these women reported receiving some type of state assistance. Furthermore, women under the supervision of criminal justice agencies were mothers of approximately 1.3 million children under the age of 18; almost 64% of these women were living with their children prior to incarceration (Greenfeld & Snell, 1999).

The negative influence of cultural stereotypes of women on vocational programming becomes problematic when one understands the economic, educational, and familial challenges experienced by these women. Some criminologists have argued that vocational programming for female inmates continues to reinforce traditional roles of women (Carlen, 1982; Carp & Schade, 1993; Chapman, 1980; Moyer, 1984).

Box 2.2

THE ECONOMIC MARGINALIZATION OF WOMEN PRISONERS

- Approximately 44% have not received a high school diploma.
- Approximately 4 in 10 were employed full-time prior to their arrest.
- Nearly 37% had incomes under $600 per month prior to their arrest.
- Almost 30% reported receiving some type of state assistance prior to their arrest.

In a study of state-run facilities for women, Weisheit (1985) reported that most of the 36 institutions surveyed provided programming that reinforced the traditional roles of women. This programming included sewing (n = 30), food services (n = 28), secretarial (n = 31), domestic work (n = 20), and cosmetology (n = 16). Some institutions, however, did offer some nontraditional programming including auto repair (n = 8), welding (n = 9), carpentry (n = 15), computer-related (n = 21), electrical (n = 15), and plumbing (n = 12) (p. 37).

Simon and Landis (1991) also conducted a survey of 40 state-run institutions for women. Compared to earlier studies (e.g., Arditi, Goldberg, Peters, & Phelps, 1973; Chapman, 1980; Glick & Neto, 1977), their study revealed that there had been an increase in vocational programs available for women. These increases, however, were not uniform across all institutions. Furthermore, the study revealed that vocational programs for women tended to reinforce traditional roles: clerical/office skills (n = 28); typing (n = 25); data processing (n = 19); cooking/domestic skills (n = 17); food service (n = 16); and cosmetology (n = 16). As with Weisheit's study, Simon and Landis (1991, p. 92) reported that some institutions did offer nontraditional programs such as computer programming (n = 10); building maintenance (n = 10); carpentry (n = 9); plumbing (n = 9); graphics/painting (n = 8); welding (n = 7); and masonry (n = 6).

In their article on programming for women and men in U.S. prisons, Morash, Haarr, and Rucker (1994) compared work and vocational training between female and male prisoners. They argued that there were disparities in work assignments, which often reflected common gender stereotypes. Women prisoners were overrepresented in janitorial and kitchen assignments, but compared to male inmates, they were underrepresented in farm and forestry, maintenance, and repair duties. In addition, the men were more often paid for this type of work when compared to women. When examining vocational programming, their study revealed that a higher proportion of male inmates were in auto repair or in construction and building trade programs; women were disproportionately represented in office training programs (pp. 204–206).

Criticisms of vocational programming for women in prison, however, have primarily focused on an organizational or institutional level (e.g., Carp & Schade, 1993; Chapman, 1980; Morash et al., 1994; Simon & Landis, 1991; Weisheit, 1985). In her study on stereotypes about vocational programming for female inmates, Schram (1998) emphasized issues pertaining to vocational programming on an individual or group level. Attitudes relevant to vocational programming for women prisoners were compared between four groups within a northeastern correctional facility: female inmates, peer counselors, correctional officers,

---

Box 2.3

TYPES OF VOCATIONAL PROGRAMS FOR WOMEN PRISONERS REPORTED IN TWO STUDIES

Weisheit (1985) *(N = 36 institutions)*		*Simon & Landis (1991)* *(N = 40 institutions)*	
Sewing	30		
Food services	28	Food services	16
Domestic work	20	Cooking/Domestic	17
Secretarial	31	Clerical/Office	28
		Typing	25
		Data processing	19
Cosmetology	16	Cosmetology	16
Auto repair	8		
Welding	9	Welding	7
Carpentry	15	Carpentry	9
Computer-related	21	Computer programming	10
Electrical	15		
Plumbing	12	Plumbing	9
		Graphics/Painting	8
		Masonry	6

Source: Adapted from R. A. Weisheit (1985), Trends in programs for female offenders: The use of private agencies as service providers. *International Journal of Offender Therapy and Comparative Criminology, 29,* 35–42; and R. J. Simon and J. Landis (1991), *The crimes women commit, the punishments they receive.* Lexington, MA: Lexington Books.

---

and prison program staff. The study revealed that the inmates had the most sexist attitudes toward women, and they were the least likely to perceive women prisoners' need to work. Schram (1998) argued that it is essential to realize that although nontraditional programs may be offered in various facilities, female inmates' participation and success in such programs may be contingent on their overall attitudes toward such programming. In this vein, just offering nontraditional programming may not be sufficient to ensure female inmates have ample opportunities to succeed (p. 262).

Another important facet to successful programming in correctional facilities is to enhance interactions between program staff and women inmates (Palmer, 1994, 1995). Koons, Burrow, Morash, and Bynum (1997) conducted a national study of correctional programs for women prisoners. The study revealed the importance of communication between staff and clients. Program participants emphasized the need for qualified and caring staff members, and the critical role of peer interactions. The program staff "served as role models to whom the women could related on an intimate level . . ." (p. 527), whereas peers placed pressure on other participants to maintain certain living standards integral to the program's success (p. 529).

Litigation Pertaining to Programming for Women Prisoners

One remedy for the lack of vocational programming for female inmates has been prisoner litigation. During the 1980s there was a relative increase in litigation from women prisoners (Herbert, 1985). By 1983, lawsuits involving the following programs were pending: education (approximately 13 states); prison industries (at least 8 states); and vocational programming (at least 12 states) (Ryan, 1984). An interesting aspect of this litigation pertaining to programming for women prisoners is the issue of parity—women receiving the same services and programs as those offered to men. Title VII of the 1964 Civil Rights Act focused specifically on eliminating racial, religious, and sexual discrimination in employment practices. Some litigation has been filed using the Title VII protections against discrimination to obtain parity in vocational, educational, and other services for female inmates.

In *Glover v. Johnson,* 478 F.Supp. 1075 ([E.D. Mich.] 1979), women incarcerated by the state of Michigan claimed that they were receiving inadequate medical services, education programs, vocational training, and law library services. Prison administrators were challenged to change these conditions that were comparably below those in male institutions. At the time the lawsuit was filed, the male prisoners had access to 22 vocational training programs; the female prisoners had access to 3 such programs. These programs were characteristically low-paying and stereotyped by sex. The female inmates did not have comparable opportunities to pursue a bachelor's or associate's degree, or to participate in apprenticeship programs, work release, and prison industries as did the male inmates. The plaintiffs argued that such inadequate services violated their constitutional rights under the Fourteenth Amendment and Title IX of the Education Amendment of 1972. The defendants, including the director of the Michigan Department of Corrections, argued that none of their policies violated the female inmates' constitutional rights. Any differences in programming were likely attributable to "economic efficiency"; providing similar services to female inmates was not economically feasible because of their relatively smaller numbers when compared to those of male inmates.

The court ruled that

> [t]he women inmates have a right to a range and quality of programming substantially equivalent to that offered the men, and the programs currently offered do not meet this standard. But additions to that program should be based on the interests and needs of the female inmates rather than short-sighted efforts to duplicate the programs offered at male institutions. While, in many cases, equal treatment may safely be achieved by requiring identical treatment, I do not believe that, in this case, identical treatment is either wise or just. (*Glover v. Johnson,* 1979, p. 1087)

The court emphasized the importance of not just improving the conditions of female inmates by providing them with the same programming opportunities as male inmates, but rather recognizing that the needs of female inmates may be different than those of their male counterparts.

In *Klinger v. Nebraska Department of Correctional Services,* 824 F.Supp. 1374 (1993), the inmates at the Nebraska Center for Women (NCW) claimed that the Nebraska Department of Corrections violated their rights as guaranteed by the Equal Protection Clause of the Fourteenth Amendment. The plaintiffs argued that the female inmates were not given "parity" of treatment, in violation of the Equal Protection Clause, because of sub-standard programs for or restricted access to employment and economic issues, educational and vocational training, the law library, and medical and dental services, as well as inadequate recreation and visitation. The court ruled that the Nebraska Department of Corrections had violated the constitutional rights of Nebraska's female inmates.

The argument for "equal" treatment of female and male inmates, however, cannot be addressed solely through mechanisms that assure "whatever the male inmates receive, the female inmates should also receive." Hunter (1984) elucidated the implications of advocating such legal remedies:

> Where policies differ between male and female institutions, there seems to be a general assumption that the policy in the male institution is most suitable, and therefore the women's institutions must adopt it. There seems to be a few instances of male institutions adopting policies of the female institution. Across-the-board policies are typically designed to accommodate the needs of the male institutions. Their effect on a women's prison can be difficult, devastating, and in some cases almost humorous. (p. 132)

In this vein, the term "gender neutral" is problematic. Criticisms of such program delivery emphasize the importance of understanding the social realities of female inmates. Fox (1984) reiterated these same concerns:

> Equality, whether a direct result of policy changes or the outcome of court-ordered adjustments, does not necessarily mean that some will be treated more kindly. It merely translates to the *same* (or similar) treatment given to male prisoners, who have constantly struggled for more humane treatment. Hence, the central issue seems to be whether or not the elimination of sexist policies will result in greater coercive restraint or social control. (p. 35)

DISCUSSION

This chapter has explored various aspects pertaining to vocational programming for female inmates within a conceptual framework that stereotypes are a form of social control. Specifically, if stereotypes of female inmates exist, do these stereotypes function as a mechanism of social control—whether on an individual, group, organizational, or institutional level—if they define as well as limit the behavior of women? As mentioned previously, Heidensohn (1985) argued that, "[o]f all the subtler constraints on the way women act and are supposed to act, few are more complex than the workings of social policies" (p. 191). Policy can be influenced, in a subtle as well as blatant manner, by stereotypes.

Furthermore, providing the opportunity for women prisoners to participate in nontraditional vocational programming does not necessarily ensure the success of such training. Schweber and Feinman's study (1985) on legislative action for women's prisons concluded that "the political reality of equality for women is that court orders and statutes are often just the beginning of the struggle" (p. 9). Litigation efforts, such as *Glover* and *Klinger,* may be just the beginning in an attempt to provide equitable opportunities in vocational programming for female inmates.

Rather, various issues need to be considered when exploring vocational programming for women prisoners, including the women prisoners' as well as correctional personnel's attitudes toward such programming, positive interactions and communication between the inmates and program staff, and appreciating the pathways of imprisonment that are a part of these women's lives.

DISCUSSION QUESTIONS

1. The author argues that traditional gender roles are replicated in prison vocational programs. Is this always negative? Why or why not?

2. Do you think that women prisoners would be more successful on release if they received training in nontraditional vocational programs, such as welding or automotive repair, compared to those who received more traditional training, such as clerical or cosmetology training? What are the strengths and weaknesses of both types of vocational programs for women prisoners?

WEBNOTES

Select a state corrections department that has a web site. Find information on vocational training for women prisoners. What kinds of training are offered? Does the site give information on the number of women who have completed the courses? Bring the information for the state to class for discussion.

REFERENCES

AMIR, D., & BINIAMIN, O. (1991). Abortion approval as a ritual of symbolic control. *Women and Criminal Justice, 3,* 5–25.

ARDITI, R. R., GOLDBERG, F., PETERS, J. H., & PHELPS, W. R. (1973). The sexual segregation of American prisons: Notes. *Yale Law Journal, 82,* 1229–1273.

BELKNAP, J. (2001). *The invisible woman: Gender, crime, and justice* (2nd ed.). Belmont, CA: Wadsworth/Thomson Learning.

BROWNMILLER, S. (1984). *Femininity.* New York: Fawcett Columbine.

CARLEN, P. (1982). Papa's discipline: An analysis of disciplinary modes in the Scottish women's prison. *Sociological Review, 30,* 97–124.

CARP, S. V., & SCHADE, L. S. (1993). Tailoring facility programming to suit female offenders' needs. In *Female offenders: Meeting needs of a neglected population.* Laurel, MD: American Correctional Association.

CHAPMAN, J. (1980). *Economic realities and the female offender.* Lexington, MA: Lexington Books.

CHUNN, D. E., & GAVIGAN, S. A. (1988). Social control: Analytic tool or analytic quagmire. *Contemporary Crises, 12,* 107–124.

COHEN, S. (1983). Social control talk: Telling stories about correctional change. In D. Garland & P. Young (Eds.), *The power to punish* (pp. 101–129). London: Heinemann.

DOBASH, R. P., DOBASH, R. E., & GUTTERIDGE, S. (1986). *The imprisonment of women.* Oxford: Basil Blackwell.

DUGGER, K. (1991). Social location and gender-role attitudes: A comparison of black and white women. In J. Lorber & S. A. Farrell (Eds.), *The social construction of gender* (pp. 38–59). Newbury Park, CA: Sage.

EDWARDS, A. R. (1989). Sex/gender, sexism and criminal justice: Some theoretical considerations. *International Journal of the Sociology of Law, 17,* 165–184.

ETZIONI, A. (1961). *A comparative analysis of complex organizations.* New York: Free Press of Glencoe.

FEINMAN, C. (1979). Sex role stereotypes and justice for women. *Crime and Delinquency, 25,* 87–94.

———. (1980). *Women in the criminal justice system.* New York: Praeger.

———. (1983). An historical overview of the treatment of incarcerated women: Myths and realities of rehabilitation. *The Prison Journal, 63,* 12–26.

FOX, J. (1984). Women's prison policy, prisoner activism, and the impact of the contemporary feminist movement: A case study. *The Prison Journal, 64,* 15–36.

FREEDMAN, E. (1981). *Their sisters' keepers: Women prison reform in America, 1830–1930.* Ann Arbor: University of Michigan Press.

GAGNE, P. L. (1992). Appalachian women: Violence and social control. *Journal of Contemporary Ethnography, 20,* 387–415.

GLICK, R. M., & NETO, V. V. (1977). *National study of women's correctional programs.* Washington, DC: U.S. Government Printing Office.

GREEN, E., HEBRON, S., & WOODWARD, D. (1987). Women, leisure and social control. In J. Hanmer & M. Maynard (Eds.), *Women, violence and social control* (pp. 75–92). Atlantic Highlands, NJ: Humanities Press International.

GREENFELD, L. A., & SNELL, T. L. (1999). *Women offenders.* Bureau of Justice Statistics Special Report. Washington, DC: U.S. Department of Justice.

HAHN, N. F. (1980). Too dumb to know better: Cacogenic family studies and the criminology of women. *Criminology, 18,* 3–25.

HEIDENSOHN, F. (1985). *Women and crime.* New York: New York University Press.

HERBERT, R. (1985). Women's prisons: An equal protection evaluation. *The Yale Law Journal, 94,* 1182–1206.

HUNTER, S. M. (1984). Issues and challenges facing women's prisons in the 1980s. *The Prison Journal, 64,* 129–135.

KLEIN, D. (1995). The etiology of female crime: A review of the literature. In N. J. Sokoloff & B. R. Price (Eds.), *The criminal justice system and women: Offenders, victims, and workers* (pp. 30–53). New York: McGraw–Hill.

KOONS, B. A., BURROW, J. D., MORASH, M., & BYNUM, T. (1997). Expert and offender perceptions of program elements linked to successful outcomes for incarcerated women. *Crime & Delinquency, 43,* 512–532.

LENGERMANN, P. M., & WALLACE, R. A. (1985). Theoretical overview: Social control. In P. M. Lengermann & R. A. Wallace (Eds.), *Gender in America: Social control and social change* (pp. 19–37). Englewood Cliffs, NJ: Prentice-Hall.

LORBER, J., & FARRELL, S. A. (1991). Principles of gender construction. In J. Lorber & S. A. Farrell (Eds.), *The social construction of gender.* Newbury Park, CA: Sage.

MANN, C. (1984). *Female crime and delinquency.* Birmingham: University of Alabama Press.

MORASH, M., HAARR, R. N., & RUCKER, L. (1994). A comparison of programming for women and men in U.S. prisons in the 1980s. *Crime & Delinquency, 40,* 197–221.

MOYER, I. L. (1984). Deceptions and realities of life in women's prisons. *The Prison Journal, 64,* 45–56.

OWEN, B. (1998). *"In the mix": Struggle and survival in a women's prison.* Albany: State University of New York Press.

PALMER, T. (1994). *A profile of correctional effectiveness and new directions for research.* Albany: State University of New York Press.

———. (1995). Programmatic and nonprogrammatic aspects of successful intervention: New directions for research. *Crime & Delinquency, 41,* 100–131.

POLLOCK-BYRNE, J. (1990). *Women, prison, & crime.* Pacific Grove, CA: Brooks/Cole.

POMEROY, S. B. (1975). *Goddesses, whores, wives, and slaves.* Pacific Grove, CA: Brooks/Cole.

RAFTER, N. (1990). *Partial justice: Women, prisons, and social control* (2nd ed.). New Brunswick, NJ: Transaction Publishers.

RYAN, T. A. (1984). *Adult female offenders and institutional programs: A state-of-the-art analysis.* Washington, DC: National Institute of Corrections.

SCHRAM, P. J. (1998). Stereotypes about vocational programming for female inmates. *The Prison Journal, 78,* 244–270.

SCHWEBER, C., & FEINMAN, C. (1985). The impact of legally mandated change on women prisoners. *Criminal Justice Politics and Women, 19,* 105–120.

SIMON, R. J., & LANDIS, J. (1991). *The crimes women commit, the punishments they receive.* Lexington, MA: Lexington Books.

SMART, C., & SMART, B. (1978). *Women, sexuality and social control.* London: Routledge & Kegan Paul.

SMITH, B. A. (1990). The female prisoner in Ireland, 1855–1878. *Federal Probation, 54,* 69–81.

WEISHEIT, R. A. (1985). Trends in programs for female offenders: The use of private agencies as service providers. *International Journal of Offender Therapy and Comparative Criminology, 29,* 35–42.

WELTER, B. (1973). The cult of true womanhood: 1820–1860. In J. E. Friedman & W. G. Shade (Eds.), *Our American sisters: Women in American life and thought* (pp. 96–123). Boston: Allyn and Bacon.

WEST, C., & ZIMMERMAN, D. H. (1991). "Doing gender." In J. Lorber & S. A. Farrell (Eds.), *The Social Construction of Gender.* Newbury Park, CA: Sage.

YOUNG, V. D. (1986). Gender expectations and their impact on Black female offenders and victims. *Justice Quarterly, 3,* 305–327.

ZUPAN, L. L. (1992). Men guarding women: An analysis of the employment of male correction officers in prisons for women. *Journal of Criminal Justice, 20,* 297–309.

3

Does Rehabilitative Justice Decrease Recidivism for Women Prisoners in Oklahoma?

Dennis R. Brewster, M.A.

❖

Almost from inception, correctional systems have struggled with the questions of the purpose of punishment, the place of rehabilitation in prison, and what the goal of imprisonment should be. Punishment for offenses is paramount in U.S. correctional history; it is recognized, however, that most offenders will be released eventually and therefore need some type of rehabilitation while incarcerated. Although various models have been in use at different times, depending on the political and social atmosphere, the rehabilitation model has been used consistently from the late 1800s to the present time, albeit in a diminished capacity (Morris, 1995). Even during periods of "getting tough on crime," correctional facilities and officials recognize their obligation to provide minimal tools to enable the prisoner, on release, to reenter society as a productive citizen.

Two key forms of rehabilitation have been used for women in correctional facilities: general education and vocational training. Education is viewed as a necessary tool for prisoners, as many are illiterate or at least severely undereducated (Lawrence, 1991, 1994). Additionally, vocational training (Vo–Tech) can provide necessary job skills that may be helpful to prisoners released back into their communities.

Primary, secondary, and higher education are the basic tools needed to help the offender become a productive citizen on release. Offenders have traditionally been one of the most undereducated groups in the United States (Egan, 1993; Lawrence, 1991, 1994). Education in prison can range from basic literacy programs to college degrees. The General Education Development or General Equivalency Diploma (GED), which provides the equivalent of a high school education, is one of the many educational programs offered and is considered one of the most valuable tools provided to prisoners.

Vo–Tech programs have been offered also to provide offenders with work-related skills in the hope that they can find meaningful employment when released. These programs have ranged from manual labor in apprenticeship positions early in correctional history to more education-based programs in the contemporary corrections period (Morris, 1995).

Thanks in large part to the feminist movement, reforms over the past 30 years mean female offenders are now provided—at least hypothetically—with many of the same educational opportunities afforded male offenders (Zedner, 1991, 1995). Not always equal, these programs at least recognize that the role of the female in society includes more than just mother and wife. Indeed, female offenders are frequently the sole providers for their family, as well as the only means of support for themselves.

This study will provide evidence of the current state of rehabilitation in the Oklahoma Department of Corrections. It will explore the effects of the two main forms of rehabilitation, GED and Vo–Tech, on female offenders. Knowledge gained from this study will be important to policy makers and correctional officials in better understanding the unique characteristics of female offenders.

EDUCATIONAL PROGRAMS AND RECIDIVISM

Educational programs have been, and continue to be, the mainstay of correctional rehabilitation. According to Kirshstein and Best, "Most states currently have some type of correctional education in most of their prisons" (1997, p. 1). Although much of the research suggests a beneficial effect on recidivism rates, the findings are somewhat mixed. For example, in the early 1970s, Martinson (1974) completed a study of all correctional programming (also see Lipton, Martinson, & Wilks, 1975) that indicated that in correctional settings, rehabilitation programs were not effective in reducing recidivism. Since that time, correctional officials and social scientists have begun to look at the effects of education on recidivism. Martinson's conclusions are not unique. In a study of the effectiveness of GED programs in North Carolina, researchers established that receiving a GED had no significant effect on recidivism (Johnson, Shearon, & Britton, 1974). Their work examined 14 factors ranging from the personal to the criminal. When controlling for these factors, rates of return to prison for those completing GED programs did not differ from the control group.

Other studies have found education to significantly effect recidivism. For example, a study of 1,983 prison releasees from 11 states indicated that those who had graduated from high school or had some college education experienced lower rates of recidivism than those who failed to complete high school. According to this study:

> Prisoners who had graduated from high school or had some college education had somewhat lower rates of rearrest, reconviction, and reincarceration than those who failed to complete high school. (Beck & Shipley, 1989, p. 5)

Similarly, Harer (1994) found that among 1,987 federal prison releasees, those who had less than a high school education had the highest rates of recidivism compared to those who had a high school education or had attended at least some college classes. He also found a relationship between the number of classes or courses taken and recidivism. Those who participated in education classes, but did not complete them, still tended to have lower recidivism than did those who attended no classes.

Gerber and Fritsch (1995) have suggested that educational programs do in fact have an inverse relationship with recidivism: ". . . prisoners exposed to education programs have lower recidivism rates than nonparticipants" (p. 123). In their analysis of educational studies, they found that the majority reported a significant relationship between education and recidivism. Similarly, the educational level of the offender is an important factor in successfully completing parole (Sims & Jones, 1997). Their work indicated that offenders who had a high school diploma or obtained a GED in prison recidivate less than those who do not.

It may be that educational level is less of a predictor than intelligence. In a study of the effects of IQ, Gendreau and colleagues (1996) found that offenders with higher IQ scores recidivate at lower rates than those with lower scores. Their research supported the work of Chown and Davis (1986), who had established that those with higher IQ scores in the Oklahoma Department of Corrections recidivated at a lower rate than Oklahoma prisoners with lower IQ scores. However, most research has focused only on the intelligence and education of male prisoners. When investigating the general effects of IQ, Gendreau and colleagues noted that, "[T]he data base was, regrettably, virtually silent on the prediction of recidivism among female offenders . . ." (p. 586).

Educational level appears to have benefits across a variety of offenses. Kernodle and colleagues (1995) found a relationship between recidivism and educational level when looking at "Driving while Impaired" offenders. In their study, the effects of their treatment group indicated a sharp decrease in recidivism with higher educational levels. In the control group, for example, those with a 9th to 12th grade level of education had a recidivism rate of 24% compared to only 13% recidivism rate for those in the treatment group.

Others suggest that the effect of education on recidivism is indirect. Batiuk and colleagues (1997) reported that a college education did reduce recidivism, but only because it facilitated finding a job postrelease, and this factor—employment—was the key to limiting new offenses.

Studies of recidivism in the Oklahoma Department of Corrections indicate that those with higher levels of education at the time of release have lower rates of return to prison. Likewise, Holley and Wright (1996) found that those who enter the department with higher levels of education had better chances of postrelease success than those who had lower levels of education.

Recidivism continues to occur at a relatively high rate, indicating the need to find programs that might work. A Department of Corrections report found that the overall recidivism rate for the department was about 26% after a 2-year period and almost 35% by 5 years postrelease (Oklahoma Department of Corrections, 1997). This data is supported by other recent studies of recidivism in the department. Holley and Brewster (1997) found that the overall recidivism rate for those released from January 1991 to December 1994 was 33.4%, and a recently released study by the Oklahoma Criminal Justice Research Center (Dean et al., 1998) put the recidivism rate at 28%; of offenders who did return, 89% were male and 11% were female.

Vo–Tech Programs

Vocational training has developed as a way to provide prisoners with marketable skills. The argument is that many prisoners lack usable job skills, and by providing vocational training during incarceration, the prison supplies the prisoner with "tools for success."

Thus, ". . . it appears that some form of vocational education programs is offered in virtually every major prison nationwide" (Khatibi & Grande, 1993, p. 152). Most of the extant literature on Vocational–Technical (Vo–Tech) programs, however, is based on men. The successful completion of Vo–Tech programs by women and its related effects are scarcely mentioned.

Gerber and Fritsch (1995) took exception to Lipton, Martinson, and Wilks' (1975) finding that "nothing works." In their analysis of 13 studies of Vo–Tech programs and their effect on recidivism, they reported that 10 of the studies did in fact indicate that "something works," to borrow Dilulio's (1991) phrase. What is most germane to success is that the education and skills are marketable (Winifred, 1996). However, more information is needed on the effectiveness of vocational training with female prisoners.

How Vo–Tech education programs are perceived by female prisoners is important to their success. One study of the perceptions of incarcerated women found that prisoners themselves favored the traditional, stereotypically female programs, such as nursing or child care, over nontraditional programs such as data entry, electrical, plumbing, or truck driving (Carlson, 1995). This finding suggests that female offenders have a traditionally "feminine" perspective, and part of the educational process of Vo–Tech may have to be helping female offenders identify their employment needs. Gina Hurley believes "[t]he primary mission of Vo–Tech is to educate, train and rehabilitate students. This often calls for a change in a person's belief system, especially about [herself] and what [she] is capable of being in society" (Winifred, 1996, p. 3).

In Oklahoma, the Vo–Tech programs are conducted in conjunction with the Oklahoma Department of Vocational and Technical Education (1998b). The *Skills Centers* operate in sixteen state-owned correctional facilities, one private prison, one state-operated juvenile center, and two private juvenile centers (Oklahoma Department of Vocational and Technical Education, 1998b).

Research on the efficacy of Oklahoma's Vo–Tech programs is mixed. One study by Chown and Davis (1986) indicated that Vo–Tech programs did not insulate offenders from recidivism, reporting that inmates who completed a Vo–Tech program reoffended at higher rates than noncompleters. On the other hand, Udell and Morton (1986) found that Vo–Tech completers did not recidivate as often as noncompleters. One problem with the Udell and Morton study was the lack of a clear-cut description of the comparison group. They found that Vo–Tech completers had a recidivism rate of 23.87%, while recidivism rate for the general population was between 45% and 77%. This is somewhat in question when compared to the work of others (see Holley & Brewster, 1997; Dean et al., 1998). The findings about the effects of Vo–Tech programs in Oklahoma are mixed; what is clear, however, is that little research has examined the relationships of Vo–Tech programs and recidivism rates among female prisoners. Considering that Oklahoma has the highest per capita female incarceration rate in the nation, this subject bears further investigation.

Female offenders.   Patriarchal ideology instills the belief that women are unequal to men and should be cared for as if they were property (Chesney-Lind & Shelden, 1998; Cockburn, 1991). Even though women have entered the workforce in great numbers and have in many cases been forced to step into the role of family provider, the ideological values of a patriarchal society still suggest it must protect the female. This ideology is often fostered and supported in the correctional setting (Chesney-Lind, 1998).

Gender roles, under a patriarchal system, also help determine the outcomes for women convicted of crimes. Women in correctional settings have been socialized to believe in the typical roles society suggests are appropriate for females. Many still believe these stereotypes (Schram, 1998; Carlson, 1995), which are also reinforced through rehabilitative efforts by correctional officials.

Early on, vocational education programs were seen as a way to "treat" the female offenders, but too often were designed to inculcate the domestic or stereotypical roles of women. Thus, many of the Vo–Tech programs centered on skills that might help the facility with maintenance problems such as laundry, tailoring, mending, flag making, and sewing (Winifred, 1996). These skills did not—and still do not—provide women with marketable skills necessary to support themselves.

Primary and secondary education programs have also been implemented in many female correctional institutions across the nation (U.S. Department of Education, 1998). These programs are designed to help the prisoner develop many educational skills that have been lost or perhaps were never acquired.

Today, in many institutions, women's needs are being examined in order to better prepare the offender for life in the "free world" (Clayton, 1997). Educational (Clayton, 1997; Winifred, 1996) and family needs (Sharp et al., 1998, 1999; Dressel, Porterfield, & Barnhill, 1998) call for better assessment of the problems facing women prisoners, who today are not only self-dependent, but also may be the sole provider for the family.

In Oklahoma, with the highest female incarceration rate in the United States, all female correctional facilities offer both Vo–Tech and educational programs. According to the Oklahoma Department of Corrections's 1997 year-end data (Oklahoma Department of Corrections, 1998b), 2,022 females were incarcerated (approximately 11% of the total prisoner population).

Within the correctional system in Oklahoma, women are afforded many of the same educational and vocational skills provided to male offenders. All female facilities offer some type of education based on offenders' requirements as well as Vo–Tech programs, based on the needs of the offender *and* availability of programs (Oklahoma Department of Corrections, 1998a).

According to the Oklahoma Department of Vocational and Technical Education (1998a, 1998c) web site, Vo–Tech programs for female offenders are limited to four programs. At the Mabel Bassett Correctional Center, a maximum/medium/minimum security facility for females, women may participate in "Business and Computer Technology" or "Horticulture/Landscape Management" programs (Oklahoma Department of Vocational and Technical Education, 1998a). At the Dr. Eddie Warrior Correctional Center for women, offenders are offered "Electronics Technology" or "Building Maintenance Technology" programs (Oklahoma Department of Vocational and Technical Education, 1998c).

Women prisoners are also provided several education programs including Adult Basic Education (ABE), General Equivalency Diploma (GED), and some "talkback" college courses (Oklahoma Department of Corrections, 1995; Holley & Brewster, 1996, 1997; Lawrence, 1991, 1994). The GED program, ". . . provides instruction in reading, math, language arts, social studies, spelling, and science for students functioning above the 8th-grade level. Prisoners passing the state GED exam are rewarded with a high school equivalency certificate" (Oklahoma Department of Corrections, 1995).

This chapter explores how completion of a GED or Vo–Tech program affected the recidivism rates of female offenders released from 1991 through 1994. Recidivism is defined as any return to the Oklahoma Department of Corrections, for any reason—a new crime or a technical violation of conditional release.

METHODOLOGY

Data for this study were a subset of data provided by the Oklahoma Department of Corrections (see Holley & Brewster, 1997). The original data set (N = 26,931) included all offenders released from the Oklahoma Department of Corrections between January 1991 and December 1994. For the purpose of this study, the data set was restricted to only female prisoners released during that time frame.

If the rehabilitation model is correct, GED and Vo–Tech educational programs should help insulate women from returning to prison. To test this concept, two hypotheses were formulated:

1. Women under the control of the Oklahoma Department of Corrections who obtained a GED program completion while incarcerated have longer survival times (the length of time the offender remains out of prison) than those who did not obtain a GED program completion.

2. Women under the control of the Oklahoma Department of Corrections who completed a Vo–Tech program while under the control of the department have longer survival times than those who did not complete a Vo–Tech program while incarcerated.

To test the first hypothesis, it was necessary to limit the analysis to those female prisoners who entered the Oklahoma Department of Corrections without a high school diploma or a GED (N = 1,233).[1]

The analysis for the second hypothesis compared those who completed a Vo–Tech program with those who did not (N = 2,811). Vo–Tech programs were assumed to help anyone who completed the Vo–Tech program equally, even those who came into the department with a high school diploma.[2]

The dependent variable was the number of months the individual stayed out of prison, or the survival (SURV) time. Because not all women had returned to the correctional setting, a cutoff date was set at July 1997, the time the data set was received. Survival (in months) was computed for all the women of the population. Because some of the women were released in 1991, it was possible for some women to have over 60 months of survival, especially if they had "survived" to the end of the study (July 1997). Using survival models, it was possible to use all of the women, including those who had reached the end of the study time, yet whose survival time was still undetermined.

Independent variables were an education (GED) and a vocational education (VOTECH). The GED program completion variable was coded 1 if prisoner had completed the GED program and 0 if the offender had not. The independent variable VOTECH was coded as 1 if the offender had completed a Vo–Tech program and 0 if the offender had not completed a program.

Control variables were used to ensure demographic, offense, and release variables were constant. The age (AGE) of the offender is an interval variable based on the years of age of the offender. The race of the offender (RACE) was a dummy variable, with black coded 1, all other groups coded 0. Marital Status (MARSTAT) was coded 1 if unmarried (divorced or single), all other categories coded 0.

Drug offense, number of prior incarcerations, and sentence length were controlled. The type of offense (OFFENSE) was coded 1 if the offender was convicted of the offenses of "Illegal Distribution of Controlled Substances" or "Illegal Possession of Controlled Substances" and 0 for all other offenses. Prior incarcerations (PRINCAR) was an interval variable measuring the number of prior incarcerations. The length of sentence (SENLEN) was measured in years.

Finally, two control variables were included. Type of release (RELTYPE) was coded 1 if the offender was "released to the streets," and 0 if the offender was released to probation or parole. The security at release (RELSEC) was coded 1 if the offender was released from an institution (a maximum, medium, or minimum security facility) and 0 if the offender was released from community supervision or probation.[3] Both models controlled for the demographic characteristics of the women. Population analyses were conducted, thus eliminating many of the problems of sampling from the population (Babbie 1995; Henry 1998).

FINDINGS

Analysis of the demographic variables (see Table 3.1) in the GED model indicated that the female population of the Oklahoma Department of Corrections was young, with 53% of the women under the age of 29. Table 3.1 also indicated that 34.5% were single. Blacks were heavily overrepresented, with 38.3% of the women black.

Table 3.1 includes 430 females (30.3%) incarcerated for drug offenses. When considering prior incarcerations, an overwhelming majority of the women were serving their first prison term (84.2%). A relatively small number were serving sentences of less than 1 year (105), whereas those serving sentences of 1 to 2.99 years and 3 to 5.99 years were almost equally divided (522 and 565 respectively). Sixteen percent of the females were serving 6 or more years. Almost 69% of the females were released from either community corrections or from probation or parole. The remaining 31% were released from an institution (maximum, medium, or minimum security). Slightly more than one third of the women were released to the street with no type of supervision.

Overall recidivism for the GED model is shown in Table 3.2. Analysis indicates that 73% of the female population released from custody between January 1991 and December 1994 had not returned to the Oklahoma Department of Corrections as of July 1997, when the data were collected. Of the 1,418 female offenders who entered the Oklahoma Department of Corrections without a high school diploma, only 180 completed a GED program while incarcerated. This suggests that only 12.7% of the eligible population either had or took the opportunity to participate (see Table 3.2).

The results of the logistic regression for the GED model are found in Table 3.3. In Model 1, age and race had statistically significant effects on recidivism; the marital status of the offender did not. The older the offender was, the more likely she was to have lower

TABLE 3.1   Description of the population of female offenders of the Oklahoma Department of Corrections

Variables	GED Model		Vo–Tech Model	
	Frequency	Percentage	Frequency	Percentage
AGE*				
13 to 19	72	5.1	125	4.0
20 to 29	682	48.5	1424	45.2
30 to 39	474	33.7	1170	37.2
40 to 49	141	10.0	340	10.8
50 and over	38	2.7	88	2.8
MARSTAT**				
Single	427	34.5	986	34.8
Married	519	42.0	1197	42.3
Divorced	291	23.5	648	22.9
RACE				
Asian	1	0.1	2	0.1
Black	543	38.3	1295	40.9
Hispanic	34	2.4	53	1.7
Native American	83	5.9	207	6.5
Other	4	0.3	9	0.3
White	753	53.1	1604	50.6
OFFENSE				
Other Offenses	696	49.1	1626	51.3
Drug	430	30.3	950	30.0
PRINCAR				
None	1194	84.2	2681	84.6
One	170	12.0	384	12.1
Two or More	54	3.8	105	3.3
SENLEN				
Less than 1 yr.	105	7.4	214	6.8
1–2.99 yr.	522	36.8	1240	39.1
3–5.99 yr.	565	39.8	1263	39.8
6–9.99 yr.	96	6.8	187	5.9
10 or more yr.	130	9.2	266	8.4
RELSEC				
Maximum	25	1.8	46	1.5
Medium	18	1.3	32	1.0
Minimum	398	28.1	808	25.5
Community	209	14.7	489	15.4
P&P	766	54.0	1792	56.5
RELTYPE				
Parole	458	32.3	1052	33.2
Probation	435	30.7	947	29.9
Discharge to Street	525	37.0	1171	36.9

*The variable AGE had 11 missing cases for GED and 23 missing cases for Vo–Tech.

**The variable MARSTAT had 181 missing cases for GED and 339 missing cases for Vo–Tech.

TABLE 3.2   Recidivism and GED/Vo–Tech Completions

Variables	GED Model		Vo–Tech Model	
	Frequency	Percentage	Frequency	Percentage
Recidivism				
No	1,044	73.6	2,328	73.4
Yes	374	26.4	842	26.6
Completions				
No	1,238	87.3	3,045	96.1
Yes	180	12.7	125	03.9

survival time. The variable race (RACE) had a positive relationship, suggesting that blacks survived longer without recidivating. There was not a statistically significant difference in those who were married and those who were divorced or single.

The offense category variables had mixed relationships with survival time. The offense (OFFENSE) of the offender was statistically significant, suggesting that women who had been sent to prison on a drug-related charge were likely to return to prison sooner than those incarcerated for other offenses, as was a prior incarceration (PRINCAR), indicating that those who had been incarcerated previously are more likely to survive longer without recidivating. The length of sentence (SENLEN) was not statistically significant.

TABLE 3.3   Cox's Survival Analysis of Survival on GED, Demographic, Offense, and Release Variables

Variables	Model 1		Model 2	
	Regression Coefficient	Odds Ratio	Regression Coefficient	Odds Ratio
GED	****	****	0.3959*	1.49
Demographic variables				
AGE	−0.0286*	0.97	−0.0302*	0.97
MARSTAT	−0.0989	0.91	−0.0969	0.90
RACE	0.4930*	1.64	0.4529*	1.57
Offense variables				
OFFENSE	−0.2645*	0.77	−0.2705*	0.76
PRINCAR	0.2398*	1.27	0.2429*	1.27
SENLEN	−0.0184	0.98	−0.0128	0.98
Release variables				
RELSEC	0.2477*	1.28	0.2739*	1.31
RELTYPE	−0.2464*	0.78	−0.2477*	0.78
−2 log likelihood	4566.26		4561.55	
N	1233		1233	

$p \leq .05$

Release security (RELSEC) of the offender was statistically significant, indicating that those released from an institution were likely to have longer survival times. The type of release (RELTYPE) was also a significant factor in the GED model. Those discharged to the street were more likely to return to prison sooner. The –2 Log Likelihood for this model is 4566.26.

In Model 2, the variable GED was added. The effect of GED was positive as predicted. The difference in the –2 Log Likelihood between Model 1 and Model 2 decreases, indicating that adding the variable GED to the demographic variables does explain more of the variance of the model. Women that came into the Oklahoma Department of Corrections without a high school diploma and completed a GED program had an odds ratio of 1.49, suggesting they have a better chance of staying out of prison for longer periods of time than those who did not complete a GED program. Figure 3.1 graphically depicts the results of the GED program.

When looking at the effect of the Vocational Education programs in Oklahoma, the analyses indicate that the demographic characteristics do not differ much from the population used in the GED model. The female population was, again, young, and 34% of the women in the population were single. Blacks were again overrepresented—1,295 of the women (40.9%). Thirty percent of the offenders had committed a drug-related offense. Prior incarcerations were almost identical to those in the GED model, and most of the Vo–Tech model females were serving from 1 to 6 years (78%) on their current charge.

The same recidivism patterns appear in this population as in the GED model. Only 26.6% of the group recidivated. Of the 3,170 female offenders, 125 (about 4% of the population) completed a Vo–Tech program while incarcerated (see Table 3.2). The results of the logistic regression for the Vo–Tech model are found in Table 3.4. Model 1 indicates that all of the demographic variables have statistically significant effects on recidivism, much like the GED model. The –2 Log Likelihood for this model is 3547.97.

In Model 2, VOTECH was added. However, the effect of VOTECH was different from the effect of GED completion. While the decrease in the –2 Log Likelihood (11434.99)

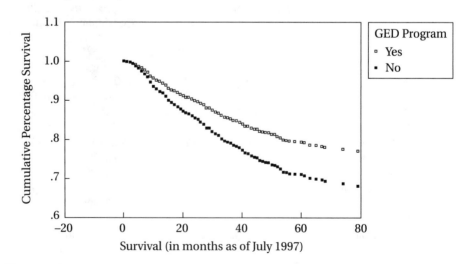

FIGURE 3.1   Effects of recidivism on survival times by GED program completions

TABLE 3.4 Cox's Survival Analysis of Survival on Vo–Tech, Demographic, Offense, and Release Variables

Variables	Model 1		Model 2	
	Regression Coefficient	Odds Ratio	Regression Coefficient	Odds Ratio
VO–TECH	****	****	–0.6098*	0.54
Demographic variables				
AGE	–0.0257*	0.97	–0.0251*	0.98
MARSTAT	–0.1774*	0.84	–0.1625*	0.85
RACE	0.5278*	1.70	0.5341*	1.71
Offense variables				
OFFENSE	–0.2838*	0.75	–0.2695*	0.76
PRINCAR	0.3175*	1.37	0.3067*	1.36
SENLEN	–0.0172	0.98	–0.0229	0.98
Release variables				
RELSEC	0.2194*	1.24	0.1842*	1.20
RELTYPE	–0.0842	0.92	–0.0922	0.91
–2 log likelihood	11448.24		11434.99	
N	2811		2811	

$p. \leq .05$

indicates significance and explains more of the variance than does Model 1, this finding indicates that those women who completed a Vo–Tech program were likely to have shorter survival times than those who did not complete a Vo–Tech program. Figure 3.2 graphically depicts the results of the Vo–Tech program.

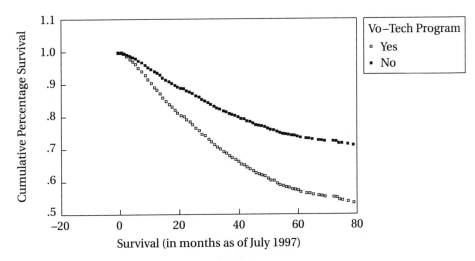

FIGURE 3.2 Effects of recidivism on survival times by Vo–Tech program completions

DISCUSSIONS AND CONCLUSIONS

The findings indicated above, although not without problems, are very instructive and enlightening. The demographic findings support the work of others (see Holley & Brewster, 1997) and follow very closely with the national trends (Greenfeld & Harper, 1990). The female population of the Oklahoma Department of Corrections is young and overrepresented with African Americans. Whereas the total African American population in Oklahoma is about 8%, the prison population is about 38% African American.

Oklahoma's female prison population includes many drug offenders, most of whom are serving their first term in prison. These findings are indicative of the still continuing "War on Drugs" being waged across the country. Many see the benefit of locking up those who are selling or using drugs, but one of the unintended consequences of the "War on Drugs" is the large numbers of felons it creates who have prison records and thus have harder times finding employment upon release. With the female population this may be even a bigger problem because many of the women are also single parents. A careful look at the effects of the "War on Drugs" continues and these findings should support efforts to explore alternative forms of punishment, especially for women.

The effect of age needs explanation. One possibility is that prisoners may suffer the effects of losing family and friendship connections on the outside. One of the keys to success in the "real world" is a support system (people who will help the offender) once released (Hairston, 1990; Light, 1993). As offenders get older they lose contact with many of the people (family and especially friends) who might provide employment opportunities and other forms of support needed to survive. Without that support, many releases fail to make the transition to a nonoffending lifestyle. This makes it even more imperative that effective programs be developed.

The shortened survival time for those convicted of drug offenses appears logical. Typically, offenders commit drug crimes for money in order to support a habit or, in the case of some female offenders, to support their family. When released, if women cannot find gainful employment and if they are the sole providers for themselves and their families, they may find the lure of the money involved in the drug market too appealing to resist.

The two major findings of the study indicate that the rehabilitative model does not always work in the way it was intended. On the positive side, a GED does provide the offender with some insulation from returning to prison, and is linked to longer periods of survival in comparison to those without a GED or high school diploma. These findings support earlier research (Chown & Davis, 1986; Holley & Brewster, 1997). The key point may be that GED completions level the playing field a little more for the ex-offender, compared to those who do not complete a GED. Across the United States, a high school education is seen as a minimum requirement for many types of meaningful employment, and these findings indicate that those who complete the program are better equipped to survive in the "free world" than those who do not.

The second key finding of the study—that those who complete a Vo–Tech program have lower survival times—is more troubling for the rehabilitative model. It supports one earlier study in Oklahoma (Chown & Davis, 1986) but is in opposition to the findings of Udell and Morton (1986).

One possible explanation of these findings may come from Winifred (1996). She believes that skills taught by Vo–Tech programs must be *marketable* when the prisoner is released. Careful examination of the programs might establish whether the women are actually employable in the Oklahoma job market once released. Another explanation along the same lines is that women may experience "rising expectations" while incarcerated. In other words, instructors and administrators may give the prisoner false or unrealistic hopes of being able to compete in the job market. When the prisoner is released she experiences the "real world" and finds that she is in competition with others with the same skills but no criminal record, thus hindering her ability to use the skills provided.

This study indicates the need for further research in the areas of education and Vo–Tech programs within the Department of Corrections in Oklahoma. It does not provide many of the facts needed to convincingly determine the value of either program—GED or Vo–Tech—but it does raise very valid concerns.

What is needed is a comprehensive study of the effectiveness of these programs. From conversations held with male and female offenders, it is apparent that offenders do not like programs in prison. If the short-term offender does not participate in a correctional program because it reinforces a feeling of over-control on the part of the prison, a selection effect may well be in play. It is very disturbing that in both programs studied, women were not utilizing the programs much. In any case, a careful examination of the complete Vo–Tech program is in order, from the selection process through release, and a suitable follow-up period.

As with research in general, this study raises further questions that must be investigated. Limitations of the data prohibit a clear-cut evaluation of the programs. Detailed longitudinal research could perhaps answer many of the important questions raised by this study. Do women actually find employment resulting from their increased education while incarcerated? Are the Vo–Tech programs offered in the Oklahoma Department of Corrections marketable for the ex-offender on release? How does being the single mother of small children hinder or prohibit the ex-offender from using the skills she has acquired in the correctional system?

This study explores the results of education for women in the Oklahoma Department of Corrections. However, comparison to male offenders is missing. Further research could explore the effects of GED and Vo–Tech programs for men as well to determine if there are gendered differences in the program effects. Women are being offered programs, but do they have the same success as men's programs?

These questions must be asked and answered to determine the success of these programs. If, for example, research indicates that those who are released cannot find work in the field they were trained for, the programs need to be altered to better fit the needs of both the incarcerated offender and the business community. A longitudinal study could also determine if the women receive the instruction close enough to time of release for their skills to be usable on release and still fresh in the women's minds.

The Oklahoma Department of Corrections is meeting the minimum requirements of the rehabilitation model of corrections for women. However, this study is only the first step in discovering how that rehabilitation is being undertaken. It is evident from this research that the Vo–Tech programs in Oklahoma's prisons for women are not working as would and should be expected. There are problems that can only be solved by closer scrutiny of the programs.

However, the results for the educational GED programs in the Oklahoma Department of Corrections are positive. Thus, the department might explore ways to enroll more women in the programs. The low number of women released with a GED completion suggests a need for recruiting in the educational arena. Additionally, longitudinal research on the graduates of the programs could provide useful answers to further enhance the program and make the ex-offenders even more marketable.

In a climate of ever changing models and moods of correctional thinking, this study indicates the continuing need to provide at least the minimum education opportunities to offenders. The findings for the GED program indicate that it does increase the survival times of prisoners, whereas the Vo–Tech program needs evaluation and retooling to provide the necessary tools to the women released from the Oklahoma Department of Corrections system.

DISCUSSION QUESTIONS

1. Why do you think the percentage of women prisoners who complete a GED program while incarcerated is low in comparison to the number without a high school education?

2. The author states that Oklahoma offers four different types of vocational training for its women prisoners. What other types of vocational programs might be beneficial for women offenders?

3. How might single-parent status affect the likelihood of recidivism, even in cases in which the parent obtains vocational training?

WEBNOTES

Read the Federal Bureau of Prisons report by Saylor and Gaes (1995) found online at http://www.bop.gov/orepg/prep95.html and their *Forum* article (Correctional Service of Canada) at http://www.csc-scc.gc.ca/text/pblct/forum/e08/e081d.shtml.

Their findings indicate that training did not reduce recidivism rates for women. Furthermore, they note in the second report that women, although they are overall less likely to recidivate, return to prison more quickly than do men if they do recidivate. How would this chapter explain these findings?

NOTES

1. All female offenders without a high school diploma or GED (1,433) were used for the demographic analysis where variables were available, but only 1,233 women were used for the survival analysis due to missing data on some variables.
2. Again, all female offenders, 3,033 women, were used for the demographic analysis, but only 2,811 women were used for the survival analysis due to missing data on some variables.
3. Cox's regression was used to analyze the data. Survival analysis indicating the survival (SURV) in months of the offender was censored by the recidivism (RECID) measure. Recidivism was determined and coded as 1 if the inmate had returned and 0 if the inmate had not returned. Because many of the women had not recidivated at the time the data was collected, it was necessary to use the Cox Regression survival method.

REFERENCES

BABBIE, E. (1995). *The practice of social research* (7th ed.). Belmont, CA: Wadsworth.

BATIUK, M. E., MOKE, P., & ROUNDTREE, P. W. (1997). Crime and rehabilitation: Correctional education as an agent of change—a research note. *Justice Quarterly, 14* (1), 167–180.

BECK, A. J., & SHIPLEY, B. E. (1989). *Recidivism of prisoners released in 1983.* Washington, DC: U.S. Department of Justice, Bureau of Justice Statistics NCJ-116261.

CARLSON, J. R. (1995). Usefulness of educational, behavior modification, and vocational programs as perceived by female inmates. *Journal of Offender Rehabilitation, 22* (3/4), 65–76.

CHESNEY-LIND, M. (1998). The forgotten offender. *Corrections Today, 60* (7), 66–73.

CHESNEY-LIND, M., & SHELDEN, R. G. (1998). *Girls, delinquency, and juvenile justice.* Belmont, CA: Wadsworth.

CHOWN, B., & DAVIS, S. (1986). *Recidivism among offenders incarcerated by the Oklahoma Department of Corrections: A survival data analysis of offenders received in 1985 and 1986.* Oklahoma City: Oklahoma Department of Corrections.

CLAYTON, S. L. (1997). Longtime educator takes teaching to a new level. *Corrections Today, 59* (6), 70.

COCKBURN, C. (1991). *In the way of women: Men's resistance to sex equality in organizations.* Ithaca, NY: ILR Press.

DEAN, N. S., HILL, C. M., SCHMITZ, K. R., CONNELLY, M., & O'CONNELL, P. (1998). *Recidivism in Oklahoma.* Oklahoma City: Oklahoma Criminal Justice Resource Center, Division of the Oklahoma Department of Public Safety.

DILULIO, J. J. (1991). *No escape: The future of American corrections.* New York: Basic Books.

DRESSEL, P., PORTERFIELD, J., & BARNHILL, S. K. (1998). Mothers behind bars: Incarcerating increasing numbers has serious implications for families and society. *Corrections Today, 60* (7), 90–94.

EGAN, S. (1993). Correctional education: An important tool in corrections. *Corrections Today, 55* (1), 10, 30.

GENDREAU, P., LITTLE, T., & GOGGIN, C. (1996). A meta-analysis of the predictors of adult offender recidivism: What works? *Criminology, 34* (4), 575–607.

GERBER, J., & FRITSCH, E. J. (1995.) Adult academic and vocational correctional education programs: A review of recent research. *Journal of Offender Rehabilitation, 22* (1/2), 199–242.

GREENFELD, L. A., & HARPER, S. M. (1990). *Women in prison.* Washington, DC: U.S. Department of Labor, Bureau of Justice Statistics. NCJ-127991.

HAIRSTON, C. F. (1990). Family ties during imprisonment: Important to whom and for what? *Journal of Sociology and Social Welfare, 18,* 87–104.

HARER, M. D. (1994). *Recidivism among federal prison releasees in 1987: A preliminary report.* Unpublished report to the Federal Bureau of Prisons. Washington, DC.

HENRY, G. T. (1998). Practical sampling. In L. Bickman & D. J. Rog (Eds.), *Handbook of applied social research methods* (pp. 101–126). Thousand Oaks, CA: Sage.

HOLLEY, P. D., & BREWSTER, D. R. (1996). The women at Eddie Warrior Correctional Center: Evaluation of a data set. *Journal of the Oklahoma Criminal Justice Research Consortium 3,* 107–114.

———. (1997). An examination of the effectiveness of GED Programs within the Oklahoma Department of Corrections. Manuscript submitted for publication.

HOLLEY, P. D., & WRIGHT, D. E., JR. (1996). Oklahoma's regimented inmate discipline program for males: Its impact on recidivism. *Journal of the Oklahoma Criminal Justice Research Consortium, 2,* 58–70.

JOHNSON, D. C., SHEARON, R. W., & BRITTON, G. M. (1974). Correctional education and recidivism in a woman's correctional center. *Adult Education, 24* (2), 121–129.

KERNODLE, J. R., JOYCE, C. C., & FARMER, R. J. (1995). Changing the behavior of DWI first offenders. *Journal of Offender Rehabilitation, 22* (3/4), 113–128.

Kʜᴀᴛɪʙɪ, M., & Gʀᴀɴᴅᴇ, C. G. (1993). Correctional education planning: A systematic approach to vocational training. *Journal of Correctional Education, 44* (3), 152–155.

Kɪʀsʜsᴛᴇɪɴ, R., & Bᴇsᴛ, C. (1996). *Survey of state correctional educational systems: Analysis of data from 1992 field test U.S. Department of Education, Office of Correctional Education.* Washington, DC: Pelavin Research Institute.

———. (1997). *Using correctional education data: Issues and strategies.* U.S. Department of Education, Office of Correctional Education. Washington, DC: Pelavin Research Institute.

Lᴀᴡʀᴇɴᴄᴇ, D. (1991). An exploratory study of the perceived role of the student–teacher relationship within correctional education. Doctoral dissertation, Department of Education, University of Oklahoma, Norman.

———. (1994). Inmate students: Where do they fit in? *Journal of the Oklahoma Criminal Justice Research Consortium, 1,* 43–51.

Lɪɢʜᴛ, R. (1993). Why support prisoners' family-tie groups? *The Howard Journal, 32* (4), 322–329.

Lɪᴘᴛᴏɴ, D., Mᴀʀᴛɪɴsᴏɴ, R., & Wɪʟᴋs, H. K. (1975). *The effectiveness of correctional treatment.* New York: Praeger Press.

Mᴀʀᴛɪɴsᴏɴ, R. (1974). What works? Questions and answers about prison. *The Public Interest, 35,* 22–54.

Mᴏʀʀɪs, N. (1995). The contemporary prison: 1865–present. In N. Morris & D. J. Rothman (Eds.), *The Oxford history of the prison: The practice of punishment in Western society* (pp. 227–259). New York: Oxford University Press.

Oᴋʟᴀʜᴏᴍᴀ Dᴇᴘᴀʀᴛᴍᴇɴᴛ ᴏғ Cᴏʀʀᴇᴄᴛɪᴏɴs. (1995). *Program description guide.* Oklahoma City: Oklahoma Department of Corrections.

———. (1997). *Recidivism.* Available at http://www.doc.state.us/docs/recidivi.htm.

———. (1998a). *Eddie Warrior Correctional Center.* Available at http://www.doc.state.ok.us/docs/alfacdes.htm#EWCC.

———. (1998b). *Inmate profile for end of month population for June 1998.* Available at http://www.doc.state.ok.us/Profiles/pop0698.htm.

Oᴋʟᴀʜᴏᴍᴀ Dᴇᴘᴀʀᴛᴍᴇɴᴛ ᴏғ Vᴏᴄᴀᴛɪᴏɴᴀʟ ᴀɴᴅ Tᴇᴄʜɴɪᴄᴀʟ Eᴅᴜᴄᴀᴛɪᴏɴ. (1998a). *Mabel Bassett Vo-Tech Skills Center.* Available at http://www.okvotech.org/scss/mbvtsc.htm.

———. (1998b). *Partnering for success.* Available at http://www.okvotech.org/scss/partner.htm.

———. (1998c.) *Taft Vo–Tech skills center.* Available at http://www.okvotech.org/scss/tbtsc.htm.

Sᴄʜʀᴀᴍ, P. J. (1998). Stereotypes about vocational programming for female inmates. *The Prison Journal, 78* (3), 244–270.

Sʜᴀʀᴘ, S. F., & Mᴀʀᴄᴜs-Mᴇɴᴅᴏᴢᴀ, S. T. (2001). It's a family affair: Incarcerated women and their families. *Women & Criminal Justice, 12.*

Sʜᴀʀᴘ, S. F., Mᴀʀᴄᴜs-Mᴇɴᴅᴏᴢᴀ, S., Sɪᴍᴘsᴏɴ, D. B., Bᴇɴᴛʟᴇʏ, R. E., & Lᴏᴠᴇ, S. R. (1998). Gender differences in the impact of incarceration on children and spouses of drug offenders. *Oklahoma Criminal Justice Research Consortium, 4.*

———. (1999). Gender differences in the impact of incarceration on children and families of drug offenders. In M. Corsianos & K. Train (Eds.), *Interrogating Social Justice,* (pp. 217–246). Toronto: Canadian Scholars' Press.

Sɪᴍs, B., & Jᴏɴᴇs, M. (1997). Predicting success or failure on probation: Factors associated with felony probation outcomes. *Crime & Delinquency, 43* (3), 314–327.

Uᴅᴇʟʟ, D. S., & Mᴏʀᴛᴏɴ, F. P. (1986). Vocational–technical education: A successful tool for rehabilitation. Unpublished manuscript, University of Oklahoma, Norman.

U.S. Dᴇᴘᴀʀᴛᴍᴇɴᴛ ᴏғ Eᴅᴜᴄᴀᴛɪᴏɴ. (1998). *Mission.* Office of Correctional Education. Available at URL: http://inet.ed.gov/offices/OVAE/OCE/mission.html.

Wɪɴɪғʀᴇᴅ, M. (1996). Vocational and technical training programs for women in prison. *Corrections Today 58* (5) 168–171.

ZEDNER, L. (1991). *Women, crime, and custody in Victorian England.* New York: Oxford University Press.

————. (1995). Wayward sisters: The prison for women. In N. Morris & D. J. Rothman (Eds.), *The Oxford history of the prison: The practice of punishment in Western society* (pp. 329–361). New York: Oxford University Press.

ZOOK, J. (1993, December 15). Amendment would cut off Pell Grants to prisoners, despite data that show education cuts recidivism. *The Chronicle of Higher Education.*

Part III

Health Care for Women Prisoners

In this section, we examine some of the issues, as well as available programs, related to the health needs of women in prison. Histories of abuse, economic marginalization, and substance abuse all contribute to making women prisoners a population with special health needs.

In Chapter 4, Tammy Anderson surveys the history of health care for women prisoners. She discusses the litigation that has occurred, pointing out that much of it has failed to benefit women in prison. She examines how the current punitive penal philosophy and tight budgets have worked against women prisoners' health needs. Anderson then explores the problems women prisoners confront in accessing health care, focusing on specific areas of concern such as obstetrical and gynecological needs, sexually transmitted diseases, and mental illness.

Chapter 5 discusses the special needs of pregnant prisoners. Diane Daane stresses the importance of a holistic perspective on pregnancy, understanding how a pregnant woman's preincarceration history affects her health. She addresses a wide range of issues common to pregnant prisoners, including homelessness, abuse histories, substance abuse, and mental health problems. She then provides a focused examination of how the prison environment itself can affect pregnancy. Finally, she turns to the birth outcomes experienced by women in prison. Daane skillfully argues that incarceration may have both positive and negative affects on birth outcomes because of the high-risk lifestyle of many inmates prior to their arrests.

The final portion of the chapter examines a range of policies and programs. Daane again presents the reader with a more holistic perspective. She stresses the need for a range of other services beyond basic medical care for pregnant prisoners. Three model programs are then examined.

Chapter 6 is devoted to an increasing threat to women's health in prison: HIV infection and AIDS. Barbara Zaitzow and Angela West outline the known extent of the problem for the reader, pointing out that nonstandardized testing policies quite likely result in nondetection of many infected women. They then present an in-depth perspective of what it is like to be HIV-positive in prison. The voices of women prisoners themselves make this compelling reading. Issues addressed range from mandatory testing policies to confidentiality and housing concerns. Other problems, such as failure to receive adequate treatment, the need for appropriate prevention programs, and compassionate release policies, are examined. Zaitzow and West stress the importance of woman-based programs that satisfy the different educational needs of women prisoners in regard to HIV/AIDS. Existing programs are reviewed with special attention paid to those that have promise.

4

Issues in the Availability of Health Care for Women Prisoners

Tammy L. Anderson, Ph.D.

❖

The considerable escalation of women sent to prison during the latter twentieth century finally helped shift attention to the various social, economic, and medical needs of this historically neglected population (Belknap, 2000). Among the concerns, and the focus of this chapter, are the numerous medical and mental health problems of today's female inmates. In comparison to their free-world female and incarcerated male counterparts, female prisoners suffer more frequent and serious disease, illness, and injuries (Maruschak & Beck, 1997) and require and utilize more medical and mental health services (Lindquist & Lindquist, 1999; Young, 1998). However, correctional institutions continue to offer inadequate health care to women inmates and far less than what they offer male offenders (Acoca, 1998; Marquart et al., 1997).

A familiar justification explains the disparity; female inmates compose a much smaller portion of the correctional population than men and, thereby, warrant less attention and investment by the state. Given the considerable growth of the female inmate population, this explanation seems increasingly problematic. The historical neglect of women prisoners, coupled with the massive increase in women's incarceration, make the health care problem increasingly salient as we begin the twenty-first century. However, two other matters promise to exacerbate it. First, the disproportionate prevalence of chemical dependencies among female offenders likely elevates physical and mental health problems, since drug offenders commonly report far more health problems than those without them. Second, and unlike their male counterparts, females' complicated reproductive systems introduce other types of health problems that current correctional systems are ill prepared to handle. For instance, female prisoners suffer considerable gynecological disease (e.g., cervical cancer), and terminal or chronic health problems such as HIV and hepatitis.

This chapter explores the health problems of female inmates, and the correctional system's responses to them, both in the past and today. It is critically important to review the health care needs of women prisoners and the correctional system's ability to deliver adequate services. Currently, a continuum of care is missing to successfully treat female prisoners' medical and mental health problems. Persistent inattention to the unique health care profiles of women offenders will likely result in an inadequate understanding of important illnesses and conditions not commonly experienced by men. Continued indifference would have great economic and social costs to society for current and future generations. According to Acoca (1999), "health care issues are a tsunami and will engulf social justice, and many other issues, within the next decade if we don't make them a priority" (p. 35).

WOMEN'S HEALTH PROBLEMS

If one were to rank population subgroups by the seriousness of their health problems, female prisoners would be located near the top of the ladder. There is a growing body of literature that shows female inmates are likely to have more serious health problems than both women and men in the general U.S. population, largely because of chronic poverty, lack of access to medical care, and problematic lifestyles. However, their health problems are also worse than those of incarcerated males (Maruschak & Beck, 1997), and the research reported below shows women often have less access to services for treatment and prevention than men.

Physical Health Problems

The differences between men's and women's physical health conditions and needs are considerable, discrepancies observable in both free society and in correctional systems. For instance, Verbrugge (1985, 1986) and Verbrugge and Wingard (1987) found that women in the general U.S. population have higher morbidity rates from acute conditions, nonfatal chronic disease, and short-term disability than men. Furthermore, the reproductive events of pregnancy, childbirth, and puerperium give women unique morbidity risks not experienced by men. Women's more complex reproductive systems increase their risks of other female-specific disorders (neoplasms of breast/genitals and genitourinary disorders, such as menstrual and menopausal symptoms). However, even when reproductive conditions are removed from consideration, significant sex differences persist in acute condition incidence and discretionary (nonhospital) health care. Compared to men, women have higher illness rates for infective disease, respiratory and digestive system conditions, injuries, ear diseases, headaches, genitourinary disorders, and skin and musculoskeletal diseases.

Nonfatal chronic diseases are also more prevalent among women. They experience twice the rate as men for varicose veins, constipation, gallbladder and thyroid conditions, chronic enteritis and colitis, anemia, migraine, and chronic urinary diseases. Women also experience more psychological distress (anxiety, depression, guilt, and conflicting demands) on a day-to-day basis and over their lifetimes than do men (Verbrugge, 1985, 1986; Verbrugge & Wingard, 1987).

The research above shows women in the general population suffer more physical and mental health problems than men. The same pattern holds true when comparing women and men prisoners (Maruschak & Beck, 1997). For instance, drug use and abuse are quite prevalent in the correctional system; however, rates tend to be higher among female prisoners than among males (Graham & Wish, 1994; Fagan, 1994; Mieczkowski, 1994; Morash et al., 1998). Moreover, women inmates are more likely than men to report IV drug use (Decker, 1992) and having HIV (Wees, 1996; Maruschak, 1997). The higher rates of substance abuse and HIV among female prisoners are, once again, due to higher percentages of women prisoners with drug offenses, many of whom exchange sex for drugs (Inciardi, Lockwood, & Pottieger, 1993).

Mental Health Problems

Marquart et al. (1997) has argued that deinstitutionalization of mental health facilities in the 1980s has contributed to the growth of mental illness among the U.S. prison population. Estimates show the percentage of inmates, both male and female, with mental health problems grew in the latter part of the twentieth century. Similar to research findings on physical health problems, women inmates' mental health problems are both more frequent and more serious than their male counterparts' (Harlow, 1999). For instance, 24% of men and 36% of women inmates surveyed reported receiving mental health services at some point in their lives, whereas 10% of men and 20% of women reported receiving them since admission (Harlow, 1999). Also, women inmates more often disclosed obtaining professional counseling or being prescribed medications for mental illness, both in their lifetimes and since entering prison (Harlow, 1999). There is considerable evidence that women are prescribed more psychotropic drugs than males (Morris, 1987; Ross & Fabiano, 1986) and that medical staff frequently prescribe these drugs without checking to determine if the inmate is pregnant (McHugh, 1980), a dangerous practice.

The leading mental illness problems among female prisoners include physical and sexual abuse/trauma, victimization, depression, and substance abuse (Young, 1998). Dual substance abuse and mental health problems are very prevalent among male and female prisoners, but more so for females (Henderson et al., 1998). Women in prison have higher rates of substance abuse, antisocial personality disorder, borderline personality disorder, post-traumatic stress disorder, and histories of sexual and physical abuse than their male counterparts. Women frequently engage in self-mutilating behaviors, are verbally abusive, and report numerous suicide attempts (Henderson et al., 1998).

HISTORICAL LOOK AT HEALTH CARE AVAILABILITY FOR WOMEN PRISONERS

Throughout time, correctional institutions have struggled to provide adequate health care and other types of health services to women prisoners. Neglect is partly responsible for the current deficit of care. Health care in women's prisons received little attention, because female offenders were a small percentage of the prison population. Professional medical groups considered them to be the responsibility of the correctional system, and prison officials were paternalistic—prioritizing making inmates "good" women and girls over treating their health care problems (Wilson & Leasure, 1991). Also, early penal reform policies embraced an ideology that women inmates must have been sick or pathological to fall from grace and participate in such male activities as crime. Although this belief encouraged treatment and rehabilitation, there was little medical care (physical and psychological) to be found. Rafter (1985, 1989), a leading expert on the history of women's incarceration, has noted that early custodial institutions often warehoused women along with men and exposed them to horrible conditions. Sexual abuse was rampant, and babies born in prison often died. Prison conditions remained like this for women until recently, when inmate-initiated lawsuits in the 1970s and early 1980s, like *Todaro v. Ward* (1977) began to force improvements.

The Todaro case was the first major court case to challenge women's access to health care in correctional institutions. It charged the entire health care delivery system in a New York women's prison was unconstitutional, arguing women had no real access to medical care or to physicians. Afterward, the American Medical Association, American Public Health Association, and the American Correctional Association became involved in creating standards for health care in prisons (Resnick & Shaw, 1981).

Other legal reforms have followed, but haven't necessarily benefited inmates. For instance, *Estelle v. Gamble* (1976) established that all prisons have an obligation to provide for serious medical needs. However, a complainant arguing he or she didn't get mandated services would have to prove it was due to deliberate indifference on the part of prison officials. This difficult standard has made it easy for prisons to avoid medical responsibility (Marquart et al., 1997) by giving them lots of room to maneuver on health care. Later, *Brown v. Beck* (1980) held that medical care provided to prisoners need not be "perfect or even very good," it only has to be "reasonable." Some have argued decisions such as these send the message that prisoners should expect a standard of health below that of the general population (Maeve, 1999).

Today, there are more legal precedents and options to enable inmates to obtain care for their health problems. Typically, cases are filed citing violations in the Eighth and Four-

---

Box 4.1

LITIGATION AND LAWS RELATED TO THE HEALTH CARE OF WOMEN PRISONERS

- *Estelle v. Gamble* (1976) created obligation for all prisons to provide for serious medical needs of their inmates.
- *Todaro v. Ward* (1977) argued that women had no real access to medical care or physicians in the New York penal system.
- *Brown v. Beck* (1980) ruled that medical care provided to prisoners needed only to be "reasonable."
- Federal Prisoner Co-Payment Act (1999) required prisoners to pay for part of their health care while incarcerated.

teenth amendments. Unfortunately, the opportunity to initiate legal action against correctional systems does not appear to be equally available to males and females. According to Morris (1987) and Rafter (1989), women have more restricted access to legal libraries and higher levels of security than men in general. Even today, and despite enduring significantly worse prison conditions and treatment, females are far less apt than males to file lawsuits against prisons and jails (Rafter, 1989; Van Ochten, 1993).

HEALTH CARE AVAILABILITY AND UTILIZATION FOR WOMEN PRISONERS

Scholarly work in the area of health care for women prisoners has trickled in slowly over the course of the twentieth century. Although more is now known about the health problems and medical needs of women prisoners, far less is known about the services prisons offer, or how they are utilized by inmate populations. A major obstacle has been the absence of data collection by prisons to keep track of proffered services. Currently, most prisons do not keep adequate medical records that would allow any systematic or thorough assessment of the health problems and utilization of services by men and women prisoners. For instance, research (American Correctional Association, 2000a) shows eighteen states collected medical data on inmates in paper form, and only five had electronic information. The federal correctional system is an exception and will be discussed in detail below. The absence of data on health care availability and utilization will likely create obstacles to effective and cost-efficient provisions for inmate health care needs. Further constraints on availability and utilization pertain to ideology and economic considerations. These are reviewed below, in addition to the limited research on use of health care services by women prisoners.

Ideology and Economics in the Current Climate

Health care availability in prisons is constrained by numerous ideological and economic considerations. Ideologically, policymakers, correctional personnel, lawmakers, and the general public have been unsupportive of equitable standards of health care for inmates and have endorsed legal action to keep things that way, as already discussed. Moreover, unlike the free-world's increasing focus on preventative care, the notion of "health" in prisons is often synonymous with the absence of disease. "Real" health problems are seen as those with visible symptoms (Maeve, 1999).

Economically, prison costs have exploded thanks to punitive crime control policies that have increasingly led to the incarceration of men and women who are more and more unhealthy (e.g., drug abusers). According to the American Correctional Association's (2000b) study of health care services offered by state departments of corrections, 41% of corrections systems spent a staggering $83 billion, or 10% of their 1997 budgets, on inmate health care. Nearly all reported health care costs had increased since the previous year, citing the expanding prison population as a primary reason (American Correctional Association, 2000b). The study also substantiated the above research showing women's health care costs exceed those of men's.

Correctional officials are all too aware that health care costs will continue to escalate and consume an ever larger portion of their budget as long as government officials continue

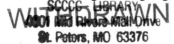

their commitment to extant drugs and crime policies. At least three major options are being considered to contain these costs, some of which promise to disproportionately disadvantage women. First is the increased use of fee-for-service or co-payment charges to cut down "illegitimate" inmate medical requests, curtail lawsuits, and raise funds to help cover expenses. The notion here is that such policies as the Federal Prisoner Co-Payment Act of 1999 will significantly reduce inmates' health care costs. However, because women inmates are more isolated from family and friends and typically have fewer financial resources than their male counterparts, prison co-pay policies may penalize them disproportionately and ultimately adversely affect their health. Second, as the correctional system moves toward increased privatization, women's facilities may be left behind because of their higher operational expense (e.g., greater health care costs and need for specialized services) and their inability to raise as much capital as men's prisons. The future of health care in prisons, therefore, will likely witness considerable change to foster cost containment. Finally, the trend toward telemedicine (Abt Associates, 1999) promises to cut prison health care costs by allowing doctors to assess health problems via advanced computer technologies, which means medical professionals can diagnose and treat inmates without having to travel to isolated medical facilities. Prisons also save financially and reduce security problems by not having to transport as many inmates out of institutions for medical care. Three issues promise to make prisons housing female inmates increasingly dependent on telemedicine services: (1) women's prisons are often more remote than men's, (2) women's prisons are more lacking in medical facilities, and (3) women inmates have more health care needs that require expensive outside contractors (e.g., childbirth). If the current situation is a valid indicator of what is to come, women inmates will continue to be disadvantaged in their access to health care in comparison to their male counterparts.

To their credit, today's correctional systems offer many more health care services than they did in the past, with more and more testing and treatment required at admission and available to inmates at their request. However, although testing and treatment at admission has increased, there remains no standard policy for routine physical exams on intake in state correctional facilities, although the Bureau of Prisons has recently implemented such a policy, discussed a little later. At the state level, for instance, the content of physical exams and the medical professionals who conduct them vary considerably by institution. Research (Reed & Lyne, 1997) has shown that the quality of health care in prisons varies

---

Box 4.2

TELEMEDICINE AND WOMEN PRISONERS

Spiraling costs for prisoner medical care are moving the correctional system toward having medical professionals diagnose and treat prisoners via computer technologies. Women prisoners are candidates for increasing use of telemedicine because of:

- Remote locations
- Lack of existing medical facilities
- Greater need for expensive outside contractors for childbirth and other health issues

greatly; much is poor quality, the low standard reinforced by the legal statutes discussed above. Doctors are often not adequately trained to do the work they face, and some fail to meet basic ethical standards. Generally, the major physical health services offered are for tuberculosis, STDs, HIV/AIDS, and obstetrics and gynecology. These services partially correspond to the types of health problems reported by inmates, but leave important gaps as well: cardiovascular problems, asthma, drug and alcohol treatment, problems especially salient for women prisoners (Young, 1998; Covington, 1998).

In general, prisoners utilize medical services at higher rates than the noninstitutionalized population (Suls, Gaes, & Philo, 1991; Twaddle, 1976). Higher utilization rates stem from inmates having greater health care needs, health care in prison being free or inexpensive, visits to clinics representing a break in prison routines, and prison clinics functioning as a safe niche for troubled inmates (Marquart et al., 1997). The most frequent medical visits are for pain stemming from a new illness. Research also shows that women in the general U.S. population utilize more health services, such as physician's offices, outpatient clinics, and hospitals, than do men. Reasons for this include that women are generally (1) more sensitive to physical discomforts, (2) more apt to label symptoms as physical illnesses, (3) more likely to possess gender traits (nurturing and compassion) that often influence them to seek medical care more often, and (4) more likely to take follow-up actions regarding a health problem and to take them sooner (see also Verbrugge 1985, 1986 for a review). The paragraphs below describe the types of medical services offered to women inmates and how they utilize them.

Services for Women

A review of existing studies reveals at least three main problems in accessibility to health care services for female prisoners. First, access to treatment for both general and drug-related health problems is seriously limited. Today, female prisoners still receive fewer health care services in comparison to their male counterparts (Acoca & Austin, 1996). Second, the health care provided to women is often mediocre. It is largely an attempt to "catch up," in that considerable effort is often necessary to raise women's health status to legally acceptable levels (Maeve, 1999). Third, women inmates have reported prison medical professionals are underskilled, often withhold medical care, and show little care or concern for them or their needs (Fletcher, Shaver, & Moon, 1993). In fact, most lawsuits filed by women in prison are for complications in receiving medical services (Belknap, 2000).

These deficiencies in health care accessibility exist despite data confirming greater health care needs among women inmates. For instance, Young (1998) found 5% of women

---

Box 4.3

PROBLEMS IN THE HEALTH CARE OF WOMEN PRISONERS

- Access to treatment is limited.
- Care is often mediocre.
- Prison medical professionals are often underskilled.

inmates received no medical services during a 4-month study period, while 50% received them twice a month, and 25% received them four times or more per month. These utilization patterns indicate that a substantial portion of female prisoners have numerous and serious medical problems (Young, 1998). In a thorough study of gender differences in prison health care utilization, Lindquist and Lindquist (1999) found women reported being in good health less often than men; the number of health care visits was considerably higher among female inmates; women were more likely than men to perceive access to health care as difficult and more often believed their quality of care was low as compared to what men received. The authors concluded gender was the stronger predictor of health problems and service utilization. The paragraphs below describe accessibility and utilization data on three of the most important health care issues of women prisoners today: pregnancy and gynecology, HIV and infectious disease, and mental illness (including substance abuse).

Pregnancy and gynecology.   In 1995, approximately 10,800 women were pregnant at the time of incarceration. However, the number of live births in prison was considerably smaller due to miscarriage, abortion, prison transfer policies, and so on (Acoca, 1998). In general, pregnant women are transported to outside medical facilities to give birth, because their correctional institutions are not medically equipped to safely provide such services. These birth transports often result in numerous medical and mental health complications; that is, security precautions increase a woman's risk of injury and stress (Young, 1998; Belknap, 2000). Moreover, after giving birth, women inmates are confronted with the loss of their child. The problem of left-behind children of incarcerated women is one of the biggest issues confronting crime policymakers today. To date, very few prisons allow newborns to remain with their mothers and, instead, typically place them with family or in foster care immediately or shortly after birth (American Correctional Association, 2000a; Belknap, 2000).

Currently, nearly all of the correctional systems housing women contain provisions for prenatal and postpartum treatment. However, such treatments are not typically required and are only offered at an inmate's request or if clinically indicated. Shortcomings in prisons' response to pregnancy-related health issues are the result. Acoca (1998) identified deficiencies in the availability of prenatal and postnatal care, prenatal nutrition, allocation of methadone maintenance, educational support for childbirth and rearing, and preparation for mother–child separation after birth. Also, she found many women who delivered babies were not given medication to dry up their breast milk, causing them to suffer painful breast engorgement.

Health care for gynecological needs is equally problematic. Annual gynecological exams are not routinely performed at admission or at any other time during incarceration. However, an American Correctional Association (2000a) study found OB/GYN services, prenatal and postpartum care, mammography, and Pap smears were available on request at nearly all institutions housing women offenders. Fewer facilities provided counseling about women's reproductive health. Provisions for such health care needs must be researched, because there is currently no information at the state and local level on when and how these services are allocated. The Federal Bureau of Prisons has recently taken the lead in creating policy for meeting the health care needs of female inmates (see below). It is too early to tell if state and local prisons and jails will follow suit. However, the exploding costs of medical care and the growth in the number of women in prison may stymie planned progress.

HIV and infectious disease.   HIV and other infectious diseases exact a considerable price on the general health care system and on those of corrections institutions as well. Funding widespread screening for the illnesses pales in comparison to providing treatment. Despite these costs, prisons today are increasingly testing for HIV/AIDS, hepatitis B and C, and tuberculosis at intake. The American Correctional Association (2000a) found that mandatory HIV testing is conducted (both men's and women's) at intake in 23 states and that a few also have follow-up testing 6 months later. HIV testing of women prisoners is conducted at intake in roughly half of facilities surveyed and/or by inmate or physician request in the others. Most prisons treat HIV-positive inmates with medications during their prison stay and will provide them with a limited supply (e.g., 30 to 60 days worth) after release. Most also refer newly released HIV-positive inmates to community resources to obtain additional medications. Specific data on treatments provided to women suffering HIV, STDs, or TB are currently not available, although the Centers for Disease Control has implemented a data collection system for correctional institutions recently.

Mental illness.   To reiterate, the leading mental health problems of female prisoners are substance abuse, trauma from physical and sexual abuse, and depression. In a study of state facilities, Morash, Bynum, and Koons (1998) found women inmates were more likely to be addicted to drugs and to have mental illnesses than their male counterparts. However, women inmates report numerous complaints about obtaining services for mental illness, including no one with appropriate credentials or diagnostic skills, not enough mental health professionals at the facility, and inadequate monitoring of psychotropic drug administration (Acoca, 1998). Furthermore, an increasingly common correctional response to women's mental health needs is prescription of antidepressants (Maeve, 1999).

CONCLUSION

This chapter has attempted to outline the major health care issues facing women prisoners and correctional facilities today. Comparisons were offered between women inmates' health care status and those of the general U.S. population and of male inmates. Evidence consistently shows women inmates suffer greater and more serious health care problems than the other groups and will present considerable demand for services from correctional institutions in the future, most often for pregnancy and OB/GYN problems, HIV, STDs, and mental illness. Despite their greater medical needs, women inmates receive fewer services and inferior care in comparison to others. Restrictions on legal resources and correctional adaptations or solutions to escalating medical costs promise to preserve this disparity well into the current century.

Recently, a glimmer of hope emerged at the federal level to reverse this situation. Although the majority of women inmates are housed in state institutions, those housed in federal prisons will likely encounter greatly improved services. For instance, the Federal Bureau of Prisons (BOP) for women provides each inmate with a complete medical exam—in other words, a medical history and a physical exam—within 30 days of admission. The physical exam includes gynecological and obstetrical history, serology for syphilis, complete blood count, urinalysis, infectious disease tests (if clinically indicated), TB screening, and an audiogram (if clinically indicated). Pregnancy tests and Pap smears are also available, but are not required for all women. Immunizations are offered for measles, mumps, and rubella (Morash, Bynum, & Koons, 1998).

The BOP has taken a leading role in meeting the specific health care needs of women inmates. They now adhere to the American College of Obstetrics and Gynecology standards for yearly exams, such as mammography. Females over 50 years old are given a complete physical exam every two years (Morash, Bynum, & Koons, 1998).

New concerns about women inmates have resulted in increased mental health services as well. For instance, the BOP has added more drug treatment slots of lasting duration (i.e., 6-month therapeutic communities) at 5 of the 11 BOP facilities. Currently, all BOP facilities have some form of psychological counseling—most often group therapy for things such as values development, recovery and sexual abuse, smoking cessation, gambling addiction, and anger management.

Although these preventive-care policies promise to reverse "symptoms-based" treatment and restore women's health to adequate levels, other improvements are still needed for the treatment of existing conditions, both chronic and acute. For instance, the BOP has few medical personnel on staff at women's institutions and still contracts out with private agencies for many inmate services. Women prisoners from all over the country suffering serious and long-term health problems are sent to Texas's medical referral center for females to receive inpatient hospitalization or long-term medical care. This typically means isolation from family and friends during an already stressful time.

Although provisions for meeting the health care needs of incarcerated men and women increased considerably during the twentieth century, the ability of correctional institutions to address and contain inmate health problems has been undercut by crime control policies that increasingly send unhealthy individuals to correctional institutions. As with many other social problems, relevant government systems have been forced to improve their health care services as a result of these crime control policies and court-based reforms following inmate-initiated legal action. Although the goal of correctional systems might be to bring inmates' health up to legally mandated standards, experts outside the system argue for vast improvements leading to a coordinated continuum of care (e.g., trained medical professionals to provide preventive care, adequate treatment for medical and mental health conditions, and coordinated community follow-up upon release) for health care needs. Absent this approach, complications are likely to result in the future, as released inmates seek high-cost medical services (e.g., emergency rooms) or disregard them completely. With continued research and additional efforts to tie findings into policy and interventions, scholars dedicated to this issue can help guide the country toward continual improvements in the future. Let us hope that such efforts are forthcoming.

DISCUSSION QUESTIONS

1. What are some of the problems faced by pregnant women in prison? What are some solutions or alternatives to issues surrounding medical care for pregnant prisoners?

2. Should prisons require mandatory HIV-testing of all entering prisoners? If so, what types of medical and mental health treatment would then be needed? If not, what are the long-term implications for women prisoners?

3. The author points out that prescription of antidepressants is an increasing response to women prisoners' mental health needs. What are the pros and cons of this type of approach?

4. At a minimum, what types of health and mental health programs are needed in women's prisons?

WEBNOTES

Read the report on women prisoner's health in California prisons at http://www.ucsc.edu/currents/99-00/08-02/stoller.htm and the state of Florida's health plan for women in prison (http://www.dc.state.fl.us/pub/females/opplan/health.html). Compare these two. Bring your comparison to class for discussion of effective programs for women's health care needs in prison.

REFERENCES

ABT ASSOCIATES. (1999). *Telemedicine can reduce correctional health care costs: An evaluation of a prison telemedicine network.* Washington, DC: U.S. Department of Justice.

ACOCA, L. (1998). Diffusing the time bomb: Understanding and meeting the growing health care needs of incarcerated women in America. *Crime and Delinquency, 44* (1), 49–70.

———. (1999). Getting healthy, staying healthy: Physical and mental health/substance abuse. In *National symposium on women offenders* (pp. 33–36). Washington, DC: U.S. Department of Justice.

ACOCA, L., & AUSTIN, J. (1996). *The hidden crisis: Women in prison.* San Francisco: National Council on Crime and Delinquency.

AMERICAN CORRECTIONAL ASSOCIATION. (2000a, October 25). Inmate health care—Part 1. *Corrections Compendium,* (10), 1–34.

———. (2000b, November 25). Inmate health care—Part 2. *Corrections Compendium,* (11), 1–35.

BELKNAP, J. (2000). *The invisible woman: Gender, crime, and justice* (2nd ed.). Belmont, CA: Wadsworth.

COVINGTON, S. (1998). Women in prison: Approaches in the treatment of our most invisible population. *Women and Therapy, 21* (1), 141–155.

DECKER, S. (1992). *Drug use forecasting in St. Louis: A three-year report* (NCJRS 14281). Rockville, MD: National Institute of Justice.

DUKE, K. (2000). Prison drugs policy since 1980: Shifting agendas and policy networks. *Drugs: Education, Prevention and Policy, 7* (4), 393–408.

FAGAN, J. (1994). Women and drugs revisited: Female participation in the cocaine economy. *Journal of Drug Issues, 24* (1–2), 179–226.

FEDERAL BUREAU OF PRISONS. (1998). *A profile of female offenders.* Washington, DC: U.S. Department of Justice.

FLETCHER, B. R., SHAVE, L. D., & MOON, D. (1993). *Women prisoners: A forgotten population.* Westport, CT: Praeger.

GRAHAM, D., and WISH, E. (1994). Drug use among female arrestees: Onset, patterns and relationships. *Journal of Drug Issues, 24* (1–2), 315–330.

HARLOW, C. W. (1999). *Prior abuse reported by inmates and probationers.* Washington, DC: Bureau of Justice Statistics.

HENDERSON, D., SCHAEFFER, J., & BROWN, L. (1998). Gender-appropriate mental health services for incarcerated women: Issues and challenges. *Family Community Health, 21* (3), 42–53.

INCIARDI, J. A., LOCKWOOD, D., & POTTIEGER, A. E. (1993). *Women and crack cocaine.* New York: Macmillan.

LINDQUIST, C., & LINDQUIST, C. (1999). Health behind bars: Utilization and evaluation of medical care among jail inmates. *Journal of Community Health, 24* (4), 285–303.

KRANE, K., PEARCE, M., & MILES, J. R. (1998, April). Managing correctional health care. *Corrections Today,* 122–126.

McHUGH, G. A. (1980). Protection of the rights of pregnant women in prisons and detention facilities. *New England Journal on Prison Law, 6* (2), 231–263.

MAEVE, M. K. (1999). Adjudicated health: Incarcerated women and the social construction of health. *Crime, Law, and Social Change, (31),* 49–71.

MARQUART, J. W., MERIANOS, D. E., HEBERT, J. L., & CARROLL, L. (1997). Health condition and prisoners: A review of research and emerging areas of inquiry. *The Prison Journal, 7* (2), 184–208.

MARUSCHAK, L. (1997). *HIV in prisons 1997.* Washington, DC: Bureau of Justice Statistics.

MARUSCHAK, L. and BECK, A. (1997). *Medical problems of inmates 1997.* Washington, DC: Bureau of Justice Statistics.

MIECZKOWSKI, T. (1994). Experiences of women who sell crack: Some descriptive data from the Detroit ethnography project. *Journal of Drug Issues, 24* (1/2), 227–248.

MORASH, M., BYNUM, T., & KOONS, B. (1998). *Women offenders: Programming needs and promising approaches.* Washington, DC: U.S. Department of Justice, National Institute of Justice.

MORRIS, A. (1987). *Women, crime, and criminal justice.* Oxford: Basil Blackwell.

RAFTER, N. (1985). *Partial justice: Women in state prisons, 1800–1935.* Boston: Northeastern University Press.

———. (1989). Gender and justice: The equal protection issues. In L. Goodstein & D. MacKenzie (Eds.), *The American Prison* (pp. 89–109). New York: Plenum Press.

REED, J., & LYNE, M. (1997). The quality of health care in prison: Results of a year's programme of semi-structured inspections. *British Medical Journal, 315,* 1420–1424.

RESNICK, J., & SHAW, N. (1981). *Prison Law Monitor, 3* (3/4), 57, 68, 83, 89, 104, 115.

ROSS, R. R., & FABIANO, E. A. (1986). *Female offenders: Correctional afterthoughts.* Jefferson, NC: McFarland.

SULS, J., GAES, G., & PHILO, V. (1991). Stress and illness behavior in prison: Effects of life events, self-care attitudes, and race. *Journal of Prison and Jail Health, 10* (2), 117–132.

TWADDLE, A. C. (1976). Utilization of medical services by a captive population: An analysis of sick call in a state prison. *Journal of Health and Social Behavior, 17,* 236–248.

VAN OCHTEN, M. (1993). Legal issues and the female offender. In *Female offenders: Meeting the needs of a neglected population* (pp. 31–36). Laurel, MD: American Correctional Association.

VERBRUGGE, L. M. (1985). Gender and health: An update on hypotheses and evidence. *Journal of Health and Social Behavior, 26* (3), 156–182.

———. (1986). Role burdens and physical health of women and men. *Women and Health, 11* (1), 47–77.

VERBRUGGE, L. M., & WINGARD, D. L. (1987). Sex differentials in health and mortality. *Women and Health, 12* (2), 103–145.

WEES, G. (1996). Inmate Health Care Part II: Women in prison accounting for an increasing percentage of HIV cases. *Corrections Compendium, 21* (11), 102–123.

WILSON, J. S., and LEASURE, R. (1991). Cruel and unusual punishment: The health care of women in prison. *Health Care Issues, 16* (2), 32–39.

YOUNG, D. (1998). Health status and service use among incarcerated women. *Family Community Health, 21* (3), 16–31.

5

Pregnant Prisoners

Health, Security, and Special Needs Issues

Diane M. Daane, Ph.D.

❖

The effect of incarceration on pregnancy and the needs of pregnant inmates are a growing concern as the population of incarcerated females increases. Some argue that incarceration has a negative impact on pregnant inmates and their fetuses; others believe that inmates may receive better prenatal care, nutrition, and housing than if they remained on the streets during their pregnancy. Although pregnant inmates theoretically are not exposed to alcohol, illicit drugs, physical and sexual abuse, and unhealthy living conditions in prison, possible past exposure must be addressed. This review of the literature explores the special health care, case management, nutritional, and mental health needs of pregnant prisoners.

The increase in the female prison population calls for programming that fits the unique needs of female offenders, particularly appropriate care and programs for pregnant inmates. About 6% of women in prison in 1991 entered the institution pregnant (Snell & Morton, 1994). High-risk pregnancies and births are expected to increase annually as the female offender population grows (Ross & Lawrence, 1998), and yet the majority of prison programs for pregnant inmates are inadequate at best.

The lack of obstetric and prenatal health care for pregnant prisoners is obvious, but their needs do not end there: A significant number of specialized programs are necessary. A healthy birth outcome and the parenting ability of the mother are essential to the well-being of the child, and to the reintegration of the mother back into society. To be effective, programs for pregnant inmates must address their educational needs, such as how to prepare for a healthy pregnancy and delivery, parenting skills, and child development. Social programs helping mothers-to-be face issues of separation and child placement must be addressed. Treatment must also be available for pregnant inmates with mental health and substance abuse problems.

PRIOR RISK FACTORS RELEVANT TO INMATE PREGNANCY

Risks Based on Previous Lifestyle

Because prisoners are often incarcerated for only a portion of their pregnancy, their living conditions prior to incarceration are an important consideration when planning for their care. Many factors of an inmate's preincarceration lifestyle can have a negative impact on pregnancy and birth outcomes. Homelessness, poverty, drug and alcohol use and abuse, and physical and sexual abuse are important issues relevant to planning comprehensive prenatal care for incarcerated women.

Homelessness.   Many women who are sentenced to prison have been disenfranchised on the streets prior to their incarceration. Even the most basic necessities of life may not have been available to them. Nearly 20% of mothers in state prison reported being homeless at some time during the year immediately preceding their incarceration (Mumola, 2000), twice the rate reported by fathers. Women in federal prison appear to have had a better situation in the community, with only 5% of them reporting periods of homelessness prior to their imprisonment (Mumola, 2000). Homelessness has been associated with multiple health problems that may have an adverse effect on pregnancy and birth outcomes (Martin, Rieger, Kupper, Meyer, & Qaqish, 1997). Living on the streets is often dangerous and unsanitary, with little hope for proper nutrition. Poor nutrition during pregnancy often leads to poor pregnancy outcomes, including low birthweights (Martin, Rieger, et al., 1997).

Poverty.   Half of all mothers in state prison reported being unemployed in the month before their arrest, and over half of all mothers in state prison reported incomes of less than $600 that month (Mumola, 2000), coming from wages, welfare, Social Security benefits, child support, and illegal sources. Many of these women were not only trying to support themselves on this level of income, but were also trying to care for their children. Over 64% of incarcerated mothers reported that their children were living with them, and over one-third had been living alone with their children in the month before their arrest (Mumola, 2000).

Drug and alcohol use.   Mothers in state prison reported more serious drug use histories than reported by incarcerated fathers. Over 65% of mothers in state prison used drugs in the month before their arrest; over 85% reported ever using drugs (Mumola, 2000). About half of women in state prison described themselves as daily users of drugs; approximately the same number reported that they had been using alcohol, drugs, or both at the time of their current offense (Greenfeld & Snell, 1999). Nearly one third of all women and all mothers in state prison reported committing the crime for which they were incarcerated in order to obtain drugs or money for drugs (Greenfeld & Snell, 1999; Mumola, 2000).

Because the fetal brain develops tolerance and dependence on drugs or alcohol, if the mother is dependent, the fetus is too. Mothers and their fetuses experience withdrawal together. This is a particularly critical issue since fetal withdrawal has a high risk of mortality (Ryan & Grassano, 1992). Healthy pregnancies and birth outcomes for addicted women require specialized prenatal care and treatment.

Physical and sexual abuse.   Over half of females in state prison and nearly 40% of females in federal prison reported being physically or sexually abused at some point in their life before incarceration (Harlow, 1999). The abuser was most often a spouse or boyfriend. One in four women in state prison were physically abused and one in ten were sexually abused before age 18, a level of abuse considerably higher than that of the general population (Harlow, 1999). Physical and sexual abuse during pregnancy may have serious consequences for the health of the woman and the fetus, and increase the risk of a poor birth outcome (Martin et al., 1997; Sable, Fieberg, Martin, & Kupper, 1999).

In addition to the risk factors posed by possible abuse during pregnancy, physical or sexual abuse prior to pregnancy also have negative consequences on the woman's health during pregnancy, and on the birth outcome. Violence also adversely affects a victim's mental health, which may have an impact on pregnancy, fetal health, and birth outcomes (Sable et al., 1999), and her risk of becoming a substance abuser. Of the women in state prison reporting abuse, 89% reported using illegal drugs regularly; of those not reporting abuse, 65% had used illegal drugs regularly (Harlow, 1999). Nearly 60% of abused female inmates reported drinking alcohol regularly, compared to 38% of women who were not abused. Abused state prisoners were also more likely to have been using alcohol or drugs at the time of their offense (Harlow, 1999). Victims of violence are less likely than nonvictims to quit abusing alcohol or drugs during their pregnancy (Sable et al., 1999).

Violence has been found to be fairly common in the lives of poor prenatal care patients, but it may be more severe among female inmates and is more likely to include both physical and sexual violence (Sable at al., 1999). Sable and colleagues found that "prisoners represent a more severely victimized group who are at extremely high risk of the multiple poor health outcomes that have been associated with severe trauma" (p. 395), and negative health and birth outcomes may be greater in women who have suffered from both sexual and physical violence than those who experienced physical violence only.

Health

Because many incarcerated women had inadequate health care prior to sentencing, it is not unusual for them to enter prison with untreated sexually transmitted diseases, high blood pressure, asthma, or diabetes (Maeve, 1999). Obviously the health and health care of the mother directly affects the health and well-being of her fetus and the birth outcome. The major organs of a fetus are at greatest risk of damage during the first 12 weeks of pregnancy (Gilmore, 2001). Because most pregnant prisoners enter the institution pregnant, their health and health care prior to incarceration are critical elements that must be evaluated to ensure healthy mothers and birth outcomes.

Mental Health

Many incarcerated women have long-standing emotional and mental health problems, especially anxiety and depression (Maeve, 1999), which may be associated with abuse experienced in their lives. Poverty, lack of education, abuse, and substance abuse often create chronic depression and chaos that can lead women to the types of behaviors that place them in jeopardy of incarceration. Maeve indicates that there is an "obvious link between violent, chaotic lives and depression" (p. 51). Most women enter prison with at least situational depression (Maeve, 1999), and incarceration is likely to add to the problem. Good mental health is associated with healthy pregnancies and birth outcomes, so it is imperative that prison systems treat women's psychological traumas.

PROBLEMS OF PREGNANCY IN PRISON

The prison environment creates a wide variety of stresses for all inmates. It is believed that these stresses may be intensified for pregnant inmates. In addition to the routine stresses of incarceration, the pregnant prisoner must also endure anxiety over whether to have an abortion, where to place the child after birth if she chooses to have the baby, and how to cope with separation once the child has been placed. If the fetus was conceived after incarceration, the prisoner may also have to explain her pregnancy to her spouse and/or family.

Prison creates an atmosphere of deprivation for all inmates. Prisoners are not free to move about society and associate with friends and family. They cannot buy their favorite foods or personal care products. They may find their environment frightening and give up any sense of personal security. This is difficult for the vast majority of prisoners, but it may be even more challenging for a pregnant inmate, who may crave the comfort of home and loved ones in this period of physical changes and uncertainty about the future of her child. She no longer has the support of those people in her life who can help her through her pregnancy. Pregnant inmates may also have physical disadvantages making it more difficult to cope with ordinary stresses of prison, such as functioning in a crowded environment.

Prison conditions and the stresses of prison life are often influenced by the size of the institution and the capacity at which it is operating. Prison capacity and the extent of overcrowding are difficult to measure because there is no uniform measure defining capacity or overcrowding. Clearly, however, many prisons in the United States are operating above capacity (Beck, 2001), a problem exacerbated by the recent growth of the female inmate population. Even in prisons that are not overcrowded, inmates have a loss of privacy.

Prison imposes dependence on inmates. The prison controls an inmate's daily activities and provides all of the necessities of life. However, obtaining some of these may humiliate an inmate. This is especially true in women's prisons. For example, female inmates are often given a monthly supply of sanitary napkins, which is expected to last for a month. If the supply is inadequate, the inmate must request additional supplies from a correctional officer, and is often required to prove that she in fact needs additional sanitary supplies (Maeve, 1999). This imposed dependence often has a debilitating affect on the prisoner. In some facilities, female inmates are given paper underwear and expected to wash them a certain number of times before new undergarments may be issued. In situations where inmates have soiled their underpants beyond the point where washing the paper will render them hygienic, they may be required to show the pants to a correctional officer to obtain a replacement. Pregnant inmates may need a greater supply of sanitary items and underwear than other inmates, but may not be given an additional allotment.

Prison uniforms are not designed for attractiveness, building the self-esteem of inmates, or even comfort or durability. Although deemed necessary for security reasons, prison uniforms may cause stress for prisoners. Pregnant inmates are often forced to wear a larger size uniform to accommodate the changes in their body, with little or no consideration to the fact that these uniforms do not fit and are uncomfortable. Wardens responding to a survey identified lack of maternity clothes as one problem of many experienced by pregnant inmates (Wooldredge & Masters, 1993).

Because most are already pregnant when they enter prison, the intake process becomes an issue in treating pregnant offenders. Admission to most correctional institutions requires a strip-search of all new inmates, and sometimes includes a pelvic exam. It has been suggested that conducting a pelvic exam on a pregnant woman without medical justification may increase the potential of vaginal and cervical irritation and infection (Ryan & Grassano, 1992).

New inmates are generally assigned to a prison based on their classification, but there are generally few choices involved in the placement of female inmates. For pregnant inmates, there is often no choice. Prenatal healthcare usually is provided only at one women's prison in a state, and it is often the maximum-security facility. Pregnant inmates who would normally be classified as medium or minimum custody may be assigned to a maximum-security institution simply because it is the only facility authorized to house them (Wooldredge & Masters, 1993).

One problem of pregnancy and birth for inmates has received special concern from nurses, who are charged with the well-being of their patients, yet are limited in their efforts by a correctional facility's security concerns. When inmates are transferred to local hospitals for labor and delivery, they are often required to be in restraints, sometimes including a belly chain, during transportation and in the delivery room. Most agencies have reviewed their policies and now require that a pregnant inmate be shackled under these circumstances only when the inmate is deemed to be a security risk. A U. S. District Court ordered the District of Columbia Department of Corrections to "develop and implement a protocol concerning restraints used on pregnant women which provides that a pregnant inmate shall be transported in the least restrictive way possible consistent with legitimate security concerns" (Pollack, 1998).

BIRTH OUTCOMES

It has been argued that the stress of prison life has a negative impact on birth outcomes. Research in the area is limited, but studies looking only at birth outcomes of incarcerated women have found very poor results in 25% of prison births (Martin, Rieger, et al., 1997). Comparing birth outcomes of prison pregnancies to those of the general population shows poorer birth outcomes for women who were incarcerated during pregnancy and delivery (Martin, Rieger, et al., 1997).

Although stress does affect the health of pregnant women and their expected infants, several studies indicate that incarceration may promote healthy pregnancies and birth outcomes by providing care that high-risk women might not receive on the streets (Martin,

Kim, Kupper, Meyer, & Hays, 1997; Martin, Rieger, et al., 1997). Studies that compare birth outcomes of women who experienced pregnancy while incarcerated and where they were not incarcerated at any point during their pregnancy found higher birth weights—one indicator of adequate prenatal care—for their "prison" babies. In fact, it has been found that the more pregnancy days spent in prison, the better the birth outcomes and the greater the infant's birth weight (Martin, Rieger, et al., 1997).

Research that compared birth outcomes of women incarcerated during pregnancy, incarcerated at a time other than during pregnancy, and women never incarcerated found that birth weights among women incarcerated during pregnancy were not significantly different than women who had never been incarcerated (Martin, Kim, et al., 1997). However, "infant birth weights were significantly worse among women incarcerated at a time other than during pregnancy than among never-incarcerated women and women incarcerated during pregnancy" (p. 1526).

The more positive birth outcomes for women who are pregnant in prison or spend more pregnancy days in prison, as compared to birth outcomes from women who have been incarcerated at another time, or who spent fewer pregnancy days in prison may be explained by a variety of factors. Certain aspects of the prison environment may offset the risk factors discussed previously. Women who were homeless or living in poverty prior to incarceration find adequate shelter and nutritionally complete meals in prison. Although (obviously contraband) alcohol and drugs may be available in prison, they may not be as easily accessible to pregnant women as they were on the streets. Prior physical and sexual abuse have an impact on women's health and pregnancy outcomes, but incarceration restricts interaction with abusive partners and may in fact provide a safer environment for these women, and therefore increase the potential for a healthy pregnancy and birth outcome.

Prenatal care in prison may not set the highest standard, but it often is significantly better than the care that impoverished or substance-abusing women may receive on the streets, and other previously overlooked health problems may also be treated in prison. In addition, prison may help pregnant women avoid strenuous physical work activity that would have been unavoidable on the outside.

PROGRAMS AND POLICIES FOR PREGNANT PRISONERS

Effective programs in prison can combat the physical and psychological problems faced by pregnant inmates, which in turn improves birth outcomes. Unfortunately, many women's prisons provide only the legally required level of medical resources and services for pregnant prisoners. Only 48% of facilities surveyed had written policies related specifically to the medical care of pregnant inmates (Wooldredge & Masters, 1993). Less than half of the facilities provided basic prenatal care, and even fewer offered additional programs and services. A nationwide survey of women's state prison wardens about available medical services for pregnant inmates reported the following: prenatal care (48%), networks with community agencies that provide other prenatal care (38%), Lamaze classes (16%), special diets and nutritional allowances (15%), abortions and abortion counseling (9%), and a full-time nurse or midwife available just for pregnant inmates (9%) (Wooldredge & Masters, 1993).

Box 5.1

MEDICAL SERVICES FOR PREGNANT INMATES IN STATE PRISONS

Prenatal care	48%
Prenatal services from community agencies	38%
Lamaze classes	16%
Special diet	15%
Abortions/abortion counseling	9%
Full-time nurse/midwife	9%
Prenatal counseling	21%
Placement counseling	15%
Lighter duties	15%
Separate quarters	13%
Postnatal counseling	11%

Source: Adapted from J. D. Wooldredge and K. Masters (1993), Confronting problems faced by pregnant inmates in state prisons. *Crime & Delinquency, 39,* 195–203.

The same survey revealed the following nonmedical programs designed for pregnant prisoners: prenatal counseling (21%), counseling to help mothers find suitable placement for their infant after birth (15%), policies for lighter work (15%), separate living quarters (13%), and postnatal counseling (11%) (Wooldredge & Masters, 1993). Although these findings may indicate improved programs for pregnant inmates in the United States, expanded programming is needed for both medical and other needs of these women.

Programming for the Needs of Pregnant Prisoners

Medical services and policies.   At a minimum, prisons housing pregnant inmates should provide prenatal and medical care and timely transportation to local hospitals for medical services not provided on-site. Prenatal care may also require special provisions for diet, exercise, housing, and work assignments to meet the particular needs of pregnant inmates. While health care must be adequate and available to all inmates, pregnant inmates should be given special consideration for health services.

Pregnant prisoners often enter prison with various preexisting risk factors that should be considered when designing programs for them. The fact that many female inmates have been homeless or living in poverty prior to their incarceration calls for proper nutrition, especially in the case of pregnant prisoners, who need a special diet high in protein, iron, milk, and vitamins (Ryan & Grassano, 1992). Preexisting health conditions must be discovered and treated. In addition, pregnant prisoners also need appropriate exercise, nonstrenuous work assignments, and noncrowded living conditions.

Special detoxification programs should be offered for pregnant women who are dependent on alcohol or drugs. Withdrawal syndromes are shared by both mother and fetus. The fetus not only experiences the mother's physical problems, but is also dependent on the substance and must also withdraw. "Since fetal withdrawal carries a high risk of mortality, it is important to prevent it through careful, slow detoxification or maintenance therapy" (Ryan & Grassano, 1992, p. 185).

Education programs and policies.   Educational programming to help prepare a pregnant inmate for pregnancy, labor and delivery, and motherhood is inadequate in most prisons for women in the United States. Educating pregnant inmates about fetal development, childbirth methods, and the effects of alcohol, drugs, and cigarettes on pregnancy and the fetus can have positive effects on pregnancy outcomes. Prenatal education classes should also include breastfeeding, especially if there is the possibility for the mother and infant to remain together after birth, and a discussion of postpartum depression can also have less devastating effects when the mother understands its causes and knows it is not abnormal.

Educational programs for pregnant inmates should also include classes on infant health, needs, and care; child development; the role of the parent; and appropriate discipline techniques. Stress and anger management, and household finances classes can also prepare an inmate for the responsibilities of parenting, increasing the likelihood that she will successfully remain in the community after her release from prison. Simple educational programs designed to help pregnant inmates become better parents may improve the chances of success for the children of incarcerated mothers and may reduce the odds of the children's incarceration in the future.

Counseling and social services.   Prenatal care in the community now focuses on and recognizes the value of education and social support, and the need for social support for pregnant inmates is even more critical. In addition to traditional prenatal counseling, pregnant inmates need help finding a safe and healthy placement for their infant in the community, and coping with this separation. This is one of the most stressful situations that a pregnant inmate must face. Whether an inmate puts her infant up for adoption, releases the child to foster care, or leaves it with relatives, there is psychological anguish for the mother, as well as potential developmental problems for her newborn (Wooldredge & Masters, 1993).

The special problems and needs of pregnant inmates should be considered when developing counseling programs. Mental health services should be provided for all inmates dealing with post-traumatic stress disorder resulting from physical and sexual abuse, but it is particularly critical for pregnant prisoners. Mental health not only affects multiple facets of physical health during pregnancy, but also increases the risk of poor birth outcome. Women who have been subjected to physical or sexual abuse are more likely to become abusive parents and to suffer mental health problems that additionally limit their ability to provide a healthy home environment for their children after release from prison (Sable et al., 1999). Other emotional and mental health problems should be detected and treated for the same reasons.

Abortion.   Abortion is a controversial topic for every woman, and an important issue that must be addressed when dealing with pregnant inmates. The Federal Bureau of Prisons' policy on birth control, pregnancy, child placement and abortion is seen by many as a model policy concerning abortion for inmates. The policy calls for providing pregnant inmates with medical, religious, and social counseling to help them to decide whether to continue with the pregnancy or to have an elective abortion (Bureau of Prisons, 1996). Under the Bureau of Prisons policy, an inmate who elects to have an abortion will have one "at Bureau expense only when the life of the mother would be endangered if the fetus is carried to term, or in the case of rape" (Bureau of Prisons, 1996). Staff members of the Bureau of Prisons may choose not to participate in arranging the abortion.

Model Programs

Santa Rita County California.   In 1989, officials in Santa Rita County, California, entered into a consent decree as the result of a lawsuit alleging inadequate medical care and inhumane conditions for pregnant inmates (Ross & Lawrence, 1998; Ryan & Grassano, 1992). This consent decree led to improvements that serve as a model for other jails and prisons in the country. A comprehensive obstetrical/gynecological (OB/GYN) unit and prenatal care services unit with a specialized medical team and casework staff was developed and implemented. Under the program, medical, social, and educational services are provided to pregnant inmates.

Women who enter the Santa Rita County Jail receive complete health appraisals, including screening for pregnancy. When a woman is identified as pregnant, she is immediately removed from the general population and placed in a special housing unit for pregnant inmates and is flagged in the institution's computer database. Pregnant women receive relevant prenatal medical and laboratory testing to screen for diabetes, human immunodeficiency virus (HIV), sexually transmitted diseases, tuberculosis (TB), and other conditions that might pose a health risk for the inmate or her fetus. All acute illnesses are identified and treated. If it is determined that a pregnant inmate is also a substance abuser, she is "immediately sent to the outpatient OB service of the hospital, evaluated and enrolled in a substance abuse treatment program" (Ross & Lawrence, 1998, p. 127). A therapeutic abortion is available if the inmate requests the procedure.

Ultrasound testing is routinely performed at 16 to 20 weeks (Ross & Lawrence, 1998; Ryan & Grassano, 1992), with follow-up tests provided as necessary. Pregnant inmates who have risk factors or illness that may complicate the pregnancy or birth may be placed in an inpatient unit with 24-hour nursing care. Delivery and other medical procedures that are beyond the scope of the institution are performed at the county hospital (Ryan & Grassano, 1992). After delivery, the inmate is returned to the institution and admitted to the infirmary for observation. A postpartum examination is conducted at the appropriate time at the facility.

In addition, the conditions of incarceration are designed to fit the needs of pregnant women and to support healthy birth outcomes. A special prenatal diet with supplemental vitamins is prescribed for the inmate. A qualified staff member conducts a structured exercise program, including outdoor walking and indoor aerobics, and all pregnant inmates who would benefit are encouraged to participate.

The housing unit for pregnant women is designed to provide them with a healthy environment that is conducive to healthy pregnancies and birth outcomes. There are two women per cell. "Each pregnant woman is assigned to share a cell with a non-pregnant woman chosen for the housing unit specifically to act as a stable, mature cellmate who can provide support for the pregnant offender" (Ryan & Grassano, 1998, p. 186). During the inmate's first 24 hours in the special housing unit, she is seen by a nurse who completes a prenatal intake, which includes a medical and social history of the offender.

Health education and pregnancy informational packets are distributed to each inmate in the pregnancy-housing unit. The special mental health and emotional needs of incarcerated pregnant women are evaluated and services are provided as necessary, including psychological counseling by mental health professionals, with special counseling for pregnancy and other health-related issues.

Other social services managed by a full-time prenatal coordinator are made available for pregnant inmates, as an integral part of the prenatal program (Ryan & Grassano, 1992). Social workers from county and state agencies also provide assistance regarding adoption procedures, resources available to single mothers, coping skills, options and skills for childcare, and foster care.

A court-appointed physician conducted follow-up evaluations of the Santa Rita County Prenatal Program and concluded that the Santa Rita program is positive and consistent with the court order (Ryan & Grassano, 1992). Their comprehensive approach to caring for pregnant inmates provides the framework other institutions can use when designing adequate programs that maximize the potential for healthy pregnancies and healthy birth outcomes. "Santa Rita's experience shows that there is little mystery regarding the operational components required for establishing credible, comprehensive, primary care services for women" (Ross & Lawrence, 1998, p. 127).

Baltimore's Healthy Start program.   The Baltimore City Health Department instituted a demonstration project to address infant mortality and low birth weight in infants in Baltimore City. In 1992, the program, including health services, was implemented at the Baltimore City Detention Center (Flanagan, 1995). "The goals of the Healthy Start program are to ensure that all incarcerated women understand and practice good health habits and are encouraged to reduce high risk behaviors; to provide pregnancy counseling and education; and to provide family planning services to nonpregnant women upon release" (p. 50).

The Healthy Start program provides educational programs on stress management, planning for a positive future, establishing a support system, developing positive relationships, the needs of an infant and infant development, and the role of a parent. Educational programs on healthy pregnancies discuss substance abuse, the effect of alcohol, caffeine, and cigarettes on pregnancy and the fetus, the importance of proper nutrition, vitamin supplements, appropriate exercise, and prenatal medical care. Women are also offered classes on budgeting, parenting and disciplining children, and ways to involve the father (Flanagan, 1995).

Center for Addiction and Pregnancy.   The Center for Addiction and Pregnancy (CAP) is offered through a branch of the Johns Hopkins Health Care system in Baltimore, Maryland. "This program has an innovative approach to helping addicted mothers and their infants deal with the physical, emotional, and social problems caused by addiction" (Flanagan, 1995, p. 50). CAP is designed to reduce the severity of obstetric complications and to help women recovering from drug and alcohol abuse deliver healthier infants. Although the program is a community residential treatment program, a nurse from CAP visits the Baltimore City Detention Center to recruit addicted pregnant inmates for the program after their release.

CONCLUSION

As the population of correctional facilities for women continues to increase, so too does the need for programs for pregnant inmates. The stress of incarceration, combined with the pre-incarceration lifestyles of many inmates, creates many risks for unhealthy pregnancies and poor birth outcomes. Although incarceration itself may be a risk factor for healthy pregnancies, many believe that the prison environment may in fact provide food, shelter, and medical care that improve the outlook for healthy birth outcomes in inmates. Appropriate programs for pregnant inmates, such as educational and social services, medical and mental health care, and special institutional provisions, may improve the chances of healthy pregnancies and birth outcomes. Few programs exist that meet the special requirements of pregnant inmates, but model programs can be used as an example. The needs of pregnant inmates cannot be ignored any longer—such neglect affects not only the inmate and child, but also diminishes the chances of society reaping the benefits of a healthy mother–child relationship.

DISCUSSION QUESTIONS

1. How are risk factors such as previous lifestyle, homelessness, poverty, substance abuse, domestic abuse histories, health problems, and mental health interrelated in women prisoners? How can these affect pregnancy outcomes for incarcerated women?

2. Incarceration may both increase and decrease the risks for pregnant women. Discuss this seeming paradox.

3. What types of social support would be beneficial to pregnant prisoners? How could these be provided to women who are incarcerated?

4. Compare the model programs described in this chapter. If you could develop a program for pregnant women in prison, what would you incorporate and why?

WEBNOTES

Read the Council of Europe Parliamentary Assembly report on the incarceration of pregnant women (http://stars.coe.fr/ta/ta00/EREC1469.HTM). How do their recommendations compare to current U.S. policies?

REFERENCES

BECK, A. J. (2001). *Prisoners in 1999.* Bureau of Justice Statistics: Special Report (Publication No. NCJ 183476). Washington, DC: U.S. Department of Justice.

BUREAU OF PRISONS. (1996). *Birth control, pregnancy, child placement and abortion.* Bureau of Prisons Programs Statement 6070.05. Washington, DC: U.S. Department of Justice. Available at http://www.bop.gov.

FLANAGAN, L. W. (1995). Meeting the special needs of females in custody: Maryland's unique approach. *Federal Probation, 59,* 49–53.

GILMORE, C. (2001, Spring). Guide to safe and healthy pregnancy. *Impressions: Spartanburg Regional Healthcare System, 2.*

GREENFIELD, L. A., & SNELL, T. L. (1999). *Women Offenders.* Bureau of Justice Statistics: Special Report (Publication No. NCJ 175688). Washington, DC: U.S. Department of Justice.

HARLOW, C. W. (1999). *Prior Abuse Reported by Inmates and Probationers.* Bureau of Justice Statistics: Special Report (Publication No. NCJ 172879). Washington, DC: U.S. Department of Justice.

MAEVE, M. K. (1999). Adjudicated health: Incarcerated women and the social construction of health. *Crime, Law, & Social Change, 31,* 49–71.

MARTIN, S. L., KIM, H., KUPPER, L., MEYER, R. E., & HAYS, M. (1997). Is incarceration during pregnancy associated with infant birthweight? *American Journal of Public Health, 87,* 1526–1531.

MARTIN, S. L., RIEGER, R. H., KUPPER, L. L., MEYER, R. E., & QAQISH, B. F. (1997). The effect of incarceration during pregnancy on birth outcomes. *Public Health Reports, 112,* 340–347.

MUMOLA, C. J. (2000). Incarcerated parents and their children. Bureau of Justice Statistics: Special Report (Publication No. NCJ 182335). Washington, DC: U.S. Department of Justice.

POLLACK, D. (1998). Pregnant inmates. *Corrections Today, 60,* 130.

ROSS, P. H., & LAWRENCE, J. E. (1998). Health care for women offenders. *Corrections Today, 60,* 122–127.

RYAN, T. A., & GRASSANO, J. B. (1992). Taking a progressive approach to treating pregnant offenders. *Corrections Today, 54,* 184–186.

SABLE, M. R., FIEBERG, J. R., MARTIN, S. L., & KUPPER, L. L. (1999). Violence victimization experiences of pregnant prisoners. *American Journal of Orthopsychiatry, 69,* 392–397.

SNELL, T. L., & MORTON, D. C. (1994). Women in prison. Bureau of Justice Statistics: Special Report (Publication No. NCJ 145331). Washington, DC: U.S. Department of Justice.

WOOLDREDGE, J. D., & MASTERS, K. (1993). Confronting problems faced by pregnant inmates in state prisons. *Crime & Delinquency, 39,* 195–203.

6

Doing Time in the Shadow of Death

Women Prisoners and HIV/AIDS

Barbara H. Zaitzow, Ph.D., and Angela D. West, Ph.D.

❖

In the last decade, both the number of female inmates and the average length of their sentences have increased dramatically. A by-product of the recent "confinement era" within criminal justice is the influx of ill and generally unhealthy female offenders into this nation's correctional institutions. In addition to tuberculosis (TB), one of the pressing public health concerns facing correctional systems today is human immunodeficiency virus (HIV)/acquired immune deficiency syndrome (AIDS). No segment of the incarcerated population is immune to this infection, but an alarming number of female inmates have tested positive for HIV, and at higher rates than male inmates (Maruschak, 1999). The high rates of HIV infection and AIDS among women offenders are essentially the result of intravenous drug use, trading sex for drugs and money, sexual abuse, living under conditions of poverty, and other gender-specific conditions, which make them more vulnerable to HIV infection (De Groot, Leibel, & Zierler, 1998). The problem of HIV infection and AIDS is especially serious for incarcerated women, who often receive the smallest piece of the criminal justice resource pie. Women in prison have different treatment needs and problems than their male counterparts; the lack of gender-specific services has prompted researchers and advocates to call for increased attention to correctional programming for women and greater use of community-based interventions and alternatives. This chapter highlights the corrections community's duty to address the unique circumstances of female inmates infected with the HIV/AIDS virus, and to acknowledge HIV/AIDS' impact on all imprisoned women in the United States.

A rising tide of infectious diseases has overtaken jails and prisons as infected inmates enter this nation's correctional systems. In addition to tuberculosis (TB), one of the pressing public health concerns facing correctional systems today is human immunodeficiency virus (HIV)/acquired immune deficiency syndrome (AIDS). Since the beginning of the HIV/AIDS epidemic, the disease has struck incarcerated populations extraordinarily hard. According to a report by the U.S. Bureau of Justice Statistics, the rate of confirmed AIDS cases is more than six times higher in state and federal prisons than in the general population (Maruschak, 1999). The "War on Drugs" has produced a prison population overwhelmingly dependent on illicit drugs, and the confluence of drug use and national drug arrest policies has made HIV infection rampant in the nation's prisons and jails.

No segment of the incarcerated population is immune, but certain populations show a higher frequency of HIV infection. Lachance-McCullough et al. (1994) note: "Minorities are disproportionately impacted by the AIDS epidemic. In fact, the sociodemographics of HIV/AIDS look strikingly similar to the sociodemographics of American prisons" (p. 200). Olivero (1992) states: "Most of those infected in prison are disproportionately members of minority groups; they tend to be black and Hispanic" (p. 50). HIV cases in prison also show a difference by sex. According to a 1997 study by the Department of Justice, male HIV cases far outnumbered those of females (20,200 compared to 2,200), but the numbers are misleading because there are so many more male prisoners. When computed as a percentage of the total population in custody, 2.2% of the male inmates and 3.5% of the female inmates were HIV-positive. The percentage of HIV-positive females has been higher than the male percentage in every year since 1991 (Maruschak, 1999). Numerous other studies support these findings.

Of course, the likelihood of infection depends largely on sets of behaviors known to place a person at risk. HIV/AIDS is primarily transmitted in one of three ways: (1) via sexual activity with an infected person; (2) through contact with infected blood via sharing an intravenous needle with an infected person; and (3) from an infected mother to a newborn infant. The Centers for Disease Control and Prevention (CDC, 1993) concluded that the high rates of HIV infection and AIDS among women offenders are usually the result of intravenous drug use and sexual activity with intravenous drug users. It is important to note that the results of the CDC's study are based on information provided by jurisdictions that are required by law or simply willing to respond to the limited scope of the survey. Some data components necessary to calculate cumulative totals (i.e., current cases, cases among released individuals, and deaths while in custody) have not been available from every jurisdiction for each year of the CDC survey. Thus, the number of HIV and AIDS cases may be much higher than reported. Additional cases may be concealed by the lengthy incubation period of the disease (sometimes as long as several years). Moreover, although levels of

---

Box 6.1

SOURCES OF HIV INFECTION/AIDS AMONG WOMEN PRISONERS

- Sexual activity with an infected person, usually a male drug user
- Sharing intravenous needles with an infected person

activity vary among facilities, many inmates continue to engage in the types of "high-risk" behavior—illicit sex and drug injection—during incarceration that pose a significant danger of viral transmission (Mahon, 1996). Thus, it is likely that there are many more AIDS cases than have actually been detected in U.S. prisons at this time.

The problem of HIV infection and AIDS is especially serious for incarcerated women, who often receive the smallest piece of the criminal justice resource pie. Effective prevention for inmates requires collaboration between inmates, corrections staff, public health agencies, and community-based service organizations. This chapter addresses the special requirements of incarcerated women relating to HIV/AIDS infection, identifies some of the barriers to meeting these needs, and articulates an initial strategy for effectively overcoming these obstacles.

FEMALE OFFENDERS

Although women make up only a small proportion of the total incarcerated population in the United States today, the numbers of women being sent to prison have increased, but disproportionate to their involvement in serious crime. Women imprisoned in state and federal correctional institutions throughout the United States totaled 84,427 (with 3,600 holdbacks for lack of beds) at year-end 1998, increasing at a faster rate during 1997–1998 than did male inmates. Moreover, the impact on women of color has been disproportionately heavy. For African American women, the incarceration rate is eight times that for white women; for Latinas, it is almost four times greater (Beck, 2000)—a reflection not only of race, but also of poverty. Despite the fact that female prisoner population growth outpaced that of males, females compose less than 7% of imprisoned offenders (Gilliard, 1999, p. 4).

Characteristics of Female Offenders

Like their male counterparts, female inmates are young (about two thirds are under 34 years old), minority-group members (more than 60%), unmarried (more than 80%), undereducated (about 40% are not high school graduates), and underemployed (Beck & Mumola, 1999). Unlike men, large majorities are unmarried, mothers of children under 18, and daughters who grew up in single-parent homes. Moreover, a distinguishing characteristic of incarcerated females is their significantly increased likelihood of having survived sexual and/or physical violence, particularly by a male relative or intimate partner (Fletcher et al., 1993; Sargent et al., 1993). Research also shows that women in prison have experienced unusually high rates of extremely abusive "discipline" from parents, involvement in drugs, and prostitution, whether they were imprisoned for these crimes or not (Harlow, 1999).

Whether as direct consequence of abuse or other contributing factors, female inmates may suffer from a loss of self-respect, hiding their pain in substance abuse (McKinney, 1994). A significant number of female inmates report substance abuse problems. Before their incarceration, women prisoners used more drugs and used those drugs more frequently than did men in prison. Women prisoners are also more likely to report that they were under the influence of drugs at the time of their current offense and to claim that they committed the offense to obtain money to buy drugs (Greenfeld & Snell, 1999).

As noted in Harlow's (1999) Survey of Inmates of State Correctional Facilities (SISCF), most of the women in prison were convicted on a nonviolent offense and had only nonviolent offenses as priors on their record. Women serving a sentence for a violent crime, including homicide, were most likely (nearly 50% of these cases) to have victimized a relative, an intimate (husband, ex-husband, boyfriend) or some other acquaintance, the result perhaps of women responding to a history of physical and psychological abuse by that person. Several studies support the theory that many women in prison for violent crimes are serving sentences for killing abusive husbands, ex-husbands, or boyfriends (see Moyer, 1993; Owen & Bloom, 1995, for reviews of the studies). The SISCF survey did not investigate this point specifically, but it did find that more women inmates (43%) than men (12%) reported having been physically or sexually abused before their current incarceration, and that women in prison were more likely to have committed their violent offense against someone close to them than were their male counterparts (36% to 16%).

The picture that emerges of the female inmate is troubling. Female criminal behavior appears to be the product of continuing social problems—the psychological repercussions of physical and emotional abuse and extreme disadvantage, exacerbated by economic problems and drug and alcohol abuse. Consequently, women come into prison with more medical needs than do men.

MEDICAL SERVICES FOR WOMEN IN PRISON

The spectrum of prison health care is as varied as in the "free world." It is impossible to generalize about conditions across one state, much less across the entire country. We do know, however, that health services delivery within prisons has been increasingly strained over the last decade, primarily because more inmates are coming into the prisons and they are less healthy than their counterparts of just a decade ago. Although research reveals improved medical services for incarcerated women during the last two decades (Lillis, 1994), the implementation of innovative in-house medical treatment for women has not kept pace with the diverse needs of the ever increasing population.

Women often require more medical attention than men, and women's prisons must deal with a greater demand for basic health care. In particular, women experience health problems related to their reproductive systems, especially true of those who are pregnant and require prenatal care when they enter prison. A host of other health care–related problems exists in women's prisons, including the availability of specific medications (Zaitzow, 1999). Because women's prisons are relatively small institutions, policymakers believe that installing extensive medical services in the prison cannot be justified. Consequently, women inmates who require greater medical attention than the prison provides must be transported to hospitals that can expand their access to care. Furthermore, when the prisons are located in rural areas, transporting inmates to urban medical centers can be problematic, posing greater risks for the inmate–patient. Such issues have been the subject of litigation. Even when the courts uphold the inmates' petition for better medical attention, however, prison administrators react slowly to court orders (Muraskin, 1993).

The quality and quantity of inmate health care have been questioned and generally found in need of reconsideration. Because women commonly require and avail themselves of more medical services than men, the problem of poor medical services is exacerbated for women inmates. The street lifestyle of many offenders (e.g., drug and alcohol abuse, poor diet, possibly indiscriminate sexual behavior, restricted access to medical services, and the tendency to neglect medical problems) means that women entering prison are likely to require significant medical attention and education to help them take better care of themselves on release to the community (Acoca, 1998).

SPECIAL NEEDS OF WOMEN PRISONERS WITH HIV/AIDS

By definition, the common condition of imprisonment is very little choice in every aspect of life. Additionally, issues and concerns become magnified within the prison environment. Crowded and highly regulated living conditions, the forced close environment, and the inability to control their own risk through personal decision-making affects all inmates. When the concern is HIV infection, the implications are even more serious. As one woman argued:

> [AIDS] is not just a white thing, it's not just a black thing, it's an everybody thing. Being in a place like this, you don't know what's good for you. So you say that we should pick things that are good for us. How can we? You can't pick and choose when you're incarcerated, they pick and choose for you. (West, 1996, p. 336)

This is also true for medical care, where prison authorities have a financial interest in limiting choice. The ability to make the most basic decisions about HIV antibody testing, HIV status disclosure, prevention education, or medical treatment often is denied to prisoners. Some persons infected with HIV may be asymptomatic, not even knowing they have the virus. Others may know they are HIV-positive but may appear just as healthy as uninfected inmates. Still others may have developed full-blown AIDS or other related health problems and may need substantial medical treatment. Inmates in the terminal stage of AIDS will need intensive medical care. Because HIV compromises the body's ability to fight infection and resist disease, those who are infected, in whatever stage of the disease, must be removed from inmates with contagious illnesses and other conditions that might overwhelm their suppressed immune systems. However, when segregation is used to isolate HIV-infected inmates, these inmates need proper care and should not be denied services or programming available to the general prison population (Zaitzow, 1999).

Counseling issues must be handled with much care and sensitivity, depending on whether the inmate is uninfected but at risk for HIV infection, is HIV-positive but asymptomatic, or has full-blown HIV infection or AIDS. The fears expressed most frequently by HIV-positive women inmates are of becoming ill, transmitting HIV to their sexual partners and children, difficulty in communicating with potential sexual partners while remaining sexually active, and being unable to bear children for fear their offspring will become infected.

Even uninfected inmates have concerns related to HIV infection that may be addressed through counseling. Programs for the "worried-well" may serve to address the fears of women who are not infected, but who interact daily with women who are. One uninfected inmate, when asked about her biggest AIDS-related fear, stated:

> I wouldn't want to die up here. My biggest fear . . . is getting sick and dying up here, because when you get sick . . . by the time you get in to see your doctor . . . then by the time they make arrangements for your [AIDS] test, you're gone. (West, 1996, p. 253)

Unlike women in the other groups, those who have symptomatic HIV infection and AIDS grieve the loss of their previous body image, sexual freedom, and potential for childbearing, and face imminent loss of their own lives. Grief and other emotions triggered by the HIV/AIDS diagnosis can be profound. Moreover, there may be as many as 80,000 mothers in local, state, and federal jails and prisons, and their dependents may total 150,000 people (Johnston, 1995). The legal and practical restrictions imposed on women prisoners infected with HIV/AIDS as they try to maintain relationships with their children significantly affect their physical and emotional well-being. The dramatic growth in the number of women in correctional settings during the past decade who either have tested positive for or are presumed to have HIV/AIDS, and their need for gender-specific services, has prompted researchers and advocates to call for increased attention to correctional programming for women and increased use of community-based interventions and alternatives.

Doing Infected Time: Issues and Challenges

Although life is rarely easy for any inmate, it is often more difficult for those who are HIV-positive. Lachance-McCullough et al. (1994) note: "That dangers exist in being a known HIV-positive prison inmate, ranging from social isolation to physical abuse, has been well documented in the literature" (p. 213). Likewise, Olivero (1992) states: "It appears that inmates and some prison administrators share society's repulsion of AIDS victims. Prisoners found to be infected with AIDS are an 'outgroup' and are stigmatized within the prison community" (p. 50).

Prisoner advocates assert that women prisoners have a harder time getting treatment than men do, but it is difficult to generalize about HIV/AIDS care in prison because it is not standardized across the nation. Each state system has its own set of policies and procedures for treating inmates, and the federal prison system operates under its own guidelines as well. Even within each state, the quality of treatment programs varies widely from facility to facility. A select few prisons provide care equal to or even better than that available on the outside. However, the majority do not even approach that level and quality of care. Some provide conditions seen only in developing countries (Zaitzow, 1999).

The prison environment clearly creates situations that these women ordinarily would not face if they were not incarcerated. Inmates have been attacked and killed for being perceived as gay and/or HIV-positive in prison. HIV/AIDS is still largely considered a "gay disease" inside. If an inmate becomes too interested in treatment or education, she may be labeled as gay, adversely affecting health, housing and life inside the concrete womb. The experiences and concerns of female inmates about the presence of HIV infection in a northeastern prison suggest that everyone in such an environment is "doing infected time" (West, 1996). Several issues must be considered when developing correctional policies and practices for HIV/AIDS.

Mandatory testing.   Perhaps the most highly charged and controversial corrections issue is the debate over forced or mandatory HIV testing for inmates. Proponents argue that identifying infected inmates facilitates administration of antiviral medications that are used for preemptive or early intervention treatment, and may help sustain better health over a period of time. Opponents argue that because any testing method may produce inaccurate results—positive cases testing negative, and negative cases testing positive—it is not possible to identify all potentially infectious inmates. This could produce a false sense of security about who may or may not have AIDS.

Although mandatory testing guidelines vary widely, all 50 states, the District of Columbia, and the Federal Bureau of Prisons (BOP) have at least one policy for prison HIV testing, the most prevalent (used in 44 of the jurisdictions in 1997) being to test inmates if they exhibit HIV-related symptoms or if they ask to be tested (Maruschak, 1999). In practice, however, the facts may be a little different. As Maggie, a former pusher explained:

> There is not mandated testing up here. Even if you ask for a test, you still don't get it. You have to fight for one. I've never shot drugs and I haven't been with a lot of men in my life, but after one of my boyfriends died, I found out he was a drug user. It scared me. It is still scary. Just to make sure that nothing is wrong with me, I went and asked for a test, and they said, "If you don't have any symptoms, we can't give it to you." What are the symptoms? That's what I want to know. But they said, "If you don't show any signs of this," or "We don't feel that you have the symptoms," or "You don't fall under this category, we can't." Why can't you? (West, 1996, p. 238)

Another common requirement is testing of inmates involved in an incident that might increase their exposure risk (29 jurisdictions). Fifteen states test inmates who belong to designated high-risk groups. Eighteen states test all inmates upon admission, and four states (as well as the BOP) test inmates at release (Maruschak, 1999).

Segregation.   Housing and segregation policies for HIV-positive or AIDS-symptomatic inmates, in which inmates are forcibly housed apart from the general population, raise a number of issues. Proponents of segregation assert that it is necessary to prevent transmission of HIV through various "high-risk" activities within the prison setting. Segregation has also been supported on grounds that HIV-infected inmates who have weakened immune systems are at greater risk of becoming ill. Therefore, they need to be protected against exposure to illnesses from the general inmate population. Civil libertarians, on the other hand, oppose segregation except for valid medical reasons or in cases involving protective custody. They argue that segregation undermines the basic public health message that HIV is not transmitted through casual contact but through "high-risk" behaviors. Moreover, it makes little sense to segregate "low-risk," HIV-positive inmates who are not ill and will complete their sentences in a relatively short period of time.

It should be noted that all HIV-infected inmates were segregated from the general population in eight prison systems in 1985, but by the year 2000, only three systems kept inmates known to be HIV-infected from the general prison population. Those three systems—Alabama, Mississippi, and South Carolina—have mandatory HIV-antibody testing for all incoming inmates, so they probably identify and segregate a large percentage of HIV-infected inmates (Greenhouse, 2000; Hammett et al., 1999). Alabama's procedure was upheld in 1999 by the United States Court of Appeals for the 11th Circuit *(Onishea v. Hopper),* and left intact by the United States Supreme Court in 2000 *(Davis v. Hopper).*

Questions about what constitutes segregation may be debated by correctional administrators and politicians, but in two women's prisons in California that have been the subject of litigation with respect to the maltreatment of incarcerated women, segregation is an obvious fact of prison life. At the California Institute for Women (CIW) in Frontera,

> Most of the HIV-positive inmates are housed in the isolated AIDS unit. HIV-positive inmates who live in the general population, live in constant fear knowing that any disciplinary infraction (physical altercation, verbal altercation, homosexual behavior) can send them to lock up for six months to a year. . . . Other women in the general population go to lock-down for thirty days for these types of infractions and then are released back into population. (an HIV-positive prisoner at C.I.W.)

And, at the Central Women's Facility at Chowchilla, one woman noted that "Most of the identified HIV-positive women live in C yard. Big signs that warn 'Beware! There are HIV-Infected Inmate Persons in this Facility'" (Siegal, 1998).

Adherence issues.   There is still much discrimination in the prison system related to HIV/AIDS, and therefore, many "positives" are not being treated for their infections. Even those who are most often do not receive the same standard of care as people on the outside. Here, access to all approved medications is limited for incarcerated persons, and many inmates who are taking combo therapy do not receive the correct dosage at the right times. Medical personnel need instruction on HIV/AIDS medication adherence and the importance of sticking to the dosing schedule.

Prisons use two methods to dispense medication: Keep-on-person (KOP) and directly-observed-therapy (DOT). With KOP, inmates are issued a day's or week's worth of medications to keep in their cells or rooms and take at the appropriate times. The prison schedule, however, may not allow for appropriate meals or fluids being available, or medications may be stolen for resale to other inmates. DOT means that the inmates must be released from their housing to stand in a pill line, where someone watches them take the medications and ensures that the pills have been swallowed. One consequence of DOT is that the inmate surrenders all chance of confidentiality. Other inmates see her routinely appear at a window and take her "meds." Another problem is lockdowns or other circumstances sometimes make it impossible for inmates to go to the pill line. To make matters worse, medication delivery often breaks down when inmates are transferred from one facility to another or taken to court. Medical records are routinely lost in the process, requiring the inmate to be retested and all medications suspended until the new results are received.

Lack of confidentiality and stigmatization.   As a result of the possible ramifications of HIV/AIDS testing, noted above, inmates often refuse to be tested or begin treatment if they know they will be separated from existing inmate friends and support systems. Despite the possibility of better medical care, a segregated inmate may lose the opportunity to hold

---

Box 6.2

METHODS OF DISPENSING MEDICATION IN PRISON SETTINGS

- KOP (Keep-on-Person): Prisoner is issued one day's to one week's worth of medication to administer to self.
- DOT (Directly-Observed-Therapy): Prison staff observes prisoner taking the medication.

a job, be considered for educational or work release, or have contact visits with family and relatives. In this instance, disclosure can lead to a longer sentence by limiting participation in programs that are viewed positively by corrections officers.

Whereas decisions to disclose the HIV status of inmates are governed by legal and policy standards and mandates, current correctional practices permit AIDS-related medical information to be provided to those with a need to know, such as correctional administrators, physicians, other medical staff, and probation officers as well as the inmate (Zaitzow, 1999). But, because there are very few secrets in a prison setting, one's medical condition—along with other personal information—is typically known by others. Thus, HIV-infected women prisoners endure additional stress because of the lack of confidentiality about their medical condition. As noted by Monica, an HIV-positive inmate:

> There is no confidentiality here once they find out you are HIV. They tell everybody to watch out for my sore. Even though we are not allowed to have sex in here, it does happen. Some of the officers tell other inmates, "watch out for her, she is HIV." They find out through the infirmary, or some kind of way, they always do. Then, if somebody says, "AIDS-dyin' bitch," we can't punch them in the face, because we will get a charge. (West, 1996, p. 239)

Moreover, some uninfected women prisoners show great concern and empathy for the HIV-positive women. As evidenced in the statements of several women, they want to help them even though they are frightened of becoming infected. Maggie said, "I don't think, 'This person may be HIV-positive' before I attempt to help or anything" (p. 237). And, Rosa eloquently related the sorrow she felt for the HIV-positive inmates:

> I worked with [AIDS] down in the infirmary. I asked to work there, but I had to let it go because it was too much strength. It is so hard to see someone die and you can't do nothing for them. You can't even give them comfort in prison. At least on the street you could hug them or give them medicine for the pain. Here you are faced with the reality that death is right around the corner and nobody is there to help them, because it gets to the point that they are so sick and they are in bed. They can't even get a swallow of water. Do you know what it is like to be thirsty, and nobody to give you water? (p. 237)

The lack of emotional support available to incarcerated women is an even greater challenge for HIV-positive women:

> You are in prison and you find out you have AIDS and you have to notify your family. You don't know how you are going to do that. You don't have nobody to stand by you . . . and it is like you are alone. You are standing in a storm by yourself and there is nobody there to help you and there is nobody there to inform you either. (p. 238)

When asked why she thought people were alone, Rosa elaborated on her previous thought by retorting, "Sweetheart, we are in prison. We can't even have physical contact, let alone sit around and tell somebody 'I have AIDS.' It is not that easy" (p. 238).

Lack of education and prevention.   Prison systems have attempted to address potential problems associated with HIV infection and incarceration by developing and implementing AIDS education programs for staff as well as inmates. Whereas almost every state has implemented some type of HIV/AIDS education program (Hammett et al., 1999), only 10% of state and federal prisons offer "comprehensive" HIV/AIDS programs that include

---

Box 6.3

Peer-led programs . . . are one of the most effective approaches, yet only 41% of systems and only 13% of facilities within those systems provide peer-led programs for their inmate populations.

"instructor-led education, peer-led programs, pre- and post-test counseling, and multisession prevention counseling" (Hammett et al., 1999, p. 27). Moreover, there are considerable differences among these programs' presentation and content, and some are viewed as more successful than others. Peer-led programs, for example, are one of the most effective approaches, yet only 41% of systems, and only 13% of facilities within those systems, provide peer-led programs for their inmate populations (Hammett et al., 1999). Many of these programs were developed and implemented hastily (Martin et al., 1993), without adequately assessing the needs of the different populations involved (e.g., male versus female, white versus nonwhite, English-speaking versus non–English speaking, etc.). As most state prison-based AIDS education programs fail to account for cultural and linguistic differences in their inmate populations, the programs may not be providing adequate, understandable, relevant, and/or feasible information (Hammett et al., 1999). A poignant scene described by Acoca (1998) highlights this challenge: "A young Hispanic inmate in this institution sits in a counselor's office struggling unsuccessfully to be understood in English. She is trying to enlist staff help in orchestrating medical services for her three-year-old who is critically ill at home. She is HIV-positive, as is the toddler from whom she is separated. She is also pregnant" (p. 49).

Figures pertaining to education programs may be misleading as prisons often advertise brief, one-time orientation sessions as HIV/AIDS education programs (West & Martin, 2000).

> This place don't give you too much information. They give you a sample movie over there [infirmary]. It's up to you to make yourself more aware. They [prison staff] don't give a shit what you know and what you don't know. (West, 1996)

Just because a facility claims to offer certain programs and services is no guarantee that they are available as promised. For example, only 57% of facilities claiming to provide mandatory intake education actually do (Hammett et al., 1999).

> We can't even educate ourselves if we wanted to, because we don't have the information. And the people here that give you information don't even know what they are talking about. (West, 1996)

Such flagrant bureaucratic misrepresentations impose potentially serious constraints on program effectiveness and on our ability to understand the reality of education programs within our correctional facilities.

Many state programs also have questionable content; they often lack crucial information, present inaccurate information, or fail to address issues relevant to prison populations in ways that are easily understood. It is also problematic that existing educational programs provide very little information to inmates about changing risk behaviors (Hammett et al., 1999; Martin et al., 1995). In fact, only 67% *claim* to provide information related to safer sex practices, 41% on negotiation skills for safer sex, 45% on safer injection practices, and 57% on triggers for behavioral relapse (Hammett et al., 1999). Lora realized that HIV-negative women who were released from prison without being properly informed ran a high risk of coming back in with the infection:

> The education here is just bad. It is poor. I mean, I know for a fact that people left from here and came back already with it. There is a couple of them, when I came up here, that didn't have it. They left . . . I mean, if they would have been more aware of it, you know, I am sure they wouldn't have gone out there and gotten it. (West, 1996, p. 248)

Obviously, education within the prison walls neither ensures success at avoiding infection upon release, nor ensures that those who are already infected will cease the behaviors that got them infected to begin with.

Compassionate release.   Stories of negligence and abuse are repeated again and again across the nation. In some cases, inmates with HIV may be sent to the nearest outside hospital, whether or not it has an infectious-disease specialist. Nevertheless, many inmates in state and federal prisons simply go untreated and find themselves in prison infirmaries or hospitals, where they are left to die.

> Linda, incarcerated at the Central California Women's Facility (CCWF) in Chowchilla in 1995, was diagnosed with AIDS. Arrested in January 1994, in Riverside County for possession of an unregistered firearm and violating her parole, Linda spent almost three years in CCWF before compassionate release sent her home in December, 1996. While at CCWF, she came down with AIDS-related herpes zoster on her leg, which looked like a series of dark-red, blistering cigarette burns. The doctor, however, did not admit her to the infirmary. The herpes spread to her eyes, and she went blind. But Linda's bad luck didn't end there. After she was returned to her old cell, she says that no one acknowledged that she could not see or taught her how to get around or even made sure that she got breakfast. When she was brought a breakfast tray, no one told her it was there. When she finally left prison in December 1996, Linda weighed 92 pounds, was unable to walk, and was convinced that she was about to die. "My care at Chowchilla?" said Linda recently, "I'll put it like this: If you were dying of thirst and I stuck you in the desert with no water, how would you feel? You would die from dehydration." She paused and then continued, "To put it even more bluntly, they didn't give a f***." (Siegal, 1998)

In California, a compassionate release policy designed for inmates dying in prison was signed into law in October 1997. But since the law became effective in January 1998, the numbers of compassionate releases have actually decreased. According to a CDC spokesperson, eight releases were granted in 1995, whereas just one was granted in 1998. So far, one release has been granted this year, under what Cynthia Chandler of the Women's Positive Legal Action Network considers disturbing circumstances.

> Tina Balagno, an HIV-positive prisoner with a history of drug addiction, started complaining of severe leg pain when she was admitted to CCWF in June 1998, and shortly thereafter discovered lumps in one of her breasts. While her leg pains were not addressed, a malignancy was found in her breast, and her family urged immediate treatment. In November, Balagno

was admitted to surgery for what she thought would be a lumpectomy, only to wake up to realize her breast had been removed. According to Chandler, Balagno received no chemotherapy or radiation treatment and got only Motrin for her pain. Falling into a coma after suffering two seizures in January, Balagno was diagnosed with metastasized bone cancer, and was released to her family just one week before her death. She was 40. (Talvi, 1993, p. 5)

Greenspan, one of the coauthors of the compassionate release legislation, finds the current overall lack of compassion toward severely ill prisoners disheartening. "The problem is that the political climate is so anti-prisoner, and prisoners have been so demonized, that they are not even getting out [on compassionate release]," she says. "The system's refusal to release dying prisoners is both inhumane and unconscionable" (p. 5).

WHAT WORKS: HOPE-FILLED EXAMPLES OF HIV/AIDS PROGRAMS

The prison setting provides a unique opportunity to present HIV/AIDS-related information, to study the results of that presentation, and to modify attempts based on deficits that may be revealed upon evaluation (Martin et al., 1995). Women inmates need the same preventive measures and level of care, treatment, and support as male prisoners. In addition, however, there is a need for initiatives that acknowledge that the problems encountered by female inmates in the correctional environment often reflect, and are augmented by, their vulnerability and the abuse many of them have suffered outside prison. The task of protecting women prisoners from HIV transmission, therefore, presents different—and sometimes greater—challenges than that of preventing HIV infection in male prisoners.

For all these reasons, the educational needs of female prisoners regarding HIV/AIDS differ from those of male prisoners, and the need for HIV prevention programs in women's prisons may be even more pressing than in men's prisons. To facilitate the development and implementation of HIV/AIDS programs for women in prison, there are particular elements that must be included to meet the needs and concerns of those they serve:

1. Voluntary HIV testing
2. On-site gynecological and obstetric along with HIV care from nurses and HIV specialists who are available several times weekly to respond to the needs of HIV-infected and at-risk women
3. State-of-the-art drug treatments, which include access to a combination of drug therapy; antiviral medication monitoring; post-exposure to prevention methods (i.e., dental dams, bleach)
4. AIDS Education and Counseling (ACE)
5. Safer-sex negotiation, skill-building, and self-esteem workshops to improve their abilities to make informed sexual choices
6. Peer-led counseling groups, drug treatment and AIDS education, and counseling
7. Discharge programming planning that includes: (a) educational and marketable skills development to provide women with the wherewithal to stay out of prison, (b) the coordination of child care with drug abuse treatment services, safe housing, and medical and educational services (De Groot et al., 1998)

The implementation of these criteria are evident in one comprehensive program, initiated by the Rhode Island Department of Health in cooperation with the Brown University AIDS Program, designed to provide multifaceted healthcare for HIV-infected inmates. The activities of the program include HIV/AIDS education, testing, and pre- and posttest counseling, medical management of HIV-infected inmates along with prerelease counseling and postrelease healthcare follow-up of HIV-positive inmates. Discharge planning links ex-inmates to community-based services. After discharge, 83% of HIV-positive women follow up with medical care, and 68% make contact with a community-based drug treatment program (Flanigan et al., 1996). Moreover, HIV-positive women who participated in the prison release program during the first year had recidivism rates of 12% and 17% at 6 and 12 months, respectively, whereas HIV-positive women released during the year prior to the availability of the program had recidivism rates of 27% and 39% at 6 and 12 months, respectively.

Another program that incorporates these criteria is the Transitional Services Unit (TSU) which was formed in 1992, in Brooklyn, to meet the needs of HIV-positive and high-risk women as they make the transition from the criminal justice system to the community. Today, it offers a continuum of services, from jail and prison through release, including stages of probation and parole, and in the community. These include HIV/AIDS education, counseling, and peer group support, coupled with comprehensive case management that helps women reunite with their children and obtain housing, medical care, public assistance, and drug treatment. Given the enormity of the need for transitional support and the diverse and complex problems involved, TSU's program is rich.

Finally, correctional systems and states are responding to the increasing numbers of terminally ill inmates—a result of HIV/AIDS and longer prison sentences. Hospice teams—made up of medical staff, chaplains, mental health staff, social workers, and trained inmate hospice volunteers—assist terminally ill inmates to make them more comfortable, provide emotional support, and offer increased family visitation. One such program that merits attention is the Federal Medical Center—Carswell (FMC) in Fort Worth, Texas. Here, women inmates from all over the country receive treatment for a wide variety of health problems, from difficult pregnancies to advanced heart disease. There are over one thousand inmates housed at FMC, many of whom are assigned there to help run the facility and support patient services. There are two skilled nursing units: one medical/surgical and one long-term unit. In addition, one of the floors houses chronically ill patients who are able to perform most of their activities of daily living. And one floor was being set up for in-patient and transitional psychiatric services. Two years ago, FMC added a hospice program for female inmates requiring end-of-life care. But, entering the hospice program does not mean that all attempts at curative treatment are abandoned. As noted by Melissa Johnson, the hospice coordinator, a young woman was transferred to Carswell in advanced stages of AIDS; she was put into the hospice program and at the same time started anti-retroviral therapy. After a reversal of her symptoms, she was transferred into general population, served her time, and went home (Seidlitz, 1999).

RECOMMENDATIONS/SUGGESTIONS

The numerous problems facing women in prison require immediate attention. Many HIV-positive women do not receive the diagnostic and treatment services that could benefit them as early as do HIV-positive men. Among the reasons for this is that women are often unaware of having been exposed to HIV by their sexual or drug-using partners and, as a result, do not seek counseling, HIV testing, and care and treatment. Second, the needs of HIV-positive women differ from those of men, and social and community support are often less frequently available and less accessible. As a consequence, women are often less educated than men about HIV infection and AIDS and do not have the support structures they need. Third, disease manifestations attributable to HIV infection or AIDS are often different in women, which has led to underrecognition or delays in diagnosis. Thus, women who are infected have often been diagnosed as HIV-infected or having AIDS later than men.

Men and women are different and obviously have different needs, and yet 35 of 42 states (83%) with programs for male and female prisoners report using the same program with both populations (Martin et al., 1993), and only one program from 27 responding states indicates any content focusing on sex-specific issues (Martin et al., 1995). Hammett et al. (1999) report that 84% of state systems have educational materials especially for women, but actual practice in the facilities may be significantly different. It is strongly suggested that any future efforts to assess and modify prison-based AIDS education programs explicitly address the needs of female inmates (Keeton & Swanson, 1998; Martin et al., 1993).

Although we lack substantial information concerning the HIV-related needs and concerns of incarcerated women in general, that deficiency is particularly striking as it pertains to women of color (West, 2001). Cultural differences also should be considered within gender-sensitive epistemologies. Stuntzner-Gibson (1991) urges that "all efforts directed at AIDS education and prevention be sensitive and appropriate to . . . ethnic and cultural beliefs, educational backgrounds, socioeconomic classes, spiritual beliefs, and sexual orientations" (p. 26). More specifically, because risk and infection rates among incarcerated women vary by race/ethnicity, it is crucial to learn more about the shared and different needs of women. In this way, enhanced prevention and education programs can be developed to address specific concerns. Behavior modification will be difficult to initiate with prisoners if these differences are not considered (Moore et al., 1995; Yeakley & Gant, 1997).

Finally, regaining control of her life after a period of incarceration is seldom easy for a woman. The need for follow-up of HIV-positive women on release from prison is particularly high. Incarcerated HIV-positive women frequently lack medical and gynecological care, substance abuse treatment, and psychosocial support after release. When a woman gets out of prison, she faces not only the task of finding a place to live and suitable work or economic support, but also the trauma of being reunited with her children and loved ones. Without much-needed support, women who fail to receive crucial transition services may be at higher risk of recidivism.

Currently, there is no established method for prisons to keep track of what happens to women after they leave, unless they violate parole or return to the same prison on a new conviction. Few services are provided in the community for the readjustment and reentry of prisoners, even though in the long run these services would pay for themselves in a reduction of crime and the cost of returning recidivists to prison. Some ex-convicts have found that self-help groups can ease their reintegration into society by providing a supportive community. Groups such as the A.C.E.–OUT, Connections, Fortune Society, LIVING-Well, Women's Prison Association, and other ex-prisoners' organizations have made a difference in the lives of many individuals.

CONCLUSION

Given the projected rise in HIV-seropositive inmates in the next decade and the continuing threat of inmate litigation, it appears that the correctional health care crisis will continue for some time. The medical and custodial needs of HIV/AIDS inmates will be one of the most, if not the single most, important consideration for correctional administrators well into the twenty-first century.

Clearly, prisons and jails have a moral and legal responsibility to prevent the spread of HIV/AIDS and other infectious diseases among inmates and to staff and the public, and to provide a level of care for inmates living with HIV/AIDS comparable to that available in the community. Whether HIV/AIDS testing should be mandatory or voluntary, whether housing should be integrated or segregated by HIV serostatus, and whether condoms/dams, bleach, and clean needles should be made available to inmates are hotly debated questions among administrative and scientific groups. It is apparent that HIV/AIDS interventions implemented in correctional settings are among those with the greatest potential to have a substantial impact on the epidemic.

The incarcerated population, like the HIV-infected population, is overrepresented by minority groups and characterized by high rates of poverty, overcrowding, injection drug use, high-risk sexual activity, and poor access to preventive and primary health care. Incarceration provides a remarkable public health opportunity for screening, counseling, and treating a "captive" audience at high risk of HIV infection and transmission, most of whom will eventually be released to their communities. Much can be done to address the issues raised by the HIV/AIDS epidemic in correctional institutions, but the implementation of effective HIV/AIDS treatment and prevention strategies in these settings is threatened by the often competing ideologies of public health and correctional officials. The inmate population and the public at large are best served by a system in which the coordinated efforts of public health and correctional systems are directed toward the development of policies and programs with the greatest likelihood of preventing the spread of HIV/AIDS among inmates while providing the highest levels of care to those already infected. In a society in which incarceration is characterized by increased risk of HIV/AIDS transmission and increased rates of disease progression in those already infected, who are the true criminals? As we are so powerfully reminded in the words of a woman who is an HIV-positive "resident" in the California prison system:

> We are in this institution for breaking the law. We are well aware that prison is a punishment for that bad judgment. We do not expect things to be pleasant or comfortable. But it is also not meant for those of us with HIV, to be faced each day of our sentence with contempt and abuse just because we have a virus. There is such a vast gap between us and the control of our health, our sanity and our sense of still being a human being. We are still a part of humanity that fears, and loves, and feels pain, both physical and emotional. We have families but many of us are separated from them. We do have real needs to be treated as you would treat someone who is not afflicted with the virus. No one should be treated this way, yet sadly we are, daily. We cannot access the intervention of our families and those who care. Doesn't anyone care? Many of us will die, we know that, and we do our best to accept the inevitable. But we also have the right to die with dignity and to know that everything was done to prolong our lives and give us some quality of life, even inside the prison walls. But, instead, we are punished for having a disease and shoved into a corner because no one wants to deal with us. (Siegal, 1998)

DISCUSSION QUESTIONS

1. What are the potential sources of HIV/AIDS for women prisoners? How are these related to their pre-prison lifestyles?

2. What are some of the ways that operation of a prison can interfere with treatment of HIV/AIDS in women prisoners?

3. What are some of the reasons HIV-positive women prisoners do not receive diagnostic services or treatment for HIV/AIDS as early in their disease as do men prisoners? Should HIV testing be mandatory for women prisoners? What are advantages and disadvantages of mandatory testing?

4. How are HIV postrelease services related to other services needed by HIV/AIDS-infected women prisoners?

W E B N O T E S

Read Dr. De Groot's story of working with women in prison who are HIV infected (http://www. prisonwall.org/hiv.htm). Then read her report on HIV-infected women prisoners (http://www. hivcorrections.org/archives/june99/index.html). What issues does she address?

R E F E R E N C E S

ACOCA, L. (1998). Defusing the time bomb: Understanding and meeting the growing health care needs of incarcerated women in America. *Crime and Delinquency 44* (1), 49–70.

BECK, A. (2000). *Prisoners in 1999.* Washington, DC: U.S. Department of Justice.

BECK, A. J., & MUMOLA, C. (1999). *Prisoners in 1998.* Washington, DC: U.S. Government Printing Office: 9.

CENTERS FOR DISEASE CONTROL. (1993, February). *HIV/AIDS surveillance quarterly report: Year-end edition.* Atlanta, GA: Centers for Disease Control.

DE GROOT, A. S., LEIBEL, S. R., & ZIERLER, S. (1998). A standard of HIV care for incarcerated women: A northeastern United States experience. *Journal of Correctional Health Care 5* (2), 139–176.

FLANIGAN, T. P., KIM, Y. J., & ZIERLER, S. (1996). A prison release program for HIV-positive women: Linking them to health services and community follow-up. *American Journal of Public Health 86,* 886–887.

FLETCHER, B. R., ROLISON, G. L., & MOON, D. G. (1993). The woman prisoner. In B. R. Fletcher, L. D. Shaver, & D. G. Moon (Eds.), *Women prisoners: A forgotten population* (pp. 15–26). Westport, CT: Praeger.

GILLIARD, D. (1999). *Prison and jail inmates at midyear 1998.* Washington, DC: U.S. Department of Justice.

GREENFELD, L. A., & SNELL, T. L. (1999). *Women offenders.* Special Report (NCJ 175688). Washington, DC: Bureau of Justice Statistics.

GREENHOUSE, L. (2000, 19 January). Justices allow segregation of inmates with HIV. *New York Times* [Online]. Available at: www.nytimes.com.

HAMMETT, T. M., HARMON, P., & MARUSCHAK, L. M. (1999). *1996–1997 update: HIV/STDs, and TB in correctional facilities.* Washington, DC: National Institute of Justice.

HARLOW, C. (1999). *Prior abuse reported by inmates and probationers.* Washington, DC: U.S. Department of Justice.

JOHNSTON, D. (1995). Child custody issues of women prisoners: A preliminary report from the CHICAS project. *The Prison Journal 75,* 222.

KEETON, K., & SWANSON, C. (1998). HIV/AIDS education needs assessment: A comparative study of jail and prison inmates in northwest Florida. *The Prison Journal 78* (2), 119–132.

LACHANCE-MCCULLOUGH, M. L., TESORIERO, J. M., SORIN, M. D., & STERN, A. (1994). HIV infection among New York state female inmates: Preliminary results of a voluntary counseling and testing program. *The Prison Journal 73* (2), 198–219.

LILLIS, J. (1994). Programs and services for female inmates. *Corrections Compendium 29* (2), 6–13.

MAHON, N. (1996). New York inmates' HIV risk behaviors: The implications for prevention policy and programs. *American Journal of Public Health 86* (9), 1211–1215.

MARTIN, R., ZIMMERMAN, S., & LONG, B. (1993). AIDS education in U.S. prisons: A survey of inmate programs. *The Prison Journal 73,* 103–129.

MARTIN, R., ZIMMERMAN, S., LONG, B., & WEST, A. (1995). A content assessment and comparative analysis of prison-based AIDS education programs for inmates. *The Prison Journal 75,* 5–7.

MARUSCHAK, L. (1999, August). HIV in prisons, 1997. *Bureau of Justice Statistics Bulletin.* Washington, DC: U.S. Department of Justice.

MCKINNEY, J. D. (1994). *A descriptive case study of the impact of social learning experiences on adult female inmates.* Paper presented at the annual meeting of the American Society of Criminology, Miami, Florida.

MOORE, J., HARRISON, J., KAY, K., & DOLL, L. (1995). Factors associated with Hispanic women's HIV-related communication and condom use with male partners. *AIDS Care 7,* 415–427.

MOYER, I. L. (1993). Women's prisons: Issues and controversies. In R. Muraskin & T. Alleman (Eds.), *It's a crime: Women and justice* (pp. 193–210). Englewood Cliffs, NJ: Regents/ Prentice Hall.

MURASKIN, R. (1993). Disparate treatment in correctional facilities. In R. Muraskin & T. Alleman (Eds.), *It's a crime: Women and justice.* Englewood Cliffs, NJ: Regents/Prentice Hall.

OLIVERO, J. M. (1992). AIDS in prisons: Judicial and administrative dilemmas and strategies. In P. J. Benekos & A. V. Merlo (Eds.), *Corrections: Dilemmas and directions* (pp. 37–55). Cincinnati, OH: Anderson.

OWEN, B., & BLOOM, B. (1995). Profiling women prisoners: Findings from national surveys and a California sample. *The Prison Journal, 75* (2), 165–185.

SARGENT, E., MARCUS-MENDOZA, S., & YU, C. H. (1993). Abuse and the woman prisoner. In B. R. Fletcher, L. D. Shaver, & D. G. Moon (Eds.), *Women prisoners: A forgotten population* (pp. 55–64). Westport, CT: Praeger.

SEIDLITZ, A. (1999, Spring). *FMC Carswell: Doing "Family" in a Women's Hospice.* [Online]. Available at: www.npha.org/6e.html.

SIEGAL, N. (1998, November). *Lethal Lottery.* POZ [Online]. Available at: www.thebody.com/poz/ survival.

STUNTZNER-GIBSON, D. (1991). Women and HIV disease: An emerging social crisis. *Social Work 36,* 22–28.

TALVI, S. (1999, August). Criminal Procedure. [Online]. Available at: www.mojones.com/info/ fnpfaq.html#fnp.

WEST, A. (1996). *Prison-based AIDS education: A comparative assessment of program impact with male and female inmates.* Unpublished doctoral dissertation, Indiana University of Pennsylvania, Indiana, Pennsylvania.

———. (2001). HIV/AIDS education for Latina inmates: The delimiting impact of culture on prevention efforts. *The Prison Journal 81* (1), 20–41.

WEST, A., & MARTIN, R. (2000). Perceived risk of AIDS among prisoners following educational intervention. *Journal of Offender Rehabilitation 32* (1/2), 75–104.

YEAKLEY, A. M., & GANT, L. (1997). Cultural factors and program implications: HIV/AIDS interventions and condom use among Latinos. *Journal of Multicultural Social Work 6,* 47–71.

ZAITZOW, B. H. (1999, November/December). *Women prisoners and HIV/AIDS.* "HIV Behind Bars," Special issue of the *Journal of the Association of Nurses in AIDS Care 10* (6), 78–89.

P A R T   I V

Issues in Mental Health and Substance Abuse

Part IV focuses on mental health and substance abuse issues. Overall, women prisoners are more likely than men prisoners to need treatment and/or counseling, but these services are limited in women's prisons, and even when present they may be ineffective.

The section begins with Joanne Belknap's chapter on the special needs of female prisoners. Belknap points out differences between men and women prisoners that affect their needs for treatment. Women prisoners' higher likelihood of having experienced abuse is one area that dictates focused and specialized treatment. Unfortunately, many prison programs were developed for male prisoners and are thus not appropriate for women. Additionally, she tells us that women, especially women of color, have been severely affected by U.S. anti-drug policies. Belknap presents a list of the ten most pressing problems faced by women prisoners, followed by proposed solutions. However, she stresses that the ultimate solution is really intervention prior to incarceration.

In Chapter 8, Susan Marcus-Mendoza and Erin Wright examine the relationship between histories of physical and sexual abuse and women prisoners' mental health issues. Using a feminist framework, they demonstrate the far-reaching effects of violence on women's lives, recovery from which is difficult in a prison setting. The needed focus on empowerment of the women is in direct conflict with the goals of most prisons, which include maintaining strict control over the inmate population. Indeed, they suggest that the prison experience often recreates a patriarchal structure that is counterproductive to recovery from abuse. They conclude that although the conditions in prisons are not optimal for therapy with abuse victims, we must find a way to treat these victims of violence. Taking a holistic approach with abused women prisoners and developing gender-specific programming is a step in the right direction.

In Chapter 9, Margaret Kelley examines one of the most necessary elements of programming for women prisoners: substance abuse treatment. In a comprehensive overview, Kelley first explores the need for substance abuse treatment before turning to the historical development of such treatment in women's prisons. Trends such as privatization, coerced treatment, and diversionary programs are examined, followed by a review of different treatment modalities. The reader is presented with evidence of the efficacy of each modality in treating women prisoners.

The latter half of the chapter is devoted to an in-depth examination of 10 model programs. These programs are diverse, and include traditional therapeutic communities, programs for addicted mothers, and nontraditional programs such as Options in Philadelphia. The chapter ends with a discussion of measures of success, cost-effectiveness, and human rights issues in prison-based substance-abuse treatment.

7

Responding to the Needs of Women Prisoners

Joanne Belknap, Ph.D.

❖

Until recent years, the efforts to address women prisoners' needs waned and ebbed, with few and short-lived cycles of meaningful advocacy for this marginalized group. This is disturbing in that the typically deplorable conditions found in men's prisons are matched or even exceeded by those in women's prisons. Over the past two decades, researchers and prison activists have raised awareness about the often traumatic histories of incarcerated girls and women, in addition to drawing attention to the inadequate facilities in which incarcerated women are housed. The purpose of this chapter is to highlight what prisons need to do to truly address incarcerated women's needs.

In most societies both women (relative to men) and prisoners (relative to nonprisoners) are marginalized. Thus, it is hardly surprising that both research about and activism for women prisoners has lagged significantly behind similar efforts for incarcerated men (see Barry, 1991; Belknap, 2001; Faith, 1993; Haft, 1980; Pollock, 2002; Rafter, 1989; Van Ochten, 1993; Wheeler, Tranell, Thomas, & Anglin, 1989). This chapter gives a better understanding of how current incarceration practices in the United States, and indeed worldwide, typically fail in responding adequately to incarcerated women, and hopefully can also offer solutions. First, however, it is important to note that (1) conditions for incarcerated women are usually significantly worse than those for incarcerated men, and (2) this chapter does not advocate for gender equality in imprisonment practices. I state the latter because, although the conditions of women's incarceration are deplorable, so are those of men's, and *all* prisons should strive to better address prisoners' needs. At the same time, we must acknowledge that the current prison system is sexist in its service to women.

A conundrum for feminists in achieving gender equality in prisons is defining what we mean by gender equality. For example, do we want men's and women's prisons to be identical? Joycelyn M. Pollock (2002) states:

> [W]hile women's prisons are still 'different,' the trend in the last decade has been to make them the same. *Parity* has been defined as *uniformity,* and that has become the mantra for the administration of women's prisons, and especially of staff who have been trained in or are coming from prisons for men, or who transfer back and forth between prisons for women and men. (Emphasis in original text.) (p. 2)

Joann B. Morton (1998) also tries to establish gender equality's specific meaning in responding to offenders and in identifying concrete solutions regarding women's incarceration. She notes:

> Where do we go from here in programming for female offenders? We need a new model for treatment for female offenders that is based on the realities of the status of women in our society and that is designed to meet their needs. In such a model, equity would mean comparable rather than the same, and programs would be evaluated on whether they are effective for women rather than whether they are useful for the supervision of men. . . . Given the growing dehumanization of offender treatment in the United States, this need is more pressing than ever before. (p. 12)

As research in recent years identified the institutional sexism within the U.S. prison system, as well as some significant gendered differences in prisons and prisoners, it clarified what good programming for incarcerated women should look like. The goal of this chapter is to present those problems and solutions.

THE RATES OF WOMEN'S IMPRISONMENT

The past few decades have seen an immense increase in the incarceration rate of both women and men in the United States. What is often left out of analyses of this phenomenon is that women's rate of incarceration is even greater than the high rate of men. One study documents that between 1980 and 1994, women's incarceration rate in the United States almost quadrupled, while men's about doubled (Phillips & Harm, 1997). According to a recent government report, over 75,000 women were in state prisons and over 9,000 women were in federal prisons at the end of 1998 (Greenfeld & Snell, 1999, p. 9). Until a little over a decade ago, women typically constituted 5% of prisoners in the United States. As of 1996, that rate increased to over 9% (Mumola & Beck, 1997). This is particularly remarkable when we recognize that men's imprisonment rate grew at a remarkable pace during that time. Notably, women in prison are less likely than their male counterparts to have previous convictions (particularly as juveniles) (Greenfeld & Snell, 1999). Finally, whereas men's incarceration offenses were typically divided equally (about 30% each) among drug, violent, and property offenses, women were predominately incarcerated for drug offenses, followed by property offenses, and women were about half as likely as men to be incarcerated for a violent crime (Greenfeld & Snell, 1999). Despite this evidence of the significant and growing number of incarcerated women, a recent book about our nation's "imprisonment binge" devotes a single page to the topic of women (Irwin & Austin, 1997).

Although women have typically made up a small proportion of prisoners, this "minority" still involves a huge number of women (as demonstrated in the preceding paragraph) and this segment of the prison population continues to grow. Thus it is not surprising that prison professionals, research scholars, and activists have all given unprecedented attention to female offenders issues in recent years. Historically, women's minority representation in the prison system has been used to justify the lack of unique programming for them. "The facilities and services offered to female inmates are based primarily on models derived from male inmates" (Coll et al., 1997, p. 11). The growing number and rate of incarcerated women in the United States and many other countries, makes effective responses to their presence more crucial than ever. However, as Pollock (2002) notes, we imprison women with no "clear mandate for what to do with them once they are incarcerated" (p. 2).

ASSESSING THE NEEDS OF INCARCERATED WOMEN

To best respond to the requirements of incarcerated women, it is important to start with an overview of their lives prior to prison, as well as an understanding of the current state of most prisons. Here we explore how incarcerated women's life experiences are often fraught with physical and psychological victimizations, chemical dependency, poverty, sexism, racism, and inadequate access to decent health care and education. Unfortunately, the prison experience itself often replicates and reinforces the victimization and marginalization of women: continued assaults or harassment (largely at the hands of the guards, but sometimes other prisoners), sexism, racism, and inadequate programming and resources for basic health care and education.

Traumatic and Abusive Histories

Although recent research suggests that incarcerated men and boys have atypically high rates of trauma and abuse, these victimization histories appear to be significantly lower than those of girls. Thus, a significant body of literature addresses the disproportionately high rates of childhood (particularly child sexual abuse) and adulthood (particularly intimate-partner abuse) victimizations in the histories of female offenders (e.g., Arnold, 1990; Browne, Miller, & Maguin, 1999; Chesney-Lind & Rodriguez, 1983; Chesney-Lind & Shelden, 1998; Coker et al., 1998; Coll et al., 1997; Fletcher et al., 1993; Gilfus, 1992; Gray, Mays, & Stohr, 1995; Greenfeld & Snell, 1999; Immarigeon, 1987a, 1987b; James & Meyerding, 1977; Klein & Chao, 1995; Lake, 1993; Owen, 1998; Pollock, 2002; Richie, 1996; Sargent et al., 1993; Silbert & Pines, 1981). Traumatic childhood events are also indicators of boys' likelihood of offending (e.g., Dembo et al., 1993; Dodge et al., 1990; Widom, 1989a, 1989b; Widom & Maxfield, 2001), but they appear to be gendered in that these incidents are more common among girls and women.

Given their extensive abuse and trauma histories, it appears that a combination of various treatments are best suited to help incarcerated women reach recovery. Clearly, a vital aspect of programming in women's prisons is to have a number of treatments available—for example, both individual and group counseling—and to recognize each woman's individual circumstances when designing her treatment at any given time. One therapist working in a women's prison in Canada found art therapy was effective in helping incarcerated women express their feelings about their abuse and "to reconnect with disowned thoughts, feelings and fantasies in a safe way" (Merriam, 1997, p. 157).

Drug and Alcohol Abuse and Dependency

A significant body of research proves anti-drug policies far more negatively affect women's incarceration rates than men's (e.g., Bush-Baskette, 1999; Chesney-Lind, 1997; Chesney-Lind & Shelden, 1998; Covington, 1997; Pollock, 2002). Notably, an in-depth study found that the war on drugs increased African American women's drug incarcerations by over 800% (double the rate of African American men), white women's by almost 250%, and Latina women's by over 300% (Mauer & Huling, 1995). Moreover, research indicates that drug use and abuse is in many ways almost inevitable when women and girls try to "self-medicate" in response to their abusive experiences (e.g., Arnold, 1990; Chesney-Lind & Rodriguez, 1983; Gilfus, 1992; Inciardi et al., 1993; Owen & Bloom, 1995; Pollock, 2002; Sargent, Marcus-Mendoza, & Yu, 1993). Thus, it is not surprising that a significant number of women in prison report substance abuse and dependency as overwhelming issues for them (e.g., Belknap, 2001; Coll et al., 1997; Gilbert, 1999; Pollock, 2002). Unfortunately, despite women's greater likelihood (relative to men) to self-medicate and to be incarcerated for drug offenses, "[h]istorically, treatment, research and recovery have been based on the male experience, often neglecting women's needs" (Covington, 1997, p. 142). Indeed, the often-used 12-step programs are problematic for many incarcerated (and nonincarcerated) women, and have even less appeal for women of color (relative to white women) (Belknap, 2000; Covington, 1997; Kasl, 1992).

Therefore, according to Stephanie Covington (1997), an ideal treatment model for addiction in women's prison must be integrated, addressing three issues. First, programs must acknowledge that, whereas traditional addiction treatment is based on a medical/disease model, many incarcerated women are raised "in an environment where drug dealing and addiction are a way of life" (p. 148). The integrated addiction treatment model should address that women's development is often gendered in the relational need to connect with others, and finally, that trauma (physical, sexual, and/or emotional) is a primary reason for developing drug addiction and relapsing back into it.

Race and Racism—Class and Classism

Similar to men's incarceration, a defining aspect of women's imprisonment in the United States and many other countries is the overrepresentation of women of color and poor women (e.g., Belknap, 2001; Binkley-Jackson, Carter, & Rolison, 1993; Goetting & Howsen, 1983; Pollock, 2002; Rafter, 1985). Research confirms that the racial and class discrimination that ends up in the prisons, begins far earlier. Women of color are processed more harshly by the police and courts than their white counterparts (e.g., Agozino, 1997; Chigwada-Bailey, 1997; Collins, 1997; Gilbert, 1999; Krohn et al., 1983; Kruttschnitt, 1981; Spohn et al., 1987; Visher, 1983), and poorer women receive worse treatment from the criminal justice system than wealthier women (e.g., Kruttschnitt, 1981). For example, even though white and black women have similar arrest rates for drugs, black women are far more likely to be incarcerated for drug offenses (Gilbert, 1999). Bush-Baskette (1999) cites government statistics examining the rise in women's incarceration between 1985 and 1995: "The rate of adult prisoners per 100,000 adult residents throughout the United States increased during this ten-year period from 27 to 68 for White females and 183 to 456 for Black females" (p. 219).

Like men's prisons, the overrepresentation of prisoners of color has been a historical constant in women's prisons (Gilbert, 1999; Rafter, 1985). Some research indicates that people of color are even more highly over-represented in women's than in men's penal institutions (Binkley-Jackson et al., 1993; Goetting & Howsen, 1983; Rafter, 1985). One recent report stated that in state and federal prisons in the United States, from 1985 to 1995, African Americans accounted for between 46% and 51% of male prisoners and 48% to 52% of female prisoners (Mumola & Beck, 1997). This same report found that Latina women's incarceration rate grew even faster than that of Latino men over the same ten years. Unfortunately, U.S. prison systems have done little to assess the representation of Native Americans in its populations. However, an analysis of Montana's prison population in 1995 found that whereas Native Americans constitute 6% of the state's population, they make up 17% of men's and *25% of women's prison populations in that state* (Ross, 1998).

It is clear from the research presented thus far that women of color face discrimination prior to their encounters with the criminal processing system (e.g., Arnold, 1990; Collins, 1990; Gilbert, 1999), and that many then face intense racism—from some prisoners, but more likely, from staff—within the prison. Ross (1998, 2000) and Diaz-Cotto (1996, 2000) write extensively on the racist conditions that Native American and Latina women face in U.S. women's prisons, respectively. Ross (1998, 2000), Diaz-Cotto (1996, 2000), and Gilbert (1999) all address the complexities of sexism, intertwined as it is with racism, classism, and sexuality issues, for incarcerated women. For example, whereas Dobash et al. (1986) and others claim that an overwhelming goal of the women's prison system is to "infantalize" inmates, and that their "success" is measured in passive women, Gilbert (1999) argues:

> From an Afrocentric perspective, the personality attributes that bring Black women into conflict with prison rules are African American culturally normative mandates for survival in American society. For example, dominance is not the feminization of masculine trait; rather it is an index of individual worth in the African American community. Specifically, the index consists of self-help, competence, confidence, and consciousness. African American women help themselves and perceive themselves as talented and worthwhile individuals. They meet challenges to their individual worth and resistance. The resistance confirms a negative stereotype of African American women advanced by the Eurocentric view of gender-role expectations. (p. 239)

Parenting

Most research about parental status of prisoners finds that about four fifths of incarcerated women are parents, and about two thirds are parents of dependent children (e.g., Belknap, 2001; Bloom, 1993; Bloom & Steinhart, 1993; Coll et al., 1997). Most incarcerated women report that worrying about their dependent children is the most stressful aspect of imprisonment (see Bloom & Steinhart, 1993; Boudin, 1997; Farrell, 1998; Henriques, 1996; Owen,

1998). Although women are eager to leave prison in order to better care for their children, it is important to remember that release from prison is not going to solve their parenting problems. These "ex-cons" have to reestablish their relationships with their children, and also face serious economic restraints. "Not only do more women plan to reunite with their children after release from prison, but their capacity to support their children is different from that of a father being released from prison" because he is likely to have more work experience (Phillips & Harm, 1997, p. 6).

A significant source of stress for imprisoned women with dependent children is who cares for the children while the woman is incarcerated. Whereas imprisoned men are likely to have their children's mothers care for them, imprisoned women may not have the other parent available to assume parenting (Enos, 1997; Rafter, 1985; Schafer & Dellinger, 1999). "The loss of maternal duties and roles is especially difficult for women who are concerned about the whereabouts and well-being of their children" (Enos, 1997, p. 59). Some researchers stress that this question of what happens to their children is particularly acute for women with few financial resources and for women of color, regarding temporary custody options and the odds that their children will be raised with self-respect and esteem (see Collins, 1997; Enos, 1997).

One mother's group in a women's prison was cofacilitated by two prisoners (and written about by one of these women [Boudin, 1997]), and here women were able to tell each other of their own troubling childhoods. "[T]hey could begin to see their children's needs, they could then begin to take on a different role in practice with their children" (Boudin, 1997, p. 110). Boudin also points out how the prison system itself exacerbates incarcerated women's dependency on their children: "Women want their children to meet their needs for connecting to the outside world and to family, even when it may be more important for a child not to visit, not to communicate on the phone or even to be distant" (p. 112).

ASSESSING PROBLEMS WITH CURRENT PRISON PRACTICES

It is difficult to "do justice" to the conditions of women's prisons in the United States in this chapter. Despite the fact that many people think prisoners should be treated horribly, we must realize that most prisoners, particularly women, do not serve life sentences, and it would behoove society as well as the prisoners to have better functioning individuals leaving the prisons. Box 7.1 is an overview of the 10 most pressing problems in women's prisons.

It is clear from research on women's prisons, that not only are basic needs not met, but prison can be and often is a terrifying victimization for many. Most poignantly, this group, consisting of individuals who are already more likely than the general population to be survivors of rape and other abuse, is at a significant risk of being sexually victimized by prison staff (e.g., Belknap, 2001; Faith, 1993; Farkas & Rand, 1999; Gilbert, 1999; Human Rights Watch Women's Rights Project, 1996; Van Ochten, 1993; Pollock, 2002). And it is likely that women of color raped in prison by staff are even less likely to be believed or addressed when reporting these immense violations (Gilbert, 1999). Notably, even when the staff do not "outright rape" women prisoners, there is some evidence that the process of body cavity searches may serve as a revictimization for rape survivors, exacerbating their trauma (e.g., Faith, 1993; Heney & Kristiansen, 1997; Pollock, 2002; Zupan, 1992).

Similar to the shortcomings already discussed of 12-step programs when applied to women, some feminist scholars question how boot camp can be an effective treatment for offending women: "Correctional boot camps teach discipline and responsibility by 'breaking down and building up' inmates so that they will no longer commit crimes. However, the assumption that female offenders commit crimes because they are lacking in discipline and responsibility has not been substantiated by research" (Marcus-Mendoza, Klein-Saffran, & Lutze, 1997, p. 174).

One of the gravest gendered injustices of U.S. prisons is that despite women's considerably worse conditions (relative to men's), they have less access to adequate law libraries and jailhouse lawyers, and thus, less chance of having their cases heard in appeal (Alpert, 1982; American Correctional Association, 1990; Carlen, 1983; Carlen &

Box 7.1
THE 10 MOST PRESSING PROBLEMS IN WOMEN'S PRISONS

1. Lack of respect from prison staff, and prison practices that reinforce powerlessness (e.g., Coll et al., 1997; Dobash, Dobash, & Gutteridge, 1986; Heney & Kristiansen, 1997; Pollock, 2002);

2. The need for safety, particularly from sexual victimization by prison staff (Belknap, 2001; Faith, 1993; Farkas & Rand, 1999; Human Rights Watch Women's Rights Project, 1996; Pollock, 2002);

3. Inadequate programs to maintain relationships with children (Owen, 1998; Pollock, 2002; Watterson, 1996);

4. Inadequate access to/availability of health care (both physical and psychological) (Belknap, 2001; Coll et al., 1997; Pollock, 2002; Watterson, 1996);

5. The need for culturally diverse programming that addresses racial/ethnic differences (Belknap, 2000; Diaz-Cotto, 1996; Ross, 2000);

6. Inadequate job training/vocational education (e.g., American Correctional Association, 1990; Belknap, 2000, 2001; Carlen, 1983; Coll et al., 1997; Diaz-Cotto, 1996; Feinman, 1983; Natalizia, 1991; Pollock, 2002);

7. Inadequate access to law libraries, lawyers, and appeal processes (whether to address the charges that led to their imprisonment or the injustices they have experienced in prison) (e.g., American Correctional Association, 1990; Wheeler et al., 1989);

8. Inadequate access to educational programming, such as college courses (American Correctional Association, 1990; Freedman, 1982; Goetting, 1987; Glick & Neto, 1982; Gray, Mays, & Stohr, 1995; Mawby, 1982; Pollock, 2002; Rafter, 1989; Sarri, 1987);

9. Inadequate access to recreational programming (American Correctional Association, 1990; Freedman, 1982; Goetting, 1987; Pollock, 2002; Rafter, 1989);

10. Inadequate access to transitional and life skills programming to help women with their release from prison and "making it" on the outside (Carlen, 1990; Pollock, 2002; Watterson, 1996).

Tchaikovsky, 1985; Haft, 1980; Wheeler et al., 1989). Another important issue is that effective transition counseling needs to be in place within the prison system subsequent to release to increase the likelihood that women will not reoffend. Many women return to prison for parole violations, and this may be because they cannot find housing (see Carlen, 1990). Moreover, if prisons are unable to offer realistic programs to help women recover from addictions and childhood and adulthood abuses and traumas, it is unlikely that releasees will manage to stay out of prison. If effective transitional programming is unavailable, released women are set up to fail. Finally, considering the inadequate medical care, educational and vocational opportunities, and life skills programming available in most U.S. prisons, it is hardly surprising that women's prisons seem to have a revolving door.

SOLUTIONS TO ADDRESSING WOMEN'S INCARCERATION

This chapter focused on the problems with women's prisons and some of the gendered differences among prisoners that indicate different approaches may be necessary for incarcerated women and men. Certainly there should be some uniformity: *both* women and men need access to adequate lawyers and legal assistance, safety, education, counseling, recreation, vocational training, and most other programming. At the same time, it is important to recognize some of the gender differences among prisoners. For example, women are more likely to be survivors of abuse (particularly sexual abuse), have different health care issues (e.g., pre- and perinatal), and are more likely to not only place a high priority on their children, but children are more likely to be affected by their mothers' than their fathers' incarceration. In striving for parity, we still acknowledge that we live in a gendered world where some programming is better suited to and more in demand in women's than men's prisons.

Before making specific recommendations about women's prison programming, it is important to state that more needs to be done to keep women from committing offenses, in particular, to responding to life crises such as sexual abuse and domestic violence cases where women's survival skills become criminalized (see, for example, Belknap & Holsinger, 1998; Richie, 1996). Morton's (1998) holistic analysis of programming for women offenders identifies eight components that, at a minimum, are necessary for effective programming: (1) incarceration should be invoked only when women are a danger to themselves or others; (2) programming and supervision should provide parity with men's prisons, but be women-centered; (3) services and programming should be based on women's individual circumstances and needs; (4) supervision and programming should be humane; (5) programs and services should take the impact of gendered acculturation into account (as well as biological differences); (6) the programs, practices, and agencies for women prisoners need to be gender sensitive; (7) staff should be carefully selected, trained and supervised; and (8) the programming, supervision, and management of women prisoners should be subject to periodic evaluation and ongoing supervision "to ensure that these areas are accomplishing the goals they were assigned to address" (pp. 12–15). I have adapted Morton's recommendations in Box 7.2, with suggestions for improved responses to incarcerated women.

The goal in this chapter was to highlight the major issues surrounding women's incarceration in terms of their programming needs. In some ways, it is useful to seek parity

---

Box 7.2

PROPOSED SOLUTIONS TO ADDRESSING INCARCERATED WOMEN'S NEEDS

1. Improvement in staff recruitment and better training around women's backgrounds
2. Improved and more consistent monitoring of all prison staff
3. Punishment (and firing if necessary) for staff who are disrespectful of, inappropriate with, or otherwise unethical with women prisoners
4. Consistent evaluations of various prison programs and services (where subsequent programming will depend on the success in the evaluations)
5. Improved individual and group counseling for childhood and adulthood traumas and other psychological needs (including groups run by and for prisoners)
6. Improved access to and quality of medical care, education, vocational, recreational and other programs
7. Improved and varied drug treatment programs
8. Improved programs and opportunities to maintain contact with children
9. More varied implementation of quality programs addressing cultural and spiritual differences and needs
10. Improved transitional and life skills programming
11. Increased use of community-based and alternative sentences
12. More community education and awareness about the plight of incarcerated women and the crisis in women's incarceration.

---

with men's prisons to ensure that women have equal access to education, health care, vocational programming, lawyers and legal libraries, and so on. But it is also important to recognize that men's prisons in the United States and other countries do not adequately serve their prisoners, even though they have access to more and better services and programming overall, relative to incarcerated women. It is also necessary to understand patterns in gender differences among the prisoners. For example, although male prisoners indicate disproportionately high levels of childhood and adulthood traumas, females' rates are significantly higher. Another example of the gendered nature of prisoners to consider in programming and services is that women prisoners tend to have far closer ties to their children and to be far more emotionally and financially responsible parents than their male counterparts; thus, a mother's incarceration generally has greater impact on both children and prisoners. Furthermore, women prisoners' increased likelihood of testing HIV positive (relative to men) (e.g., Clark & Boudin, 1990; Greenfeld & Snell, 1999; Hankins et al., 1994; Lawson & Fawkes, 1993; Pollock, 2002) and their pregnancy and postnatal needs require gender differences in medical facilities and care in prisons. Finally, it is crucial to slow down the incarceration of both women and men, and doing so will likely result in better communities, children less likely to turn to crime, and offenders who are more able to maintain jobs, education, treatment, and parenting. "Community-based sanctions such as probation, work release, electronic monitoring, community service, and treatment programs are potentially less disruptive to the lives of children whose mothers are involved in the criminal justice system" (Phillips & Harm, 1997, p. 5). Although prison is an appropriate, necessary place for violent, repeat, and/or serious offenders, many of the inhabitants in U.S. women's prisons have not committed serious offenses or proved themselves to be dangerous, and these women are served poorly by their incarceration. It is more than possible to take what we've learned from the vast increase in recent research on female offenders and provide more adequate programming and treatment for incarcerated women as well as to question current decisions and practices in incarceration.

DISCUSSION QUESTIONS

1. How do women prisoners' personal histories affect their needs for prison programs? Why does the author suggest that a variety of treatments are needed?

2. How have anti-drug policies affected women? How does the impact differ from that on men? What role do race and ethnicity play? What issues need to be addressed to make drug treatment programs for women prisoners more effective?

3. The author suggests that many women return to prison because of circumstances beyond their control. What measures could be taken to reduce female recidivism?

4. What are some potential solutions to the problems of incarcerated women? How are these similar to the problems faced by men prisoners? In what ways do they differ?

WEBNOTES

Go to the web site for the California Coalition for Women Prisoners: http://www.prisonactivist.org/ccwp. Find the Theresa Cruz story and read it. What types of prison programs do you think would be effective for women like Theresa?

REFERENCES

AGOZINO, B. (1997). *Black women and the criminal justice system.* Aldershot, England: Ashgate.

ALPORT, G. (1982). Women prisoners and the law: Which way will the pendulum swing? In B. R. Price and N. J. Sokoloff (Eds.), *The criminal justice system and women* (pp. 171–182). New York: Clark and Boardman.

AMERICAN CORRECTIONAL ASSOCIATION. (1990). *The female offender: What does the future hold?* Arlington, VA: Kirby Lithographic Company.

ARNOLD, R. (1990). Processes of victimization and criminalization of black women. *Social Justice, 17,* 153–166.

BARRY, E. M. (1991). Jail litigation concerning women prisoners. *The Prison Journal, 71,* 44–50.

BELKNAP, J. (2000). Programming and health care responsibility for incarcerated women. In J. James (Ed.), *States of confinement: policing, detention, and prisons* (pp. 109–123). New York: St. Martin's Press.

———. (2001). *The invisible woman: Gender, crime, and justice* (2nd ed.). Belmont, CA: Wadsworth.

BELKNAP, J., & HOLSINGER, K. (1998). An overview of delinquent girls: How theory and practice have failed and the need for innovative changes. In R. T. Zaplin (Ed.), *Female crime and delinquency: Critical perspectives and effective interventions* (pp. 31–64). Gaithersburg, MD: Aspen.

BINKLEY-JACKSON, D., CARTER, V. L., & ROLISON, G. L. (1993). African–American women in prison. In B. R. Fletcher, L. D. Shaver, & D. G. Moon (Eds.), *Women prisoners: A forgotten population* (pp. 65–74). Westport, CT: Praeger.

BLOOM, B. (1993). Incarcerated mothers and their children: Maintaining family ties. In *Female offenders: Meeting the needs of a neglected population* (pp. 60–68). Laurel, MD: American Correctional Association.

BLOOM, B., & STEINHART, D. (1993). *Why punish the children?* San Francisco: National Council on Crime and Delinquency.

BOUDIN, K. (1997). Lessons from a mother's program in prison. *Women and Therapy, 21* (1), 103–125.

BROWNE, A., MILLER, B., & MAGUIN, E. (1999). Prevalence and severity of lifetime physical and sexual victimization among incarcerated women. *International Journal of Law and Psychiatry, 22,* 301–322.

BUSH-BASKETTE, S. R. (1999). The "War on Drugs": A war against women? In S. Cook & S. Davies (Eds.), *Harsh punishment: International experiences of women's imprisonment* (pp. 211–229). Boston: Northeastern University Press.

CARLEN, P. (1983). *Women's imprisonment: A study in social control.* London: Routledge & Kegan Paul.

———. (1990). *Alternatives to women's imprisonment.* Milton Keynes, UK: Open University Press.

CARLEN, P., & TCHAIKOVSKY, C. (1985). Women in prison. In P. Carlen, J. Hicks, J. O'Dwyer, & D. Christina (Eds.), *Criminal women* (pp. 182–186). Cambridge: Polity Press.

CHESNEY-LIND, M. (1997). *The female offender: Girls, women and crime.* Thousand Oaks, CA: Sage.

CHESNEY-LIND, M., & RODRIGUEZ, N. (1983). Women under lock and key. *The Prison Journal, 63,* 47–65.

———. (1998). *Girls, delinquency, and juvenile justice.* Belmont, CA: Wadsworth.

CHIGWADA-BAILEY, R. (1997). *Black women's experiences of criminal justice.* Winchester, England: Waterside Press.

CLARK, J., & BOUDIN, K. (1990). Community of women organize themselves to cope with the AIDS crisis: A case study from Bedford Hills Correctional Facility. *Social Justice, 17,* 90–109.

COKER, A. L., PATEL, N. J., KRISHNASWAMI, S., SCHMIDT, W., & RICHTER, D. L. (1998). Childhood forced sex and cervical dysplasia among women prison inmates. *Violence Against Women, 4* (5), 595–608.

COLL, C. G., MILLER, J. B., FIELDS, J. P., & Matthews, B. (1997). The experiences of women in prison: Implications for services and prevention. *Women & Therapy, 20* (4), 11–28.

COLLINS, C. F. (1997). *The imprisonment of African American women.* Jefferson, NC: McFarland & Company.

COLLINS, P. H. (1990). *Black feminist thought.* Boston: Unwin Hyman.

COVINGTON, S. (1997). Women in prison: Approaches in the treatment of our most invisible population. *Women & Therapy, 21* (1), 141–153.

DEMBO, R., WILLIAMS, L., & SCHMEIDLER, J. (1993). Gender differences in mental health service needs among youths entering a juvenile detention center. *Journal of Prison & Jail Health, 12* (2), 73–101.

DIAZ-COTTO, J. (1996). *Gender, ethnicity, and the state: Latina and Latino prison politics.* Albany: The State University of New York.

————. (2000). Race, ethnicity, and gender in studies of incarceration. In J. James (Ed.), *States of confinement: Policing, detention, and prisons* (pp. 123–131). New York: St. Martin's Press.

DOBASH, R. P., DOBASH, R. E., & GUTTERIDGE, S. (1986). *The imprisonment of women.* Oxford: Basil Blackwell.

DODGE, K. A., BATES, J. E., & PETTIT, G. S. (1990). Mechanisms in the cycle of violence. *Science, 250,* 1678–1683.

ENOS, S. (1997). Managing motherhood in prison: The impact of race and ethnicity on child placements. *Women & Therapy, 20* (4), 57–74.

FAITH, K. (1993). *Unruly women: The politics of confinement and resistance.* Vancouver: Press Gang.

FARKAS, M. A., & RAND, K. R. L. (1999). Sex matters: A gender-specific standard for cross-gender searches of inmates. *Women & Criminal Justice, 10* (3), 31–56.

FARRELL, A. (1998). Mothers offending against their role: An Australian experience. *Women & Criminal Justice, 9* (4), 47–69.

FEINMAN, C. (1983). An historical overview of the treatment of incarcerated women: Myths and realities of rehabilitation. *The Prison Journal, 63,* 21–26.

FLETCHER, B. R., ROLISON, G. L., & MOON, D. G. (1993). The woman prisoner. In B. R. Fletcher, L. D. Shaver, & D. G. Moon (Eds.), *Women prisoners: A forgotten population* (pp. 15–26). Westport, CT: Praeger.

FREEDMAN, E. (1982). Nineteenth-century women's prison reform and its legacy. In D. K. Weisberg (Ed.), *Women and the Law,* Vol. I (pp. 141–157). Cambridge, MA: Schenkman.

GELSTHORPE, L. (1989). *Sexism and the female offender.* Aldershot, England: Gower.

GILBERT, E. (1999). Crime, sex, and justice: African American women in U.S. prisons. In S. Cook & S. Davies (Eds.), *Harsh punishment: International experiences of women's imprisonment* (pp. 230–249). Boston: Northeastern University Press.

GILFUS, M. E. (1992). From victims to survivors to offenders: Women's routes of entry and immersion into street crime. *Women & Criminal Justice, 4,* 63–90.

GLICK, R. M., & NETO, V. V. (1982). National study of women's correctional programs. In B. R. Price & N. J. Sokoloff (Eds.), *The criminal justice system and women* (pp. 141–154). New York: Clark and Boardman.

GOETTING, A. (1987). Racism, sexism, and ageism in the prison community. *Federal Probation, 49,* 10–22.

GOETTING, A., & HOWSEN, R. M. (1983). Women in prison: A profile. *The Prison Journal, 63,* 27–46.

GRAY, T., MAYS, G. L., & STOHR, M. K. (1995). Inmate needs and programming in exclusively women's jails. *The Prison Journal, 75,* (2), 186–202.

GREENE, PETERS, & ASSOCIATES. (1998, October). *Guiding principles for promising female programming.* Nashville, TN: The Office of Juvenile Justice and Delinquency Prevention, 94.

GREENFELD, L. A., & SNELL, T. L. (1999, December). *Women offenders.* Washington, DC: U.S. Department of Justice, Bureau of Justice Statistics: Special Report.

HAFT, M. G. (1980). Women in prison: Discriminatory practices and some legal solutions. In S. K. Datesman and F. R. Scarpitti (Eds.), *Women, Crime, and Justice* (pp. 320–338). New York: Oxford Press.

HANKINS, C. A., GENDRON, S., HANDLEY, M. A., RICHARD, C., TUNG, M. T. L., & O'SHAUGHNESSY, M. (1994). HIV infection among women in prison. *American Journal of Public Health, 84,* (10), 1637–1640.

HANNAH-MOFFAT, K. (1994). Unintended consequences of feminism and prison reform. *Forum on Corrections Research, 6,* 7–10.

HENEY, J., & KRISTIANSEN, C. M. (1997). An analysis of the impact of prison on women survivors of childhood sexual abuse. *Women & Therapy, 20* (4), 29–44.

HENRIQUES, Z. W. (1996). Imprisoned mothers and their children: Separation–reunion syndrome dual impact. *Women & Criminal Justice, 8* (1), 77–96.

HUMAN RIGHTS WATCH WOMEN'S RIGHTS PROJECT. (1996). *All too familiar: Sexual abuse of women in U.S. state prisons.* New York: Human Rights Watch.

IMMARIGEON, R. (1987a). Women in prison. *Journal of the National Prison Project, 11,* 1–5.

———. (1987b). Few diversion programs are offered female offenders. *Journal of the National Prison Project,* 12, 9–11.

INCIARDI, J., LOCKWOOD, D., & POTTIEGER, A. E. (1993). *Women and crack-cocaine.* New York: Macmillan.

IRWIN, J., & AUSTIN, J. (1997). *It's about time: America's imprisonment binge* (2nd ed.). Belmont, CA: Wadsworth.

JAMES, J., & MEYERDING, J. (1977). Early sexual experiences and prostitution. *American Journal of Psychiatry, 134* (12), 1381–1385.

KASL, C. (1992). *Many roads, one journey.* New York: HarperCollins.

KLEIN, H., & CHAO, B. S. (1995). Sexual abuse during childhood and adolescence as predictors of HIV-related sexual risk during adulthood among female sexual partners of drug users. *Violence Against Women, 1* (1), 55–76.

KNIGHT, B. (1992). Women in prison as litigants: Prospects for post-prison futures. *Women & Criminal Justice, 4,* 91–116.

KROHN, M., CURRY, J. P., & NELSON-KILGER, S. (1983). Is chivalry dead? An analysis of changes in police dispositions of males and females. *Criminology, 21,* 417–437.

KRUTTSCHNITT, C. (1981). Social status and sentences of female offenders. *Law & Society Review, 15,* 247–265.

LAKE, E. S. (1993). An exploration of the violent victim experiences of female offenders. *Violence and Victims, 8* (1), 41–51.

LAWSON, W. T., & FAWKES, L. S. (1993). HIV, AIDS, and the female offender. In *Female offenders: Meeting the needs of a neglected population* (pp. 43–38). Laurel, MD: American Correctional Association.

MARCUS-MENDOZA, S. T., KLEIN-SAFFRAN, J., & LUTZE, F. (1997). A feminist examination of boot camp prison programs for women. *Women & Therapy 21* (1), 173–185.

MAUER, M., & HULING, T. (1995). *Young black Americans and the criminal justice system: Five years later.* Washington, DC: The Sentencing Project.

MAWBY, R. I. (1982). Women in prison: A British study. *Crime & Delinquency, 28,* 224–239.

MERRIAM, B. (1997). To find a voice: Art therapy in a women's prison. *Women & Therapy, 21* (1), 157–171.

MORTON, J. B. (1998). Programming for women offenders. In J. B. Morton (Ed.), *Complex challenges, collaborative solutions: Programming for adult and juvenile female offenders* (pp. 1–18). Lanham, MD: American Correctional Association.

MUMOLA, C. J., & BECK, A. J. (1997, June). *Prisoners in 1996.* Washington, DC: U.S. Department of Justice, Bureau of Justice Statistics.

NATALIZIA, E. (1991, Fall). Feminism and criminal justice reform. *Odyssey,* 19–20.

OWEN, B. (1998). *"In the mix": Struggle and survival in a women's prison.* Albany: State University of New York Press.

OWEN, B., & BLOOM, B. (1995). *Modeling gender-specific services in juvenile justice: Policy and program recommendations.* Final Report submitted to the Office of Criminal Justice Planning of the State of California.

PHILLIPS, S. D., & HARM, N. J. (1997). Women prisoners: A contextual framework. *Women & Therapy, 20* (4), 1–10.

POLLOCK, J. M. (2002). *Women, prison, and crime* (2nd ed.). Belmont, CA: Wadsworth.

RAFTER, N. HAHN. (1985). *Partial justice: Women in state prisons, 1800–1935.* Boston: Northeastern University Press.

———. (1989). Gender and justice: The equal protection issues. In L. Goodstein & D. MacKenzie (Eds.), *The American prison* (pp. 89–109). New York: Plenum Press.

RICHIE, B. E. (1996). *Compelled to crime: The gender entrapment of black battered women.* New York: Routledge.

ROSS, L. (1998). *Inventing the savage: The social construction of Native American criminality.* Austin: University of Texas Press.

———. (2000). Imprisoned native women and the importance of native traditions. In J. James (Ed.), *States of confinement: Policing, detention, and prisons* (pp. 132–144). New York: St. Martin's Press.

SARGENT, E., MARCUS-MENDOZA, S., & YU, C. H. (1993). Abuse and the woman prisoner. In B. R. Fletcher, Shaver, L. D., & Moon, D. G. (Eds.), *Women prisoners: A forgotten population* (pp. 55–64). Westport, CT: Praeger.

SARRI, R. (1987). Unequal protection under the law. Women and the criminal justice system. In J. Figueira-McDonough and R. Sarri (Eds.) *The trapped woman: Catch-22 in deviance and control* (pp. 394–426). Newbury Park, CA: Sage.

SCHAFER, N. E., & DELLINGER, A. B. (1999). Jailed parents: An assessment. *Women & Criminal Justice, 10* (4), 73–91.

SHAW, M., WITH RODGERS, K., BLANCHETTE, J., THOMAS, L. S., HATTEM, T., & TAMARACK, L. (1990). *Survey of federally sentenced women.* Ottawa: Ministry of the Solicitor General, Corrections Branch.

SILBERT, M. H., & PINES, A. M. (1981). Sexual child abuse as an antecedent to prostitution. *Child Abuse and Neglect, 5,* 407–411.

SPOHN, C., GRUHL, J., & WELCH, S. (1987). The impact of the ethnicity and gender of defendants on the decision to reject or dismiss felony charges. *Criminology, 25,* 175–191.

VACHON, M. M. (1994). It's about time: The legal context of policy changes for female offenders. *Forum on Corrections Research, 6,* 3–6.

VAN OCHTEN, M. (1993). Legal issues and the female offender. In *Female offenders: Meeting the needs of a neglected population* (pp. 31–36). Laurel, MD: American Correctional Association.

VAUGHN, M. S., & SMITH, L. G. (1999). Practical penal harm medicine in the United States. *Justice Quarterly, 16* (1), 175–232.

VISHER, C. A. (1983.) Gender, police arrest decisions, and notions of chivalry. *Criminology, 21,* 5–28.

WATTERSON, K. (1996). *Women in prison: Inside the concrete womb.* Boston: Northeastern University Press.

WELLISCH, J., PRENDERGAST, M., & ANGLIN, M. D. (1996). Needs assessment and services for drug-abusing women offenders: Results from a national survey of community-based treatment programs. *Women & Criminal Justice, 8* (1), 27–60.

WHEELER, P. A., TRAMMELL, R., THOMAS, J., & FINDLAY, J. (1989). Persephone chained: Parity of equality in women's prisons. *The Prison Journal, 69,* 88–102.

WIDOM, C. S. (1989a). The cycle of violence. *Science 244,* 160–166.

———. (1989b). Child abuse, neglect, and adult behavior: Research design and findings on criminality, violence, and child abuse. *American Journal of Orthopsychiatry, 59* (3), 355–367.

WIDOM, C. S., & MAXFIELD, M. G. (2001, February). *An update on the "cycle of violence."* Washington, DC: National Institute of Justice, Office of Justice Programs, Research in Brief.

ZUPAN, L. A. (1992). The progress of women correctional officers in all-male prisons. In I. L. Moyer (Ed.), *The changing roles of women in the criminal justice system* (2nd ed.), (pp. 232–244). Prospect Heights, IL: Waveland Press.

8

Treating the Woman Prisoner

The Impact of a History of Violence

Susan T. Marcus-Mendoza, Ph.D., and Erin Wright, M.A.

❖

Numerous studies have shown that the majority of female inmates suffer some form of abuse before they are incarcerated. Many experience more than one type of violence, and have been abused as both children and adults. Violence against women can leave its victims with myriad psychological problems that require treatment. We will examine the types of violence women inmates have experienced and their resulting psychological problems. We will also explore some of the better treatments available in prison and discuss the pros and cons of prison-based treatment for abuse issues.

A HISTORY OF VIOLENCE

Violence against women is an ever present reality in the United States. For many, abuse starts early in life and continues into adulthood. The effects of violence on women are devastating and nowhere is this seen more clearly than in women's prisons in the United States, where the vast majority of inmates have been victims of abuse. This chapter describes the types of violence women inmates endure prior to their incarceration and the resulting psychological impact. We also explore available treatment for abused women in prison, and the implications of prison-based treatment.

The Devastation of Violence against Women

Researchers finally have turned their attention to the plight of female inmates in sufficient numbers to produce a substantial literature. We are beginning to understand the etiology of female criminality and the findings are striking. Environmental factors, as opposed to biological determinism, appear to play a huge role in the genesis of women's criminal behavior. Study after study has shown that factors such as economic marginalization, substance abuse, sexual and physical abuse, and parenting without adequate financial resources are part of what motivates women to commit crimes (Chesney-Lind, 1997; Girshick, 1999; Owen, 1998; Simon & Landis, 1991; Sommers, 1995). Of these issues, a history of violence may be the most important as it often directly leads to other problems such as substance abuse and juvenile delinquency. This section examines the prevalence of violence reported by women in prison and its effects. Although we will discuss different types of violence, it is important to note that it is impossible to truly separate them (i.e., a battered women may experience physical, emotional, *and* sexual violence).

Researchers have found that up to 90% of women in prison have experienced one or more types of abuse: emotional, physical, sexual, and psychological (American Correctional Association, 1990; Browne, Miller, & Maguin, 1999; Girshick, 1999; Marcus-Mendoza, Sargent, & Chong Ho, 1994; Owen, 1998; Owen & Bloom, 1995). These statistics vary widely because of methodology. For instance, some researchers look at only sexual and physical abuse or only abuse before or after the age of 18. Overall, these studies' estimates of the incidence of sexual abuse before the age of 18 range from 13% to 59%, and estimates of physical abuse before the age of 18 range from 29% to 70%. The incidence of emotional abuse under the age of 18 ranges from 40% to 55%, and estimates of emotional abuse over the age of 18 range from 48% to 83%. The number of women sexually assaulted under the age of 18 ranges from 17% to 23%, and over 18 from 31% to 46%. The majority of women in prison (58% to 85%) have experienced domestic violence. A government study on women in prison found that 64% percent of the mentally ill women in state prisons and 78% of the mentally ill women in federal prisons had a history of physical or mental abuse (United States General Accounting Office, 1999).

No matter how researchers define it, the incidence of abuse experienced by women before they go to prison is high. According to Watterson (1996),

> New research in the 1980s and 1990s has confirmed that, in fact, an enormous proportion of women in prison have been victims of abuse. In a survey published in 1990, the American Correctional Association found that over half of the women it surveyed had been physically abused and 36 percent had been sexually abused. Women in prison say the figures are far greater than that, and a study in Massachusetts confirmed their perceptions. It showed that 88 percent of the women inside prison in that state had experienced traumatic episodes of violence—childhood sexual or physical abuse, or adult rape or battering—before their first arrest. (p. 36).

Clearly, a history of abuse and battering is very prevalent among women in prison.

Box 8.1

Researchers have found that up to 90% of women in prison have experienced one or more types of abuse: emotional, physical, sexual, and psychological.

These results are even more compelling when compared to other populations of women. In a study of the incidence of sexual abuse of women in the general population, Russell (1984) found that 25% had been raped as adults and one third had been sexually abused as children. Walker (1994), in a comprehensive literature review, reported that approximately 25% of adult women had been battered by a partner. Overall, Walker found that about 50% of women had experienced some form of physical, sexual, or psychological abuse, and further research on psychiatric patients revealed that 68% of female outpatients had experienced physical or sexual abuse, and 50% to 80% of hospitalized male and female patients had experienced some form of physical, sexual, or psychological abuse (Walker, 1994). Again, although statistics on abuse often vary because of differences in definitions and methodology, women in the United States experience a high percentage of abuse. The fact that there is a higher incidence of abuse among psychiatric populations and inmates than among the general population of women demonstrates the devastating effects of violence against women.

Given the prevalence of a history of violence, it is not surprising that most women in prison are still dealing with the aftershocks of abuse. A substantial number may be experiencing post-traumatic stress syndrome (PTSD). According to the Diagnostic and Statistical Manual of Mental Disorders (DSM–IV; American Psychiatric Association, 1994), PTSD is an illness precipitated by a traumatic event and characterized by a number of distressing symptoms including flashbacks, intrusive thoughts, difficulty sleeping and concentrating, avoidance of people or things that arouse recollections of the trauma, recurring dreams about the event, and psychological and physical reactions to events that symbolize or resemble the traumatic experience. Although there are not many studies that systematically examine the incidence of PTSD, Zlotnick (1997), in her review of the existing literature, reported that PTSD rates among women prisoners are twice that of women in the general population. Research also shows that 78% to 85% of women inmates have experienced at least one traumatic event, compared to 69% of women in the general population (Zlotnick, 1997). Teplin, Abram, and McClellend (1996) report that 33.5% of female jail detainees had experienced PTSD sometime during their life, while 22.3% were currently experiencing it. Zlotnick's study found rates of 48.2% for current PTSD and 20% for lifetime PTSD.

There are other consequences of abuse experienced by girls and women, some of which directly relate to their criminality. According to Sommers (1995), "When children are sexually abused, they experience an invasion of their personal boundaries and they are unable to maintain a sense of their own identity" (p. 73). This abuse is just the beginning of a loss of self that begins a downward spiral if nothing is done to help the victims. One result is a lack of self-esteem.

Box 8.2

PTSD AND WOMEN PRISONERS

- 78% to 85% have experienced at least one traumatic event
- 48.2% are experiencing current symptoms of PTSD

> Abuse is what kicked off alcohol or drug addiction in many of these women; it's what made them run away from home and get into trouble with the law in the first place when they were juveniles; it's what has made so many of them attempt suicide; it's what has kept their self-esteem at a low ebb; it's what has kept them in trouble with the law as grown women who bear the label of "criminal." (Watterson, 1996, p. 36)

Essentially, childhood abuse is a major catalyst toward criminality for many women.

Belknap and Holsinger (1998) see a pattern emerging from the research on delinquent girls in the 1980s and 1990s that suggests that childhood victimization results in aberrant behavior. They report a connection between abuse and running away and drug and alcohol misuse; then to survive and feed their drug habits, girls resort to prostitution, selling drugs, and robbery. Zaplin (1998) echoes these sentiments. She reports that

> . . . the life experiences of female offenders give them a distorted view of empathy and caring. As a result of their childhood experiences, they do not feel self-worth. They are not able to develop empathic and caring attitudes towards themselves. Nor are they able to develop empathic and caring attitudes towards others. (p. 67)

This, according to Zaplin, leads to ongoing emotional stress, characterized by self-hatred, anxiety, depression, and aggressive and impulsive behavior.

Widom (2000) studied sexually abused children from ages 0–11 to age 33 and described the girls as being "derailed" by abuse into the criminal justice system. Girls in her study became runaways to escape an abusive environment, scored lower on IQ and reading-ability tests, were likely to be raised in homes with alcoholic or drug-abusing parents, had friends and relatives who had been arrested, and consequently lacked important social and psychological resources needed to deal with adult life in a healthy manner. In Widom's study, 8% of the girls became chronic, persistent offenders, whereas none of the control group of nonabused girls fell into this category. These findings are mirrored by researchers and continue to be an important focus of research on girls in the juvenile justice system (Chesney-Lind, 1997; Heney & Kristiansen, 1998; Pepi, 1998).

Traumas suffered as a child can also affect women into adulthood. As noted earlier, many women in prison have suffered or are suffering from PTSD. Those not diagnosed with PTSD may still be profoundly affected by childhood trauma. One area that is being addressed increasingly by researchers is women's sense of power. Sommers (1995) relates Jean Baker Miller's work on relational theory and women offenders who have been abused. According to Sommers, Miller implies that "Healthy, mutually empathic relationships empower women to interact within society as if it were a growth fostering environment" (p. 118). However, women who have been abused have not had the benefit of such healthy, empowering relationships:

> It is when a woman is disempowered in this way that she feels unable to make an impact on her personal or her social world; she is unable to develop the capacity to become fully functional in the world and retreats into unhealthy relationships and behaviours, through which she intermittently experiences the illusion of power. (p. 118)

She concludes that in an effort to feel empowered, women break the law.

This sense of disempowerment may also lead to domestic violence. Walker (1984), in her study of battered women, found that almost two thirds had either seen their father batter their mother, or had been battered as a child. Further, she found almost half of her sample had been sexually abused as children, a higher rate than is reported among women in the general population. This, again, suggests that violence leads to more violence, which may lead to incarceration.

Dougherty (1998) also looks at women's view of their power in relation to trauma to explain female criminality. She has posited a power-belief theory, as yet untested. She claims that women who have been abused feel helpless. Despite an internal feeling of power-lessness, they will define themselves as 'tough' and often commit crimes to survive. And, according to Dougherty, although these women acknowledge being abused, they often min-imize or refute its impact on them. Similarly, Fishman (2000) suggests that slavery, a prod-uct of a patriarchal and racist society in which women and men were abused in every way imaginable, led to criminal resistance among black men and women, setting the stage for black women's criminal activities today. Owen (1998) agrees that women's power, espe-cially in the criminal justice system, is limited. "Beyond the patriarchy that defines and lim-its the options and personal choices of all women in contemporary society, women within the criminal justice system are also women on the social, racial, and economic margins of conventional society" (p. 41). Although theories about the relationship between trauma and crime differ and details of traumas experienced vary, it appears that trauma's relationship to a feeling of power, in a society where women have limited options, may indeed be another casualty of abuse and a pathway to crime.

Widom (2000) does leave some room for hope. In her longitudinal study of abused children followed into adulthood, she found that while abused children are at high risk for criminal behavior, 70% did not become offenders. Therefore, she concludes that crime is not the inevitable result of abuse. However, the plight of women who commit crime is pretty grim before they even enter the prison gates.

Programming for Women in Prison

The majority of women in prison are dealing with the aftermath of violence that for many of them has been a way of life since they were children. They have been abused by the very people who should care the most about them—parents, spouses, and other family mem-bers. This situation presents unique challenges for working with these women, as they may not trust, thanks to their history of familial abuse. In a recent government report, Ritchie (2000) cautions, "Important considerations challenge the work of several communities of practitioners. Domestic violence advocates and sexual assault service providers need new information about the effects of abuse against women and the ways in which abuse influ-ences women's participation in illegal activity" (p. 8). As noted previously, abuse both makes women harder to connect with and leads them to criminal activity. Breaking through these barriers is indeed, as Ritchie claims, a challenge.

Ritchie (2000) concludes that those who design programming for women need to consider several issues, including this connection between abuse and crime. We would add that this must be a comprehensive overhaul, taking into account the unique etiology of women's crime and their needs and hopes as women and mothers. Therapeutic intervention strategies and indeed all programming should be designed with this often distrustful and hard-to-reach population of women suffering from the effects of violence and abuse in mind. Ritchie calls for gender-specific approaches to programming that help empower women and lead to positive life changes once they are released.

Despite calls for a change in prison programming, we have not made significant progress. The National Institute of Justice sponsored a nationwide survey of state prisons in 1993 and 1994. Morash, Bynum, and Koons (1998) surveyed departments of corrections in all states and at least one women's prison in each state. They found problems at several levels. First, their study revealed that about one in four administrators surveyed felt that current assessment and classification protocols did not provide adequate information about women's programmatic needs. Indeed, in 39 states, the same instrument was used for men and women. In seven states, the instrument was adapted for women, and in only three states was there a special instrument designed to capture women's needs. When asked about specific programming for women, 242 programs were mentioned. However, most of these programs were clustered in the same states, as only 16 states had programs cited as highly or considerably innovative. Of these programs, only 90 fell into the mental health category (which includes treatment for abuse and domestic violence). About one third focused on substance abuse, which is an important problem. However, for many women, it may be just one more consequence of emotional, psychological, and physical abuse. Interestingly, administrators cited an emphasis on self-esteem, empowerment, and self-sufficiency as programmatic elements related to success in victimization programming. These issues mirror those cited as psychological consequences of abuse and show that these important issues must receive attention for women to become psychologically healthy.

There was some progress in prison programming for women from the 1800s and 1900s, when women inmates were solely taught to be feminine, submissive, and domestic, so they could become better women (Freedman, 1981). However, many prison systems still base their treatment of women on male offending patterns and programming. And, according to Morash, Haarr, and Rucker (1994), vocational programming for female inmates still reflects gender stereotyping. Women learn horticulture, typing, and food preparation, whereas men learn more marketable skills, such as assembly work or mechanics. Therefore, women are at a disadvantage when they re-enter the job market. The gender-stereotyped programming also suggests that prison administrators continue to see female offenders as "fallen women," as they were considered in the 1800s and 1900s (Freedman, 1981). By preparing women inmates to be better at "women's work," prisons perpetuate the idea that if women can learn to assume gender-stereotyped roles, they will stay out of trouble. This strategy ignores the reality of women's criminality as it relates to violence and social and economic marginalization, and justifies a continued focus on punishment, rather than gender-specific programmatic intervention.

Prison practices are also in direct conflict with the need for a gender-specific approach to treatment. Marcus-Mendoza, Klein-Saffran, and Lutze (1998), in their feminist examination of boot camp prison programs, argue that the practices of boot camps, and indeed much prison programming for women, are diametrically opposed to those of feminist therapy, which as conceptualized by Brown (1996) helps a woman resist dominant cultural norms and attend to her own voice. Resistance, rather than a form of lawlessness or unfeminine behavior, is positive and healthy given the social and political context. The therapist and client work "toward strategies and solutions advancing feminist resistance, transformation, and social change in daily personal life, and in relationships with the social, emotional, and political environment" (p. 22). Interventions are devised to help solve problems in the social context in which they were created, whereas prisoners must work on their issues apart from the normal settings in which they live. Feminist therapy encourages resistance and personal integrity, self-directedness, and self-esteem. Boot camps and other forms of programming often create confusing dual-role relationships, in which the same person is the correctional officer and counselor, oppressor, and confidant. This dynamic is similar to that of the abusive relationships experienced by women inmates that created their initial feelings of powerlessness and low self-esteem. Therefore, Marcus-Mendoza et al. conclude that feminist therapy is difficult to practice in a prison setting where resistance is usually punished, not valued. Covington (1998) states that prisons often create relational disconnection and violation—a microcosm of our patriarchal society inside the prison wall. She advocates programs guided by the principles of relational theory (Jordan, Kaplan, Miller, Stiver, & Surrey, 1991).

Despite the difficulty of the task, there are some successful gender-specific programs that are being used to treat abuse survivors. It is important to note that although not all the programs described here focus specifically on abuse, they all acknowledge abuse as contributing to the problems that face incarcerated women and design interventions to fit the needs and emotional states of abuse survivors. Some programs, based on the tenets of relational and other feminist theories, are being used successfully in women's prisons. Merriam (1998) describes case studies of incarcerated women in which therapists employ art therapy to help women express feelings related to trauma that they have been unable to verbalize. She asserts that art therapy empowers women in an otherwise punishing environment by providing a highly personal activity controlled by the women that has structure and boundaries (the edge of the paper). They can explore their feelings about their traumatic experience in the safe confines of the artwork.

Covington (1998) uses relational theory to develop guidelines for working with incarcerated women with substance abuse problems that takes note of their history of abuse. In doing so, she acknowledges that women cannot be treated in a vacuum, issue by issue, as if each were disconnected; women's histories of trauma must be faced when treating addiction. Most important, she focuses on Herman's (1992) guidelines for trauma therapy, which advocate for a safe environment in which women can heal. Although this may be difficult in a prison setting where inmates may distrust each other and staff, Covington maintains that therapists working on addiction issues with abused women in prison can and must create a safe group environment in which healing can take place.

Zaplin (1998) edited a book that presents a feminist perspective on problems facing incarcerated women and proposes gender-specific treatments. In every chapter in which specific programming is discussed, abuse and its consequences are addressed. Velasquez (1998) advocates a gender-specific, holistic approach to working with women in prison that avoids the traditional myths about women offenders (i.e., women offenders need moral correction) and focuses on an integrative approach that includes assessment and diagnosis, and supportive, educational, and custodial service. She contends that failure to take a holistic approach has led to frustration and failure. All aspects of programming for women must therefore address issues in a way that acknowledges women's histories of violence and marginalization.

Henriques and Jones-Brown (1998) present Self-Taught Empowerment and Pride (STEP), based on relational theory, as a way to help African American women transition into the community. This model focuses on both individual and community empowerment. Central to this program is the assertion that oppression of African American women "has led to her historical and current sexual exploitation and her overrepresentation among those who are victims of multiple forms of psychological and physical abuse" (p. 311). Although the focus of the program is reintegration, addressing violence is a central component.

Zaplin and Dougherty (1998) discuss programming for mothers in prison. Key components to these programs are modules on dealing with emotions and stress, promoting self-esteem, and teaching parenting skills. These are areas that are traditionally needed by abused and battered women to become healthy. Besides needing healthy coping skills and self-esteem, as discussed earlier, abused women need to learn parenting skills. Children who are parented by abusive adults do not learn how to parent in a healthy manner based on example. They need instruction regarding expressions of feeling and discipline that do not involve violence. Therefore, parenting programs offer corrective education for abuse survivors. Bradley and Moschella (1998) examine the history and needs of prostitutes, which are also tied to violence. They argue that prostitutes, many of whom have a history of sexual abuse, are engaging in a continued exploitation of their bodies that started in childhood. The first step one in their treatment model involved understanding the causes of prostitution. Sexual abuse is noted as the primary risk factor and a key issue to be considered in the treatment program.

CONCLUSIONS

Can abuse survivors be treated in prison? The answer seems to be that we do not have a choice, so we must figure out how to do it. Since the majority of women in prison have been victims of one or more types of violence, it is imperative that all prisons implement gender-specific programming for violence. Appropriately designed interventions should take a holistic view of women's lives instead of treating each issue separately, as if they are unrelated. All interventions should also be mindful of the specific needs of survivors of abuse or they will be ineffective. However, addressing these difficult issues is an overwhelming task, especially in prison.

Watterson (1996) appropriately subtitles her chapter on entering prison "leave your dignity at the door" (p. 65). She goes on to describe the humiliations suffered by women in prison. It is hard to imagine a more inappropriate setting to heal and empower women; the goals of relational and other feminist approaches to trauma work with women are poorly suited to a setting where women have little dignity or control over their lives. In fact, prison creates its own scars and traumas, and women would be much better served by "doing their time" in the community (Bloom & Chesney-Lind, 2000).

Women in prison, given their history of abuse, will not trust others easily. "Treatment providers will need to establish the kind of trust with their clients—many of whom will be predisposed *not* to trust authority figures who offer help—that will enable them to convince these women and girls that the maladaptive behaviors they relied on to cope and, in many instances, to survive, can be safely abandoned" (Dougherty, 1998, p. 242). This will be especially difficult in an environment such as prison that does not feel safe and where women, healthy and otherwise, may need all of their resources to cope. However, the theoretical and practical progress outlined here inspires hope. Although helping women heal wounds from abuse in an abusive environment would seem impossible, scholars and practitioners are working, and must continue to work together to achieve this ambitious goal.

DISCUSSION QUESTIONS

1. What types of environmental factors contribute to women's criminality? What roles do violence and abuse play?

2. What is the underlying principle of power-belief theory? How does it attempt to explain female criminality?

3. How do women's abuse histories affect their receptiveness to treatment?

4. What issues should be considered in developing programs for women prisoners?

5. How does the operation of prisons conflict with the mental health needs of women prisoners? In particular, how does feminist therapy conflict with prison life?

WEBNOTES

Go to the site for Oregon's WICS Lifeskills training for women offenders (http://wics.org/ femoff.htm) and read the report. What types of programs are included in the WICS Lifeskills Program? Do they address the issues of women prisoners? How effective are they?

REFERENCES

American Correctional Association. (1990). *The female offender: What does the future hold?* Arlington, VA: Kirby Lithographic.

American Psychiatric Association. (1994). *Diagnostic and statistical manual of mental disorders* (4th ed.). Washington, DC: American Psychiatric Association.

Belknap, J., & Holsinger, K. (1998). An overview of delinquent girls: How theory and practice have failed and the need for innovative changes. In R. Zaplin (Ed.), *Female offenders: Critical perspectives and effective interventions.* Gaithersburg, MD: Aspen.

Bloom, B., & Chesney-Lind, M. (2000). Women in prison: Vengeful equity. In R. Muraskin (Ed.), *It's a crime: Women and justice* (2nd ed.). Upper Saddle River, NJ: Prentice Hall.

Bradley, L., & Moschella, L. (1998). Programs that work: Working with prostitutes. In R. Zaplin (Ed.), *Female offenders: Critical perspectives and effective interventions.* Gaithersburg, MD: Aspen.

Brown, L. S. (1996). *Subversive dialogues: Theory in feminist therapy.* New York: Basic Books.

Browne, A., Miller, B., & Maguin, E. (1999). Prevalence and severity of lifetime physical and sexual victimization among incarcerated women. *International Journal of Law and Psychiatry, 22* (3–4), 301–322.

Chesney-Lind, M. (1997). *The female offender: Girls, women, and crime.* Thousand Oaks, CA: Sage.

COVINGTON, S. S. (1998). The relational theory of women's psychological development: Implications for the criminal justice system. In R. Zaplin (Ed.), *Female offenders: Critical perspectives and effective interventions.* Gaithersburg, MD: Aspen.

DOUGHERTY, J. (1998). Power-belief theory: Female criminality and the dynamics of oppression. In R. Zaplin (Ed.), *Female offenders: Critical perspectives and effective interventions.* Gaithersburg, MD: Aspen.

FISHMAN, L. T. (2000). " Mule-headed slave women refusing to take foolishness from anybody": A prelude to future accommodation, resistance, and criminality. In R. Muraskin (Ed.), *It's a crime: Women and justice* (2nd ed.). Upper Saddle River, NJ: Prentice Hall.

FREEDMAN, E. B. (1981). *Their sisters' keepers.* Ann Arbor: University of Michigan Press.

GIRSHICK, L. (1999). *No safe haven.* Boston: Northeastern University Press.

HENEY, J., & KRISTIANSEN, C. M., (1998). In J. Harden and M. Hill (Eds.). *Breaking the rules: Women in prison and feminist therapy.* Binghamton, NY: Harrington Park Press.

HENRIQUES, A. W., & JONES-BROWN, D. (1998). Self-taught empowerment and pride: A multimodal/dual empowerment approach to confronting problems of African American female offenders. In R. Zaplin (Ed.), *Female offenders: Critical perspectives and effective interventions.* Gaithersburg, MD: Aspen.

HERMAN, J. L. (1992). *Trauma and recovery.* New York: Basic Books.

JORDAN, J. V., KAPLAN, A. G., MILLER, J. B., STIVER, I. P., & SURREY, J. L. (1991). *Women's growth in connection.* New York: Guilford Press.

MARCUS-MENDOZA, S. T., KLEIN-SAFFRAN, J., & LUTZE, F. (1998). A feminist examination of boot camp prison programs for women. In J. Harden and M. Hill (Eds.), *Breaking the rules: Women in prison and feminist therapy.* Binghamton, NY: Harrington Park Press.

MARCUS-MENDOZA, S. T., SARGENT, E., & CHONG HO, Y. (1994). Changing perceptions of the etiology of crime: The relationship between abuse and female criminology. *Journal of the Oklahoma Criminal Justice Research Consortium, 1,* 13–23.

MERRIAM, B. (1998). To find a voice: Art therapy in a women's prison. In J. Harden and M. Hill (Eds.), *Breaking the rules: Women in prison and feminist therapy.* Binghamton, NY: Harrington Park Press.

MORASH, M., BYNUM, T. S., & KOONS, B. A. (1998). *Women offenders: Programming needs and promising approaches,* Research in Brief (NCJ 171668). Washington, DC: National Institute of Justice.

MORASH, M., HAARR, R. N., & RUCKER, L. (1994). A comparison of programming for women and men in U.S. prisons in the 1980s. *Crime & Delinquency, 40* (2), 197–221.

OWEN, B. (1998). *In the mix: Struggle and survival in a women's prison.* Albany: State University of New York Press.

OWEN, B., & BLOOM, B. (1995). Profiling women prisoners: Findings from national surveys and a California sample. *The Prison Journal, 72* (2), 165–185.

PEPI, C. L. O. (1998). Children without childhoods: A feminist intervention strategy utilizing systems theory and restorative justice in treating female adolescent offenders. In J. Harden and M. Hill (Eds.), *Breaking the rules: Women in prison and feminist therapy.* Binghamton, NY: Harrington Park Press.

RITCHIE, B. E. (2000). Exploring the link between violence against women and women's involvement in illegal activity. In *Research on women and girls in the justice system,* Research Forum (NCJ 180973). Washington, DC: National Institute of Justice.

RUSSELL, D. E. H. (1984). *Sexual exploitation: Rape, child sexual abuse, and sexual harassment.* Beverly Hills, CA: Sage.

SIMON, R. J., & LANDIS, J. (1991). *The crimes women commit, the punishments they receive.* Lexington, MA: Lexington Books.

SOMMERS, E. (1995). *Voices from within: Women who have broken the law.* Toronto: University of Toronto Press.

TEPLIN, L. A., ABRAM, K. M., & McCLELLAND, G. M. (1996). Prevalence of psychiatric disorders among incarcerated women: Pretrial jail detainees. *Archives of General Psychiatry, 53,* 505–512.

UNITED STATES GENERAL ACCOUNTING OFFICE. (1999). *Women in prison: Issues and challenges confronting the U.S. correctional systems.* (GAO/GGD–00–22). Washington, DC: U.S. General Accounting Office.

VELASQUEZ, A. (1998). An integrated systems approach to program development and implementation. In R. Zaplin (Ed.), *Female offenders: Critical perspectives and effective interventions.* Gaithersburg, MD: Aspen.

WALKER, L. E. A. (1984). *Battered woman syndrome.* New York: Springer.

———. (1994). *Abused women and survivor therapy.* Washington, DC: American Psychological Association.

WATTERSON, K. (1996). *Women in prison: Inside the concrete womb* (rev. ed.). Boston: Northeastern University Press.

WIDOM, C. S. (2000). Childhood victimization and the derailment of girls and women to the criminal justice system. In *Research on women and girls in the justice system,* Research Forum (NCJ 180973). Washington, DC: National Institute of Justice.

ZAPLIN, R. (1998). Female offenders: A systems perspective. In R. Zaplin (Ed.), *Female offenders: Critical perspectives and effective interventions.* Gaithersburg, MD: Aspen.

ZAPLIN, R., & DOUGHERTY, J. (1998). Programs that work: Mothers. In R. Zaplin (Ed.), *Female offenders: Critical perspectives and effective interventions.* Gaithersburg, MD: Aspen.

ZLOTNICK, C. (1997). Posttraumatic stress disorder (PTSD), PTSD comorbidity, and childhood abuse among incarcerated women. *The Journal of Nervous and Mental Disease, 185* (12), 761–763.

9

The State-of-the-Art in Substance Abuse Programs for Women in Prison

Margaret S. Kelley, Ph.D.

❖

The development of substance abuse programs in women's prisons in the United States has not kept up with the rapidly growing number of women entering prison, a large percentage of whom are committed on drug-related offenses or as drug-involved inmates. Drug treatment programs are sorely deficient and do not meet the diverse needs of women inmates. This is not a problem unique to the United States: research in Australia, Britain, and Canada parallels our trends (Kerr, 1998; Long, Langevin, & Weekes, 1998; Maden, Swinton, & Gunn, 1994; Mason, Birmingham, & Grubin, 1997). Currently, less than 4% of substance abuse spending by U.S. states funds prevention, treatment, and research (Center for Substance Abuse Research, 2001).

Male and female prisoners have much in common, but they differ in some significant ways, including types of offenses committed, individual characteristics, living situations prior to incarceration, and relationships with children. Successful treatment programs take these diverse factors into account. This chapter surveys existing substance abuse programming for women in prison and summarizes its effectiveness, evaluates state-of-the-art programs, and provides suggestions for improvement. Despite the scarcity of programs designed specifically for women inmates, some model programs are identified and reviewed.

One overwhelmingly consistent finding, however, is that there are not enough programs or information about what makes existing programs successful. This chapter is a beginning step toward bridging this gap in the literature by providing a comprehensive review of available research about substance abuse treatment programs for women in prison. Finally, the provision of treatment for women in prison is discussed in the framework that the protection of human rights in the United States must include access to medical care and drug treatment for the many women in prison who need it.

SIGNIFICANCE OF THE PROBLEM

Women are the fastest-growing segment of the U.S. prison population, even though their crime rate is not increasing dramatically (Owen, 2001). They currently make up about 6% of the prison population (Greenfeld & Snell, 1999). There have always been women drug offenders, but their numbers rose substantially in the past decade because of increased drug-related crime, federal and state legislation, and mandatory sentencing. Mandated sentencing for drug convictions, with no parallel development of services to address the needs of this population, has had devastating consequences for women prisoners, as women are most often incarcerated for drug convictions (Kaplan & Sasser, 1996; Prendergast, Wellisch, & Falkin, 1995). The growing trend to criminalize illicit drug use while *in* prison through monitoring and drug testing (Kassebaum & Chandler, 1994) has compounded drug treatment problems. Women prisoners have complex issues in addition to drug addiction (Austin, Bloom, & Donahue, 1992; Phillips & Harm, 1998), including family disruption; cultural and ethnic considerations; health problems such as HIV/AIDS, tuberculosis, and mental disorders; sexual abuse; and violence (Maden et al., 1994).

Treatment for women inmates is in great demand, yet perhaps fewer than 20% get the help they need (Kaplan & Sasser, 1996; Mason et al., 1997), with some estimates much lower (National Center on Addiction and Substance Abuse, 1998). What programs do exist often operate on principles derived from male offender programs, and consequently do not take account of women's complex needs. For example, Young (1994) argues that "[traditional male] treatment often operates to adjust women to dominant gender, race, and class structures and depoliticizes and individualizes their situations" (Young, 1994, pp. 33–34). Addiction is really a health problem for women, not specifically a criminal justice problem. However, because so many addicts are in the care of the criminal justice system, their incarceration provides an opportunity for intervention (Young, 1994).

Beginning in the 1980s, concerns about treatment for women grew apace with the number of women incarcerated for drug offenses (Lockwood, McCorkel, & Inciardi, 1998; Morash, Haarr, & Rucker, 1994). Problems specific to women in the criminal justice system garnered some attention from researchers in the early 1990s, but interest has since declined. Those early reports were dominated by calls for new programs and the evaluation of existing programs. The 1994 Violent Crime Control and Law Enforcement Act appropriated millions of dollars in 1998 through 2000 to increase the number of prison-based drug treatment programs (Farabee et al., 1999). Research has identified a number of barriers to implementing successful programs in prison, and despite the funding, too few women's programs are developed and evaluated.

BRIEF PROFILE OF THE FEMALE OFFENDER AND ASSESSMENT OF SPECIAL NEEDS

As noted in previous chapters, the average female offender is poor, uneducated, and unskilled. Female offenders are disproportionately young African Americans and Latinas with children (Greenfeld & Snell, 1999; Kaplan & Sasser, 1996; Phillips & Harm, 1998; Seldin, 1995). More female than male prisoners are parents, and more had custody and lived with their children before prison than did male prisoners—78% compared to 50.5% (Phillips & Harm, 1998). Many have severe physical and mental health problems (Kaplan & Sasser, 1996). Strikingly, as many as half have a history of physical, emotional, and sexual abuse (Greenfeld & Snell, 1999; Kaplan & Sasser, 1996; Owen, 2001; Seldin, 1995). Finally, of special importance here, women offenders are more often and more extensively involved with drugs (Greenfeld & Snell, 1999; Kassebaum & Chandler, 1994).

One of the most crucial steps toward addressing drug-related problems for incarcerated women is assessing their drug problems when they enter prison. Knowing a woman's background and current health can aid in understanding motivations and behavior both inside and upon release from prison (Pollock, 1998). Typically, the same classification scales are used for men and women without evaluating their applicability to individual circumstance (Pollock, 1998). Assessment takes many forms, including self-report, the Drug Misuse Scale, and various drug tests, such as urinalysis or hair analysis.

A person's treatment is best guided by assessed needs, but there is little guidance in the literature on how to match prisoners with programs (Farabee et al., 1999). In one study, three out of five respondents being transferred from jail to prison said they believed drug treatment would be beneficial to them (Lo & Stephens, 2000). Another study, including men and women prisoners, found that about half the requests for treatment from inmates entering prison were for residential rehabilitation and about half were for counseling (Brooke, Taylor, Gunn, & Maden, 1998). Very few requested drug maintenance therapy, such as methadone maintenance. One overview of available programs, using data from 53 prison programs, found that most failed to use a standardized assessment protocol, suggesting there is tremendous variation in information obtained about client needs (Prendergast et al., 1995). The sheer volume of women entering the criminal justice system hampers further the assessment of their special needs. According to Morash,"[prison] administrators at all levels said that classification and screening procedures did not provide needed information, were not adapted to women, and were not useful in matching women's needs for programming" (Morash, Bynum, & Koons, 1998, p. 3).

Although it has long been recognized that women have special needs when it comes to drug treatment (National Institute on Drug Abuse, 2001), three merit extra consideration here: pregnancy and motherhood, dual diagnosis, and history of violence. First, most women with children had custody before they entered prison and must face broken bonds with their children during incarceration. Whereas children of men in prison are usually cared for by their family, children of women in prison are often taken into state custody and put into foster homes (Snyder-Joy & Carlo, 1998). Incarcerated drug-using women who are pregnant require special consideration and additional services (Wesson, 1995). Family-centered interventions are needed to enable women prisoners to confront and resolve family issues and reintegrate back into the community (Phillips & Harm, 1998). Parent education classes have been shown to benefit drug-using women when they are released from prison and rejoin their families (Harm, Thompson, & Chambers, 1998; Snyder-Joy & Carlo, 1998).

Second, many incarcerated women suffer from more than substance abuse problems, and report a wide range of diagnosed mental illness (Peters, Strozier, Murrin, & Kearns, 1997). This issue of co-morbidity, or presenting with multiple problems, is receiving more attention from treatment providers and policymakers (Ditton, 1999; Wexler, 1995). Accurate assessment is crucial for identifying the numerous needs of this population, of which women make up the greater part.

Finally, most studies estimate at least one-third and more likely 50% to 60% of adult women in prison have survived physical abuse, with as many as one-third having been sexually abused (Greenfeld & Snell, 1999; Moon, Thompson, & Bennet, 1993; Pollock, 1998; Sargent, Marcus-Mendoza, & Yu, 1993; Seldin, 1995). These early experiences of violence shape women's adult lives (Chesney-Lind & Shelden, 1992; Owen, 1998, 2001) and negatively affect their chance of entering and successfully completing drug treatment (Kelley, Rosenbaum, Knight, Irwin, & Washburn, 1996). In sum, these factors demonstrate the broad but unique treatment needs of female offenders.

TREATMENT IN PRISON: HISTORY AND TRENDS IN WOMEN'S PROGRAMMING

Prisons have diverse populations and any one program cannot magically solve the problems of drug addiction for all women. Since the early 1980s, nearly all state prisons for women offer some form of drug and alcohol treatment programs (Weisheit, 1985). Estimates vary on the prevalence of women in treatment, but all suggest a continued dearth of available treatment programs, both in prison and in the community. For example, in California in 1994, there were only 120 slots for drug treatment for 7,700 female inmates (Bloom, Chesney-Lind, & Owen, 1994). Before identifying types of programs for women in prison, there are several treatment trends to consider that influence programming, including improved diversion programs, privatization, and coerced treatment.

Prior to Imprisonment: Drug Courts and Diversion Treatment Programs

Prior to imprisonment, women may participate in drug courts and diversion treatment programs. A number of studies have evaluated these community-based treatment programs for women offenders (Austin et al., 1992; Newbern, Dnasereau, & Pitre, 1999), but they are limited and difficult to compare because of variations across settings and program fidelity. In an assessment of outpatient treatment programs for adult offenders, outcomes indicated mixed results (Chanhatasilpa, MacKenzie, & Hickman, 2000). Increased supervision, monitoring, or control over offenders in the community does not reduce recidivism. However, community programs that followed up prison residential therapeutic communities did show encouraging results. There are currently over 300 drug courts in operation, in virtually every state (Blanchard, 1999). Evaluations of these drug courts are also encouraging.

Community-based sanctions help keep families together (Phillips & Harm, 1998), and given the less serious nature of women's crime, community interventions are preventative and cost-efficient (Owen, 2001). One of the most impressive and evaluated diversion efforts is the Treatment Alternatives to Street Crime (TASC), which matches drug-dependent offenders to treatment programs. The programs use a number of methods to motivate participation, including deferred prosecution, community sentencing, and pretrial intervention (Anglin, Longshore, & Turner, 1999; Anglin et al., 1996).

Privatization

Many prisons simply do not have the resources to implement programs internally and so must contract out for drug treatment, reflecting a general trend for the provision of state substance abuse services (U.S. Department of Health and Human Services, 2000; Weisheit, 1985). According to Wexler (1995), using independent contractors is a key consideration in designing residential programs in prison (Wexler, 1995). Morash (1998) found that "nearly all States contract out to the private sector for at least some services for women offenders" (Morash et al., 1998, p. 5). Most prison and jail administrators who responded to the Morash survey believed the use of outside contractors improved their programming. Contracts reduced conflict between prison and treatment staff, improved programs, promoted new ideas, contained costs, and strengthened continuity with aftercare. This is a positive trend in providing support services, because corrections personnel cannot be expected to have the necessary training to deal with the complex problems of drug-involved women offenders.

Coerced Treatment

Many inmates do not take advantage of drug treatment programs even when available. Thus, policy has shifted toward the idea of using the coercive power of the criminal justice system to mandate offenders into treatment (Blanchard, 1999). This often happens in the form of diversion programs, but it also occurs in prisons. California prison officials are reportedly proud of their forced treatment programs, which they claim have reduced recidivism drastically, although 80% of the inmates resisted the forced treatment (Alcoholism and Drug Abuse Weekly, 1999). Coercion in prison can take many forms, from withholding good-time credits and privileges such as family visits to preventing or delaying parole and release. Other reports recommend positive incentives such as reduced sentences for those who voluntarily enter and complete treatment while in prison (National Center on Addiction and Substance Abuse, 1998).

Forced treatment raises many ethical and practical considerations. Research has consistently found mixed results about the effects of coercion on treatment outcomes (Farabee et al., 1999). These variations in coerced-treatment outcomes may result from flawed consistency in terminology for referral, neglected emphasis on internal motivation, and deviation from program implementation (Anglin, Prendergast, & Farabee, 1998). Overall, those coerced into treatment show "low intrinsic motivation to participate, are less ready for treatment, and are consequently more problematic to treat and less satisfied with their treatment than are voluntary clients" (Sia, Dansereau, & Czuchry, 2000, p. 459). Other research indicates that time in treatment has been found to be a stronger predictor of treatment success than motivation for treatment (De Leon, Andrews, Wexler, Jaffe, & Rosenthal, 1979; De Leon, Hawke, Jainchill, & Melnick, 2000; Simpson, 1981; Simpson, Joe, & Rowan-Szal, 1997; Wellisch, Anglin, & Prendergast, 1993), and many sources do report that coerced treatment is better than no treatment (U.S. Department of Justice, 1996b). What is needed is more information about the determinants of seeking treatment, both in prison and after release. Motivation is still an important factor, and success in programs is more likely when clients are involved in developing their own program of recovery than when one is forced on them (Lipton, 1998).

TREATMENT IN PRISON: TYPES OF PROGRAMS

Most prisons have some type of treatment program, but these vary drastically in content and implementation. Programs are difficult to adapt to prison environments for many reasons, including conflicts between treatment providers and prison authorities (Weinman & Lockwood, 1993). Treatment most often consists of drug education classes and some type of self-help meetings, which are provided to the general prison population (not in specialized units dedicated to drug treatment) (Prendergast et al., 1995). Commonly available programs include: drug education, individual and group counseling, cognitive therapy, self-help and 12-step programs, acupuncture, methadone maintenance, case management, and therapeutic communities. Drug education is designed to provide information to offenders about the physiological and psychological effects of the drug, development of addictive behaviors, stages of recovery, aspects of the addictive lifestyle, and relapse warning signs (Peters, 1993). Because drug education and counseling components (group, individual, and family level) are incorporated into most other programs, they are not discussed separately here.

Cognitive Therapy

Cognitive therapy is individualized and highly structured, with the goal of undermining dysfunctional belief systems about inability to control drug use (Pollock, 1998). There are many strengths to this approach but little information about how widely available it is in prisons. The history of this type of treatment, conducted with African American female heroin-using inmates in the 1970s, found that psychotherapy "marathon groups" were effective in "altering the perceptions of black female heroin addicts toward the future, counseling, and themselves" (Page & Kubiak, 1978, p. 414; Page, Richmond, & De La Serna, 1987), indicating their potential as a counseling strategy (Kilmann, 1974; Ross, McReynolds, & Berzins, 1974). Marathon group and cognitive therapy methods have been incorporated into some therapeutic communities. This approach does not utilize a social learning model with behavioral components.

Twelve-Step Programs

For many incarcerated women, 12-step programs—Alcoholics Anonymous and Narcotics Anonymous—are the only intervention available at most prisons. In 1997, 16.1% of state prisoners reported participating in self-help or peer-counseling programs since admission (Mumola, 1999). Although these programs have proved successful in some cases, they are limited in scope and unable to address the comprehensive problems of illicit drug use, criminality, and inadequate social support. Twelve-step programs are less structured than other treatment options and depend upon member involvement to be successful (Wellisch et al., 1993). Their wide variation in content and structure makes their success difficult to evaluate. Therapeutic communities grew out of the 12-step model.

Acupuncture

Usually a component of a larger drug treatment program, along with drug testing and counseling, acupuncture apparently reduces craving for drugs and alcohol while increasing a patient's level of relaxation. According to one report, acupuncture is popular in prisons and jails because it is inexpensive (Wallace, 1992). However, there has been very little evaluation of acupuncture treatment in the general population (Moner, 1996), much less in prisons. One published study of an outpatient adult probation program that included acupuncture reported mixed levels of success in drug use and criminal behavior outcomes (Moon & Latessa, 1994). A short-term, two-week intensive program in Baltimore targets women in jail awaiting trial (Kassebaum, 1999)—women with less extensive criminal histories and those likely to be released back into the community after trial. Program members who remain incarcerated do receive some aftercare, as do those who choose to continue treatment upon release. Although promising, there are no available evaluations of the Baltimore program. Some community-based therapeutic communities make referrals for acupuncture, but these are not a standard part of most programs. Support for these types of supplementary programs is tenuous and their availability often depends upon funding sources.

Methadone Maintenance Treatment Programs

Methadone maintenance is an effective treatment for heroin-addiction (Magura, Rosenblum, Lewis, & Joseph, 1993), yet the U.S. criminal justice system has not fully utilized its benefits, and methadone treatment is difficult to get while in prisons and jails. Some short-term detoxification programs are available, including methadone and other drug replacement therapies (Peters, 1993). In 1997, only 0.2% of state prisoners reported participating in a maintenance drug therapy since admission (Mumola, 1999). There are no established programs for women in prison to evaluate. One jail-based program for men, KEEP (Key Extended Entry Program), at Rikers Island in New York City, has reported positive results (Magura et al., 1993).

Case Management

Case-management approaches feature individualized treatment plans based on a thorough needs assessment of inmates (Austin et al., 1992). Clients are often involved in treatment planning, and services are wide-ranging. Counselors work with inmates in developing and working toward treatment goals (Peters, 1993). A case manager

> is the single accountable individual who provides assessment, case planning, advocacy, linkage/coordination, and monitoring . . . the case manager is the best guarantor of continuity of treatment across the operating elements of the criminal treatment system. (Lipton, 1998, pp. 7–8)

Case-management programs are less common in prisons as the sole treatment option, but elements of case management are often incorporated into therapeutic communities. Substance abusers are the criminal justice population most likely to receive case management services (Healey, 1999). Because the range of services can vary tremendously (Martin & Inciardi, 1993), these types of programs are difficult to evaluate, but existing studies of case management for substance abusing offenders are promising, indicating lower recidivism upon release.

The Current Model of Choice: Therapeutic Communities

By far the most common programs available to women in prison settings that are discussed in the literature are therapeutic communities (Wexler, 1995). Community-based therapeutic communities were initiated in the 1950s, beginning with Synanon in California (Siegal et al., 1999). Now their strongest influence is in jails, prisons, and post-release community facilities. Both prison- and community-based therapeutic communities have shown the best long-term results in reducing criminality and drug use for men and women (Chanhatasilpa et al., 2000; Lockwood et al., 1998; Wexler, 1995; Wexler, Cuadrado, & Stevens, 1998), although less research has been done with women prisoners. Prison-based therapeutic communities are usually in isolated areas of the prison (Koski-Jannes, 1997), and they use the community itself as the healing agent (Groom, 1999).

Prison-based therapeutic communities began to develop in the early 1960s but did not become entrenched until the 1980s (Pan, Scarpitti, Inciardi, & Lockwood, 1993). Federal therapeutic communities lost support in the late 1970s, as did early state prison programs. Project REFORM, a program of the Bureau of Justice Assistance from 1987 to 1991, was initiated to help design state prison drug treatment programs (Wexler & Lipton, 1993). It served as a critical route for expansion of prison therapeutic communities and produced guidelines for developing prison programs, including the importance of program evaluations. Project RECOVERY continued the work of Project REFORM through 1992.

Prison-based therapeutic communities are usually voluntary programs in which "the residents, with the guidance and supervision of trained staff, are the primary therapists for one another" (Groom, 1999, p. 118). They vary in organizational design (Melnick, De Leon, Hiller, & Knight, 2000), but usually include a group involvement approach in all aspects of daily life. They are based in confrontation, especially in the early days of treatment. All residents are involved in monitoring their peers, and treatment progresses through peer pressure and role modeling (McCorkel, Harrison, & Inciardi, 1998). Days are filled with work, house meetings, classes, and group processes. The curriculum tends to be informal and based on oral tradition (Wexler, 1995), and lacking in theory of behavior change (Pan et al., 1993). Duration of inmate participation in these treatment programs varies, with many offenders averaging treatment stays of over a year. Therapeutic communities offer a "stronger support mechanism to enable individuals opportunities for self-disclosure whilst enhancing skill deficits, such as poor self-esteem, that are identified as being misuse triggers" (Wolstenholme, McHugh, & Jennings, 1995, p. 57). The "traditional" therapeutic community is one in which patients exert control over their own recoveries in a self-help modality (U.S. Department of Justice, 1996b). A "modified" therapeutic community puts greater emphasis on professional staff rather than recovering drug users, exhibits a decreasing reliance on community-as-method, and has a reduction in group therapy (Melnick et al., 2000; Newbern et al., 1999). Traditional therapeutic communities place more emphasis on changing the person and reducing relapse and substance abuse, and use work as part of the process of building self-esteem and social responsibility. Modified programs involve shorter stays and may serve distinct populations, such as adolescents or offenders. Therapeutic communities are being modified and used for offenders with mental illness and dual diagnoses with promising results (Sacks, 2000).

Overall, both types of therapeutic communities agree about the fundamental nature of therapeutic community treatment (Melnick et al., 2000). Prison-based therapeutic communities are considered modified versions and they are "shaped by the unique features of the correctional institution," including the focus on security, limited physical and social space, and the prison culture itself (Therapeutic Communities of America, 1999, p. 3). Whereas retention rates were similar across the two types of therapeutic communities, they tend to serve different clienteles: Traditional therapeutic communities serve more "hard core" clientele—those abusing harder drugs and arrested for more serious crimes—while modified programs typically help offenders who have abused alcohol and have been arrested for less serious crimes (Melnick et al., 2000).

Despite the literature being dominated by discussion of the importance and impact of therapeutic communities in prisons, in 1997, only 5.7% of state prisoners reported participating in residential treatment since their incarceration (Mumola, 1999). However, in a survey of prison facilities in the same year, administrators reported that 31% of those receiving treatment were placed in a dedicated, specialized unit (Department of Health and Human Services, 2000).

Postrelease: Continuity of Care

One of the most promising trends in drug treatment for offenders is the attention being paid to their needs after prison. Transition back into the community is difficult for drug offenders, and women receive inadequate discharge planning before their release (Kaplan & Sasser, 1996). Continuing treatment upon release into the community is perhaps the greatest predictor of success in preventing relapse and recidivism (National Women's Law Center, 1995). Relapse rates are consistently high without appropriate support during the transition (Peters & Schonfeld, 1993). Women would have higher success rates if treatment programs continued into the community, and they had access to additional services, such as child care, transportation, and housing (Peugh & Belenko, 1999).

Women do not always volunteer to continue with treatment after prison. The relatively low rates of treatment continuity reduce the effectiveness of prison drug treatment, as research indicates that continuing care reduces overall drug use and criminality. A continuum of care would ease women's transitions back into the community (Owen, 2001). Even after completing a treatment program in prison, many women relapse into illicit drug use because they return to the same problems that helped put them in prison (Pollock, 1998). Twelve-step programs are the most easily continued in the community as most communities have some form available. But again, individual programs vary substantially and it is difficult to predict success rates. Therapeutic communities for offenders clearly have demonstrated successful results. But few community treatment programs let women keep their children with them (Pollock, 1998), which could partly explain why women do not volunteer for treatment at release.

WHAT WORKS? THE STATE-OF-THE-ART IN PRISON-BASED SUBSTANCE ABUSE PROGRAMS

In a 1995 nationwide survey of existing programs for women offenders, researchers identified 242 innovative and promising substance abuse programs for women offenders that warranted further study (Morash & Bynum, 1995; Morash et al., 1998; National Institute of

Justice, 1998). Of these, only 18 had been evaluated, and many states had *no* promising programs for incarcerated women. Evaluating the evaluation literature can be confusing and overwhelming. Programs take place in different settings, with different target populations and different results. The primary objective of this overview of model programs is to identify the type of treatment that is most effective for women in custody. The focus here is on prison-based programming and outcomes for drug use, recidivism, and family maintenance. There is one jail-based program included because of its unique focus on women. Programs were excluded if they focused only on alcohol dependence, such as Alcoholics Anonymous, and if they were integrated into shock incarceration, or boot camp, settings. A thorough review of the literature was conducted using electronic methods, with a focus on sociological and public health sources. The review consisted of primarily published studies, included conference proceedings and occasional papers. To be confident in the results of a literature overview such as this, all of the possible evaluation studies must be included and they must be free of weaknesses. Here, although few cases met the criteria of having published evaluations with strong research designs, it is reasonable to expect that programs discussed below represent the most relevant programs for women in prison. With so few cases, however, and with some of them lacking rigorous evaluations, it is difficult to generalize about the effectiveness of these programs for women.

MODEL PROGRAMS

Very few prison-based programs have been designed specifically for women and their needs. Some of the programs below were designed for men and eventually incorporated women into existing programs. Table 9.1 identifies and briefly describes the selected model programs. Research and outcomes are summarized along with key program information.

Stay'n Out. This program, originally designed for men in 1977 and modeled after the Phoenix House program, helped define the model prison therapeutic community for future programs (Pan et al., 1993). It was the first prison therapeutic community to be extensively evaluated (Lipton & Johnson, 1998; Peugh & Belenko, 1999; Wallace, 1992; Wexler, 1995; Wexler & Williams, 1986). The women's program operates at the Bayview Correctional Facility, New York City, with a capacity of 40 beds, and averages 30 women per day, for 9 to 12 months. The goal of the original program and evaluation was to test the "time-in-treatment" hypothesis. In one report, parole outcomes are compared among three therapeutic community groups: Stay'n Out members (n = 247); a counseling group—inmates who participated in other types of prison-based drug treatment programs (n = 113), and a no-treatment control group—those who volunteered for Stay'n Out but never participated (n = 38) (Wellisch et al., 1993). Data were collected from 1977 to 1984. Results provided convincing evidence that the program is effective in reducing recidivism, a finding that increased as time in the program increased. Other outcomes, including positive parole completion, no arrest, and time until arrest, also increased with time in the Stay'n Out group but did not increase for the other interventions.

BWCI Village. The parent program, KEY–CREST, was started in 1988 in Delaware. It is a long-term, residential program, emphasizing resocializing behavior change. The overall program has been extensively evaluated (Farrell, 2000; Hooper, 1997; Inciardi, Martin, Butzin, Hooper, & Harrison, 1997; Inciardi, Martin, Lockwood, Hooper, & Wald,

TABLE 9.1   The State of the Art: Model Substance Abuse Programs for Women Offenders

Program Title	Program Location	Program Description	Research Description	Research Outcomes
Stay'n Out Program	Bayview Correctional Facility, New York City, began in 1977.	Residential prison-based therapeutic programs for women and men.	Numerous outcome evaluations. Parole outcomes are compared among three groups: Stay'n Out members (247), a counseling group—inmates who participated on other types of prison-based drug treatment programs (113), and a no–treatment control group—those who volunteered but never participated (38). Data was collected from 1977 to 1984.	Results show that the program is effective in reducing recidivism, a finding that increased as time in the program increased. Positive parole completion, no arrest, and time until arrest increased with time in the therapeutic community but did not increase for the other interventions.
BWCI Village	Baylor Women's Correctional Institution, New Castle, Delaware. The only women's correctional facility in Delaware. Started in 1994 with funding from the Center for Substance Abuse Treatment.	Multistage residential prison- and community-based therapeutic community associated with the KEY–CREST program. Unique in a number of ways in its adaptation to women. They have all women staff and the programming content is geared to women's needs. They have a children's visiting center.	One evaluation compared 279 people in four groups: CREST dropouts, CREST graduates without aftercare, CREST graduates with aftercare, and a control group assigned to traditional work-release program with drug treatment. Qualitative analysis of women's perceptions of treatment in order to understand the high dropout rate.	At an 18-month followup, those graduating and completing aftercare were much more likely to remain drug-free, 76% compared to 19%. Three years later, one third of treatment offenders remained drug-free, compared to 5% of the comparison group. The qualitative study found that even modified programs have difficulty recruiting and retaining women.

continued

TABLE 9.1 *(continued)*

Program Title	Program Location	Program Description	Research Description	Research Outcomes
Forever Free Substance Abuse Program	California Institution for Women (CIW), Frontera, California. California Department of Corrections. Started in 1991. The state has contracted with Mental Health Systems, Inc., to run the program.	Residential prison-based therapeutic community. Designed specifically for women in prison and with women-centered programming. Less confrontational model of group therapy.	Several outcome evaluations. The most recent evaluation compared four groups: all women who entered the program (1995–1996), women who dropped out of the program, women who received only the in-prison program, and women who continued to receive treatment after being paroled. They found very high program retention during these years, at almost 95%.	It was found that only 9% of women receiving 120 days or more of community treatment were reincarcerated. Two years after parole, only 25% were reincarcerated. Both percentages are much lower than for the comparison groups.
TAPESTRY	Ohio Department of Alcohol and Drug Addiction Services. Ohio Reformatory for Women, Marysville, Ohio. Begun in 1990.	Residential prison-based therapeutic program for women only (there is a similar men's program, OASIS, at the Pickaway Correctional Institution, which started in 1992). Very limited information about program content, not women-specific.	The purpose of the evaluation study was to evaluate Ohio's prison-based therapeutic community system. Outcome data came from rearrest and charge after release from prison. Included inmates originally interviewed between 1991–1995. Sample of women was 193 inmates (no treatment) and 350 therapeutic community residents.	It was reported that length of time in therapeutic community is crucial to outcome. Those with 180 days or more in therapeutic community were much less likely to be rearrested or charged with violent or drug-related crime one year later.

Turning Point Alcohol and Drug Program	Columbia River Correctional Institution, Portland, Oregon. Minimum security prison. Operated by ASAP Treatment Services, Inc. Started in 1990.	Residential prison-based therapeutic community that houses 50 men and 50 women, in separate facilities. Programming takes a holistic approach, with life skills training, drug education, relationship development, anger management, case management, and a family component.	Female clients have presented with increasing number of mental health issues. The program hired a mental health staff. The women's unit is exceptionally good at identifying issues specific to the population and responding to the needs of women participating in treatment.	Overall outcomes included a 48% decrease in arrests, 61% decrease in convictions, and 28% decrease in incarcerations. The program has a 45% treatment completion rate.
Dismas Charities	Owensboro, Kentucky. Started in 1994. Operated by Dismas Charities.	Residential prison-based therapeutic community, at a private community center and prison for female offenders. The program uses an integrated approach that addresses all aspects of their lives, including on-site supervised visitation of children during incarceration.	Evaluation not published. Results based on internal evaluation.	Inmates believe they have better skills regarding parenting, better emotional balance, more confidence, and knowledge about their families well-being.
Discovery	Rhode Island Department of Corrections Women's Facilities, Cranston, Rhode Island. Started in 1994. Run by Talbot Treatment Centers, a community-based drug treatment agency.	Residential prison-based therapeutic community. Programming is holistic and women-specific, and includes a physical education and a furlough program that facilitates aftercare.	Internal evaluation, report to U.S. Department of Justice. Average length of stay is 3 months, but participants may stay until their release from prison.	The furlough program is important because women are more likely to continue treatment after release if they are familiar with the staff and surroundings. The recidivism rate for women completing the treatment program has dropped to about 20%, compared with 45% for the general population.

continued

TABLE 9.1 *(continued)*

Program Title	Program Location	Program Description	Research Description	Research Outcomes
Taconic Correctional Facility Nursery Program	New York, started in 1990. Taconic Correctional Facility, a minimum security facility.	Nursery program for inmates with substance abuse histories who give birth while incarcerated.	Evaluation conducted by the New York State Division of Parole, followed up the program's first 27 participants.	81% of the children were living with their mothers, 15% with grandmothers, and only 1 child was in foster care.
Options	Philadelphia Prison System. The Women's Therapeutic Center. Opportunities for Prevention and Treatment Interventions for Offenders Needing Support.	Jail-based therapeutic community that uses a communal, noncompetitive approach rather than the traditional, hierarchical structure. All female staff. Will treat pregnant inmates.	Internal evaluation, report to U.S. Department of Justice.	55% who leave the program receive community-based treatment.
Marilyn Baker Program	Connecticut Department of Corrections. Niantic Correctional Institution. Began in 1992.	Residential, prison-based therapeutic community. Started with 32 inmates, isolated from the general population. Increased to a capacity of 85 in 1995. Mostly female staff and 60 hours of programming a week for the participants. Six month program.	Evaluation conducted by faculty at Central Connecticut State University, comparing program participants and a control group, both in prison and postrelease. Data collected from 140 group participants and 40 follow-up assessments in 1995.	Preliminary findings indicate that participants showed a significant increase in knowledge of drug addiction, self-efficacy, awareness of spirituality, and self-esteem. In addition, those completing the program had significantly lower rates of return to custody. Results also indicated improvement in readiness to change after program completion.

1992; Martin, Butzin, & Inciardi, 1995; Martin, Butzin, Saum, & Inciardi, 1999; Nielsen, Scarpitti, & Inciardi, 1996; U.S. Department of Justice, 2000a), but the women-specific components have not. The Delaware Department of Corrections contracts with Spectrum Behavioral Services to run all components of the program. The first phase of the men's program is called KEY and is located at the Multi-Purpose Criminal Justice Facility for Men in Wilmington, with the corresponding women's program (BWCI Village) at Baylor Women's Correctional Institute in New Castle. This is the only women's correctional facility in Delaware. It was started as a demonstration project in 1994 with funding from the Center for Substance Abuse Treatment. The program has forty-two beds in a separate building. Women may enter voluntarily or be sentenced to the unit, and they usually spend 6 to 18 months in the program. Eligibility requires that only 6 to 18 months of an inmate's sentence remain at admission to the program and there can be no severe mental disorder diagnosis.

As with other therapeutic communities, BWCI Village is based on the twelve-step model, but it is uniquely adapted for women in a number of ways. It has all women staff, and the programming content is geared to women's needs, including topics such as parenting, domestic violence, overall health, sexuality, codependency and vocational training. BWCI Village also has a children's visiting center; women well advanced in the program are allowed occasional overnight visits with their children. Participants leave the program with an aftercare plan. The next phase, CREST, consists of a work release therapeutic community outreach center and aftercare. This phase was developed in 1992 to help inmates make a smooth transition back into society. It consists of 6 months of treatment with work reintegration and mixes men and women together. After completing CREST, there are another 6 months of aftercare.

One evaluation, focusing on the total Delaware program, compared 279 people in four groups: CREST dropouts, CREST graduates without aftercare, CREST graduates with aftercare, and a control group assigned to a traditional work-release program with drug treatment (U.S. Department of Justice, 2000a). At an 18-month follow-up, those graduating and completing aftercare were much more likely to remain drug-free—76% compared to 19%. Three years later, one third of treatment offenders remained drug-free, compared to 5% of the comparison group.

Another study compared a subgroup of 448 KEY–CREST clients at an 18-month follow-up (Inciardi et al., 1997). The comparison group consisted of those who were placed in the conventional work-release setting and received neither prison-based nor community-based therapeutic community treatment. The KEY group received the primary therapeutic community treatment while in prison but no secondary or tertiary treatment. A third group received treatment only at CREST, and finally, the KEY–CREST group were those who received their primary treatment at KEY/BWCI followed by CREST. The comparison and both CREST groups included men and women, while the KEY group did not because BWCI has a shorter history in Delaware. Both groups assigned to treatment at CREST significantly improved drug and arrest outcomes.

There are no published outcome evaluations focusing only on BWCI, although there have been some qualitative analyses of women's perceptions of treatment at BWCI trying to understand the high drop-out rate. It was reported that even modified programs have difficulty recruiting and retaining women (Kassebaum, 1999; Lockwood et al., 1998; McCorkel et al., 1998), primarily because of institutional and structural barriers.

In an analysis of CREST focusing on the experiences of women only at an 18-month follow-up, the program failed to produce significant differences in recidivism or relapse (Farrell, 2000). The small sample size (79) could have made it difficult to detect significant differences. On other outcome variables, such as degree of social support, the CREST program did produce positive results, leading to stable ties in a supportive community. When used as a predictor of recidivism and relapse, social support was a strong predictor of success. The CREST program was not designed specifically for women, and the women in this study did not attend BWCI Village during incarceration. Thus, it appears that CREST by itself, although effective for the general population of offenders, may not be effective for women.

Forever Free. The Forever Free program, located at the California Institution for Women in Frontera, is overseen by the California Department of Corrections. Started in 1991, the state has contracted with Mental Health Systems, Inc., of San Diego to run the program. Forever Free is a demonstration project sponsored by the Center for Substance Abuse Treatment. What began as a 120-bed residential unit is now at a 240-bed capacity. The program is based on a 12-step philosophy, and includes individualized counseling, education, and an aftercare component. It averages 720 women annually, and consists of an intensive 4 to 6 months of treatment. This is probably the most extensively evaluated program designed *specifically* for women (Jarman, 1993; Prendergast, Wellisch, & Baldwin, 2000; Prendergast, Wellisch, & Wong, 1996; U.S. Department of Justice, 2000a). Most women enter the program voluntarily. There are two treatment tracks, for 4 or 6 months, depending upon length of incarceration, but women may remain in the program longer if they choose. The program components focus on women's needs and include individual counseling, educational seminars, 12-step programs, and parole planning. The relapse prevention groups are less confrontational than in men's programs. Participants are highly encouraged to voluntarily enter treatment after release.

Jarman (1993) evaluated Forever Free outcomes at 6 months following release (paroled in 1992), comparing 196 treatment respondents, 107 in treatment from other prisons, and 110 with no treatment. Control groups were matched on a number of variables in the quasi-experimental study. For Jarman, outcomes included disciplinary actions and parole revocation. Length of time in treatment was found to be critical in predicting outcomes. Prendergast and colleagues (1996) compared three groups at the 1-year follow-up: graduates from Forever Free who entered residential treatment, graduates who did not enter residential treatment, and women who applied to Forever Free but were not able to enter. The Prendergast study assessed treatment experiences, needs, and services received, and drug use and parole outcomes at 1-year follow-up (release from prison). They found services lacking for relapse prevention and retention. Women who participated in the community-based therapeutic community after release had lower self-reported drug use and higher levels of successful parole discharge than the other women.

A more recent evaluation compared four groups: all women who entered the program (1995–1996), women who dropped out of the program, women who received only the in-prison program, and women who continued to receive treatment after being paroled. It found very high program retention during these years, at almost 95% (U.S. Department of Justice, 2000a). Only 9% of women receiving 120 days or more of community treatment were reincarcerated. Two years after parole, only 25% were reincarcerated. Both percentages were much lower than for the comparison groups.

TAPESTRY. Started in 1990, TAPESTRY is located at the Ohio Reformatory for Women, Marysville, and is operated by the Ohio Department of Alcohol and Drug Addiction Services. In 1992 the state initiated OASIS, a comparable program for men, at the Pickaway Correctional Institution. The purpose of the evaluation study used here was to evaluate Ohio's prison-based therapeutic community system across a number of facilities (Siegal et al., 1999). Researchers had a total sample of 729 respondents. Outcome data came from rearrest and charge after release from prison. Inmates were originally interviewed between January 1991 and December 1995. The sample of women consisted of 193 "no treatment inmates" and 350 therapeutic community residents. Results indicated that length of time in the therapeutic community was crucial to outcome. Those with 180 days or more in a therapeutic community program were much less likely to be rearrested or charged with violent or drug-related crime one year later.

Turning Point Program. This program is located at the Columbia River Correctional Institution in Portland, Oregon, a minimum security prison with 500 total inmates, of which 160 are women. Turning Point is operated by ASAP Treatment Services, Inc., and was started in 1990. It is a therapeutic community that houses 50 men and 50 women in separate facilities (Federal Bureau of Prisons, 2000; Morash et al., 1998; Peugh & Belenko, 1999; U.S. Department of Justice, 1998a). There is a minimum of 9 months required in the program. Aftercare continues for 6 months, with the offender paying for the treatment after two months. The program averages 40 women per day. Turning Point takes a holistic approach, with life skills training, drug education, relationship development, anger management, case management, and a family component. It includes a work release phase, and program staff assist in arranging aftercare. There are five phases, beginning with a 30-day assessment and evaluation and ending with work release and parole. Ideally, residents participate 6 to 12 months prior to parole.

In an internal evaluation, it was reported that female clients presented with an increasing number of mental health issues. In response, the program hired professional mental health staff. The women's unit was exceptionally good at identifying issues specific to the population and responding to the needs of women participating in treatment. Overall promising outcomes include a 48% decrease in arrests, 61% decrease in convictions, and 28% decrease in incarcerations. The program has a 45% treatment completion rate (U.S. Department of Justice, 1998a).

The first Turning Point outcome evaluation studied participants by time spent in prison but did not include a nontreatment control group (Field, 1995). The midpoint for predicting treatment success, measured by reduced recidivism, was more than 180 days in prison. A recent evaluation, which also did not include a control group, found that at a 1-year follow-up, women who participated in treatment had lower rates of drug use and criminal activity than they did prior to treatment (Falkin & Straus, 2000).

Dismas. This program, located in Owensboro, Kentucky, was started in 1994. Dismas Charities is a 100-bed private community center and prison for female offenders, most of whom are sentenced on drug offenses. The program uses an integrated approach that addresses all aspects of their lives, including on-site supervised visitation of children during incarceration. Program goals are to successfully reintegrate female offenders into society, reduce recidivism, lower incarceration rates among their children, and empower female offenders to be independent and productive citizens. Program components include family-oriented topics, alcohol and drug education and treatment, counseling, education, vocational training, and more. There are no published evaluations, but the results based on an internal evaluation are promising. In interviews conducted after participation in the program, inmates reported believing they had better parenting skills, better emotional balance, more confidence, and improved knowledge about their family's well-being (U.S. Department of Justice, 1998a).

Discovery. Discovery is a therapeutic community located at the Rhode Island Department of Corrections Women's Facilities in Cranston. The facility is a minimum security prison for women. The program, based on a 90-day, intensive treatment model, is a 24-bed residential unit run by Talbot Treatment Centers, a community-based drug treatment agency. It was started in 1994 with bilingual counselors. The overall goal of the program is to educate and counsel women about the disease of addiction. Discovery consists of four phases: orientation, recovery, relapse, and transition. The average length of stay is 3 months, but participants may stay until their release from prison. The program emphasizes planning for release and utilizes case management techniques. It also integrates physical activities into group and individual sessions. Talbot Treatment Centers, Inc., provides a continuum of care on release. A furlough programs allows women to leave the facility for treatment one night each week, an important feature because women are more likely to continue treatment after release if they are familiar with a program's staff and surroundings. In an internal evaluation, the recidivism rate for women completing the treatment program was reported to have dropped to about 20%, compared to 45% for the general population (Nichols, 1997; U.S. Department of Justice, 1998a).

Taconic Correctional Facility Nursery Program. Located at a minimum security facility in the state of New York, Taconic is a nursery program started in 1990 (U.S. Department of Justice, 1998a). Targeted toward inmates with substance abuse histories who give birth while incarcerated, it is modeled after the well-established nursery and parenting program at Bedford Hills Correctional Facility. Taconic is the only female correctional facility in the state of New York that operates this program. Its goal is to provide drug counseling services for incarcerated mothers identified as substance abusers. Program staff works exclusively in the nursery and includes a number of specialist drug treatment counselors, pediatric nurses, and a psychologist. Inmates must submit an application to be considered for the program, which includes a parenting curriculum, access to a public health nurse, psychologist services, medical care, and infant care. Participants must simulate single-parenting in the community, and are therefore required to manage scheduling the child's care while still meeting the program requirements. That is, they must have the babies ready for daycare by the time the program begins and they must pick up the child immediately after the program ends for the day. The program is able to foster the development of a strong bond between mother and child and give the mother incentive to change. The program includes continuing care after release. An evaluation conducted by the New York State Division of Parole followed up with the program's first 27 participants. It reported that 81% of the children were living with their mothers, 15% with grandmothers, and only one child was in foster care. This is an especially promising result given the overarching goal of keeping families of offenders intact.

Options. Part of the Philadelphia Prison System, Options is located at the Women's Therapeutic Center, and operates within a larger framework of drug treatment efforts known as Opportunities for Prevention and Treatment Interventions for Offenders Needing

Support (OPTIONS). It is a jail-based program with a capacity of 70 beds. Program objectives are to interrupt the cycle of addiction, criminal activity and incarceration, with programming designed for women's needs. Assessment uses a modified version of the Addictions Severity Index. Options uses a communal, noncompetitive approach rather than the hierarchical structure typical of therapeutic communities, and so is considered a nontraditional therapeutic community. It includes group and individual therapy, 12-step meetings, and family support. Women can attend classes at the Community College of Philadelphia, OPTIONS Campus, on topics such as abuse, violence, and drug education. Options houses an all-female staff and will provide treatment for pregnant inmates. The program has two important initiatives that affect success rates. First, a counselor develops community resources for the clients, such as educational seminars and services. Second, the program has access to community treatment slots, many specifically designed for female offenders. In an internal evaluation, it was reported that 55% who leave the program receive community-based treatment (U.S. Department of Justice, 1998a). This is important given the consistent research indicating that those inmates who continue with aftercare following release have higher success rates in terms of relapse and recidivism.

Marilyn Baker House. The Marilyn Baker House, in the Niantic Correctional Institution for Women, is part of the Connecticut Department of Corrections. It is a residential therapeutic community, and was initiated in 1992 with a capacity of 32 inmates who were isolated from the general population. In 1995, accompanied by a change in facilities, the program capacity increased to 85. While initially disruptive to the program, the move reportedly resulted in improved facilities and increased program satisfaction. The staff is about 90% female, and many are bilingual. The program is highly structured, with 60 hours of programming a week for the participants, and cycles through a wide variety of elective components every 6 weeks. The overall emphasis is on a balance of 12-step and cognitive restructuring strategies while focusing on women's lives. With that in mind, the elective components include parenting, leisure education, communication skills, surviving sexual abuse, grief and loss, HIV support, anger management, domestic violence awareness, spirituality, and a collection of other discussion groups. Phase I, which lasts for 3 weeks, provides basic addiction education. In Phase II (15 weeks), women work on specific topic groups that help them identify and meet their recovery support needs. Phase III (4 weeks) focuses on relapse prevention and the fine-tuning of skills obtained in earlier parts of the program. It is a 6-month program, and many women return to the general population upon completion. However, they may request to stay until their release. This is referred to as Phase IV, the "Life Management" phase, in which they continue as part of the treatment community.

In an evaluation conducted by faculty at Central Connecticut State University, program participants were compared with a control group of women offenders who did not receive treatment (Pease et al., 1996). Both in-prison and postrelease data were collected from 140 group participants in 1995. Researchers also conducted 40 follow-up assessments. Preliminary findings indicate that participants have significantly more knowledge of drug addiction, self-efficacy, awareness of spirituality, and self-esteem. In addition, those completing the program had substantially lower rates of return to custody, and demonstrated an improvement in "readiness to change" after program completion, meaning they were well prepared to continue their recovery.

COMMON CHARACTERISTICS OF WOMEN'S PROGRAMS

Despite the lack of research addressing the effectiveness of women-specific programming, many in the field are willing to speculate about women's needs (Federal Bureau of Prisons, 2000). The modification of the treatment programs to meet the needs of women offenders is complicated, and much more research is needed to adequately address what female-specific components improve treatment success for women. For example, numerous research studies have suggested that women do not respond well to traditional confrontational and attack therapy approaches (Finkelstein, 1996; Nelson-Zlupko, Kauffman, & Dore, 1995; Zweben, 1991), and that program structure and philosophy affect client compliance and involvement (Kelley, 2001). Yet many of the programs cited above continue to use traditional approaches. When modifications are made to programs they must be rigorously evaluated.

Adapting the therapeutic community model for women has produced encouraging results, as highlighted by the model therapeutic programs discussed here and their early evaluations. In an important study of women's experiences in a prison-based drug treatment program, it was found that "clients who completed the program had a more favorable perception of staff and felt empowered by the experience in treatment" (Strauss & Falkin, 2000, p. 2127). Programs staffed with women capable of serving as strong female role models are the ones that get the best reports from clients. One study found that women participating in a prison therapeutic community found the groups and individual counseling session to be the most helpful part of the program (Prendergast et al., 1996). The women felt the least helpful components were the strict structure and rules imposed on them by the programs. Elements found to be conducive to women's needs include staff that provide strong role models, supportive peer networks, and attention to women's parenting roles and histories of abuse (Morash et al., 1998).

Ironically, one of the biggest obstacles to developing substance abuse treatment programs for women in prison is that women often serve sentences too short to accommodate a complete treatment program. The majority of the model programs identified this as a barrier to successful treatment. At Forever Free, the program staff tries to engage women as soon as they enter the system. Women are allowed to participate even if they have only a few months to serve, as long as they agree to continue with treatment upon release. Other barriers to implementation, again mentioned by the majority of programs, include conflict between program staff and prison personnel and misinformation about the program resulting in low recruitment.

Success in Reduced Recidivism and Drug Use

Both men and women offenders who are addicted to drugs are more likely to become repeat offenders if they do not receive drug treatment. Numerous studies have found that women benefit from drug treatment programs in prison as measured by reduced recidivism and drug use. Modified therapeutic community programs in prisons also are effective in reducing recidivism and relapse for women; their effectiveness is enhanced when the programs include continuous aftercare. Those who remain longer in prison-based therapeutic communities are significantly less likely to be rearrested or charged with violent or drug-related crimes 1 year after release. It is difficult to recruit and retain women participants in prison programs. However, all of the model programs reported some success, which increased with duration and aftercare.

Success in Maintaining Families

To the extent that future evaluations will become more women-centered, questions about families will be included in outcome measures. In terms of improving the quality of life for their clients, several of the women-specific featured programs cited family integrity as a main treatment goal. In particular, evaluation of the Taconic program will enable an examination of the effectiveness of this treatment goal. In addition, those programs with family visitation components, such as BWCI Village, Taconic, and Dismas, will likely foster family preservation, because visitation is crucial to maintaining family ties. Research would benefit from including the children and family of offenders to find out what comprehensive services are needed.

DRUG TREATMENT AND HUMAN RIGHTS

Over and over again the literature points to the special needs of women in drug treatment. There are many published lists of what treatment programs should include, ranging from relevant topics to skills-based programming. Yet there is little published about the success of these programs because there are so few to evaluate. In simple terms, there is an unmet need for treatment for women in prison. Although some promising trends and results have been identified in substance abuse programming for women in prison, the U.S. criminal justice system is far from developing an overarching theoretical and analytical model of treatment for this population. First, the cost-effectiveness of treatment is reviewed in light of its overarching benefits for all of society. Second, the human rights framework of treatment is developed. Finally, empowering women in treatment leads to individuals capable of independent and productive lives outside of prison. Empowerment, integrated with a wraparound approach, is proposed as a promising approach to treatment for women offenders, one that may incorporate and expand upon existing programs for women.

Cost-Effectiveness of Prison Treatment Programs

The cost-effectiveness of drug treatment has been well documented. Incarceration is more expensive than residential treatment. Prison treatment programs could save billions of dollars and reduce crime, with substance abuse treatment for offenders paying for itself in a short time (National Center on Addiction and Substance Abuse, 1998). According to one report,

> if just ten percent of inmates given one year of residential treatment stay sober and work during the first year after release, prison-based drug treatment would more than pay for itself in one year. (Blanchard, 1999, p. 27)

And according to another recent report,

> the cost of treatment in conjunction with education, job training, and health care averages $6,500 per year. The benefit of each inmate who completes the program and becomes a

law-abiding, tax-paying citizen would—after 1 year—add up to 10 times the amount spent on the inmate's rehabilitation. (U.S. Department of Justice, 2000b, p. 21)

Clearly, it makes sense to both improve existing programs and make more programs available to women in prison.

Despite the overwhelming evidence that drug treatment is cost-effective, the percentage of inmates who receive treatment while in prison has continued to drop over the past decade (Office of National Drug Control Policy, 2001; U.S. Department of Justice, 2000a). It is more expensive to incarcerate women than to incarcerate men (Seldin, 1995). It costs taxpayers on average almost $21,000 per year to incarcerate one person in a state facility (Office of National Drug Control Policy, 2001), plus additional dollars per year for each of the children put in state care. According to Shapiro (1998), "[parental] drug abuse is one of the most common factors leading to a child's entry into the welfare system" (p. 2). When effective treatment helps bring about long-term recovery, the benefits for women and families are tremendous.

Recent efforts have focused on finding economic support for drug treatment programs. Funding for some prison-based programs comes from the Residential Substance Abuse Treatment (RSAT) for State Prisoners Formula Grant Program (Lipton, Pearson, & Wexler, 1999; U.S. Department of Justice, 1998b, 2000b). This funding is intended for the development or enhancement of comprehensive substance abuse treatment programs in prisons. Programs must last a minimum of 6 months, be held in a separate facility, focus on the substance abuse problems of the offender, and be cognitive-behavioral in nature. The RSAT program was created by the Violent Crime Control and Law Enforcement Act of 1994 (the Crime Act) and is administered by the Corrections Program Office. Outcomes and process evaluations of these programs are funded by the Corrections Program Office.

EMPOWERING WOMEN IN TREATMENT

An encouraging trend in program curriculum, illustrated by a number of the model programs, is the goal of empowering women in treatment. To succeed, drug treatment for pregnant women should include a wide variety of health and social services (Young, 1994), consciousness-raising, client participation and evaluation, meaningful work, and community network ties. But empowerment models usually view women as victims. And while intended to increase self-efficacy, it is unclear that overall effects of such a model address the complex areas of need for women. A relatively new theoretical treatment approach, the Wraparound model, views women as holding a unique position in society (Office of Justice Programs, 1999), one characterized by distinct needs and experiences, and is a long-term approach to planning and coordinating the provision of formal and informal services to the incarcerated woman and her family. Adapted from models used with children, including some juvenile offenders (Brown, Borduin, & Henggeler, 2001; Epstein et al., 1998; Kamradt & Meyers, 1999), it consists of a network of coordinated local services that are "wrapped around" the woman and her family (Malysiak, 1997; Skiba & Nichols, 2000). Modified to apply to adult women and women offenders, this model helps women function in the mainstream, while accentuating the positive individual strengths of each participant (Wingfield & Klempner, 2000). The use of empathy in the Wraparound model is potentially empowering for women and should be emphasized in treatment programs for women offenders (Morrison-Velasco, 2000). Crucial to the success of the Wraparound model is the development of community and criminal justice linkages, which are difficult to achieve but are necessary for women's transition back into the community. One evaluation of the Wraparound model in use at some Comprehensive Substance Abuse Treatment and Rehabilitation program facilities, including some with "Women with Children" programs, found positive outcomes, which increased with length of time in treatment (Evenson, Binner, Cho, Schicht, & Topolski, 1998). Despite the encouraging findings, wraparound services are often cut because of funding pressures (Room, 1998).

THE HUMAN RIGHTS APPROACH TO TREATMENT

Under the Equal Protection Clause of the Fourteenth Amendment, no state shall deny any person equal protection of the law. As such, the courts must provide equal access to treatment for men and women in segregated prison facilities. Differences in access to all kinds of prison programming have been challenged under this provision, and unequal prison conditions are found to be a gender-based classification in violation of the Equal Protection Clause (Seldin, 1995). Yet, at the same time, states claim they cannot make provisions for *more* treatment for women, despite their greater need, without subverting the intent and violating the Equal Protection Clause. Given the separate facilities, "courts may not consider that a higher percentage of women are incarcerated for drug offenses than men and that women have higher rates of addiction before entering prison than men" (Seldin, 1995, p. 16). In other words, policy should be gender-neutral to avoid discrimination. However, without gender-specific language, it is difficult to get programming geared toward special needs, and there is the danger, according to some critics, of viewing women as victims. Self-empowerment models of drug treatment, with gender-specific language, are contrary to prison policy and the interest of prison official to control inmates (Smith & Dailard, 1994). However, the trend with programming has been to move in the direction of noting women's special needs, because without gender-specific language, they are overlooked.

Perhaps another way to conceptualize the gender-specific language necessary to justify funding for special programming is to consider access to treatment as a basic human right. The United Nations (1990) advocates that "prisoners should have access to the health services available in the country without discrimination on the grounds of their legal situation." Yet, in 1997, the Human Rights Project found that many incarcerated individuals suffered from inadequate medical and mental health care (Human Rights Watch, 2001a, 2001b). Women prisoners have been denied the same facilities and services as men prisoners, partly due to economic constraints, but also because of an "ideology of sexism" (Hancock, 1986, p. 101), but women's human rights should include responding to their differences in order to meet their needs for treatment (Seldin, 1995). Many prisons cover up human rights violations in prisons by not allowing visitors and journalists full access to prison facilities (Human Rights Watch, 2001a). Given the lack of funding and the current governmental response to punish rather than treat (Pollock, 1998), it is not at all clear that women and their families will have their human rights protected in the development of treatment programs for prisons. While important for all inmates, access to drug treatment is especially crucial for women, given their high incarceration rates for non-violent drug offenses. To reunite women with their families and children and supply the skills to function in society, their right to treatment in prison must be recognized and their unique needs met. Once that happens and the structure is in place to ensure their basic right to treatment, an Empowerment Wraparound model as a theory of the state-of-the-art in treatment will envelop all offenders and their families.

DISCUSSION QUESTIONS

1. How have recent imprisonment trends, such as coerced treatment and privatization, affected substance abuse treatment in prison?

2. What are the different types of treatment programs used in prisons?

3. Compare the model programs discussed in this chapter. What are the strengths of each? Of those that have been evaluated, how effective are they?

4. What does the author say about substance abuse treatment in women's prisons and human rights issues?

5. What is the Wraparound model? Why does the author believe this is a good treatment modality for women prisoners?

WEBNOTES

Choose a state and go to the web site for the department of corrections for that state (if available). What types of substance abuse treatment programs are available for women prisoners?

NOTES

The author thanks Hallie Stephens for her tireless efforts in the library. An earlier version of this chapter was presented as a paper at the Society for the Study of Social Problems annual meeting, in Anaheim, California, August 2001.

REFERENCES

ALCOHOLISM AND DRUG ABUSE WEEKLY. (1999). California prison officials overcome inmate resistance to treatment. *Alcoholism and Drug Abuse Weekly, 11,* 3.

ANGLIN, M. D., LONGSHORE, D., & TURNER, S. (1999). Treatment alternatives to street crime: An evaluation of five programs. *Criminal Justice and Behavior, 26,* 168–195.

ANGLIN, M. D., LONGSHORE, D., TURNER, S. T., MCBRIDE, D., INCIARDI, J., & PRENDERGAST, M. (1996). *Studies of the functioning an effectiveness of treatment alternatives to street crime (TASC) programs.* Los Angeles, CA: UCLA Drug Abuse Research Center.

ANGLIN, M. D., PRENDERGAST, M., & FARABEE, D. (1998). The effectiveness of coerced treatment for drug-abusing offenders (Paper presented at the ONDCP Consensus Meeting on Treatment in the Criminal Justice System). Washington, DC: Office of National Drug Control Policy.

References

AUSTIN, J., BLOOM, B., & DONAHUE, T. (1992). *Female offenders in the community: An analysis of innovative strategies and programs.* Washington, DC: U.S. Department of Justice, National Institute of Corrections.

BLANCHARD, C. (1999). Drugs, crime, prison and treatment. *Spectrum: The Journal of State Government, 72* (1), 26–27.

BLOOM, B., CHESNEY-LIND, M., & OWEN, B. (1994). *Women in California prisons: Hidden victims of the war on drugs.* San Francisco: Center on Juvenile and Criminal Justice.

BROOKE, D., TAYLOR, C., GUNN, J., & MADEN, A. (1998). Substance misusers remanded to prison—a treatment opportunity? *Addiction, 93* (12), 1851–1856.

BROWN, T. L., BORDUIN, C. M., & HENGGELER, S. W. (2001). Treating juvenile offenders in community settings. In J. B. Ashford, B. D. Sales, et al. (Eds.), *Treating adult and juvenile offenders with special needs* (pp. 445–464). Washington, DC: American Psychological Association.

CENTER FOR SUBSTANCE ABUSE RESEARCH. (2001). Less than 4% percent of substance abuse spending by U.S. states used to fund prevention, treatment, and research. *CESAR FAX, 10* (18), 1.

CHANHATASILPA, C., MACKENZIE, D. L., & HICKMAN, L. J. (2000). The effectiveness of community-based programs for chemically dependent offenders: A review and assessment of the research. *Journal of Substance Abuse Treatment, 19,* 383–393.

CHESNEY-LIND, M., & SHELDEN, R. (1992). *Girls and delinquency.* Belmont, CA: Wadsworth.

DE LEON, G., ANDREWS, M. P. A., WEXLER, H. K., JAFFE, J., & ROSENTHAL, M. S. (1979). Therapeutic community dropouts: Criminal behavior five years after treatment. *American Journal of Drug & Alcohol Abuse, 6,* 253–271.

DE LEON, G., HAWKE, J., JAINCHILL, N., & MELNICK, G. (2000). Therapeutic communities: Enhancing retention in treatment using "senior professor" staff. *Journal of Substance Abuse Treatment, 19,* 375–382.

DEPARTMENT OF HEALTH AND HUMAN SERVICES. (2000). *Substance abuse treatment in adult and juvenile correctional facilities: Findings from the uniform facility data set 1997 survey of correctional facilities.* Rockville, MD: Substance Abuse and Mental Health Services Administration.

DITTON, P. M. (1999). *Mental health and treatment of inmates and probationers.* Washington, DC: U.S. Department of Justice.

EPSTEIN, M. H., JAYANTHI, M., MCKELVEY, J., FRANKENBERRY, E., HARDY, R., DENNIS, K., & DENNIS, K. (1998). Reliability of the wraparound observation form: An instrument to measure the wraparound process. *Journal of Child & Family Studies, 7* (2), 161–170.

EVENSON, R. C., BINNER, P. R., CHO, D. W., SCHICHT, W. W., & TOPOLSKI, J. M. (1998). An outcome study of Missouri's CSTAR alcohol and drug abuse programs. *Journal of Substance Abuse Treatment, 15* (2), 143–150.

FALKIN, G. P., & STRAUS, S. M. (2000). *Reductions in drug use and criminal activity among women treated at Turning Point.* New York: National Development and Research Institutes.

FARABEE, D., PRENDERGAST, M., CARTIER, J., WEXLER, H., KNIGHT, K., & ANGLIN, M. D. (1999). Barriers to implementing effective correctional drug treatment programs. *The Prison Journal, 79* (2), 150–162.

FARRELL, A. (2000). Women, crime and drugs: Testing the effect of therapeutic communities. *Women and Criminal Justice, 11* (1), 21–48.

FEDERAL BUREAU OF PRISONS. (2000). *TRIAD drug treatment evaluation project final report of three-year outcomes: Part I.* Washington, DC: Federal Bureau of Prisons, Office of Research and Evaluation.

FIELD, G. (1995). *Turning Point alcohol and drug program outcome study.* Salem: Oregon Department of Corrections.

FINKELSTEIN, N. (1996). Using the relational model as a context for treating pregnant and parenting chemically dependent. In B. L. Underhill & D. G. Finnegan (Eds.), *Chemical dependency: Women at risk* (pp. 23–65). New York: Haworth Press.

GREENFELD, L. A., & SNELL, T. L. (1999). *Women offenders.* Washington, DC: U.S. Department of Justice.

GROOM, B. (1999). Handling the triple whammy: Serious mental illness, substance abuse, and criminal behavior. *Corrections Today, 61* (4), 114–118.

HANCOCK, L. (1986). Economic pragmatism and the ideology of sexism: Prison policy and women. *Women's Studies International Forum, 9* (1), 101–107.

HARM, N. J., THOMPSON, P. J., & CHAMBERS, H. (1998). The effectiveness of parent education for substance abusing women offenders. *Alcoholism Treatment Quarterly, 16* (3), 63–77.

HEALEY, K. M. (1999). *Case management in the criminal justice system.* Washington, DC: U.S. Department of Justice, National Institute of Justice.

HOOPER, R. M. (1997). Attacking prison-based substance abuse. *Behavioral Health Management, 17* (6), 28.

HUMAN RIGHTS WATCH. (2001a). Ending the abusive treatment of prisoners (Human Rights Watch Prison Project). Human Rights Watch. Available at http://www.hrw.org/prisons.

————. (2001b). Prisons in the United States of America (Human Rights Watch Prison Project). Human Rights Watch. Available at http://www.hrw.org.

INCIARDI, J. A., MARTIN, S. S., BUTZIN, C. A., HOOPER, R. M., & HARRISON, L. D. (1997). An effective model of prison-based treatment for drug-involved offenders. *Journal of Drug Issues, 27* (2), 261–278.

INCIARDI, J. A., MARTIN, S. S., LOCKWOOD, D., HOOPER, R. M., & WALD, B. M. (1992). Obstacles to the implementation and evaluation of drug treatment programs in corrections setting: Reviewing the Delaware KEY experience. In C. G. Leukefeld & F. R. Tims (Eds.), *Drug abuse treatment in prisons and jails* (pp. 176–191). Washington, DC: U.S. Government Printing Office.

JARMAN, E. (1993). An evaluation of program effectiveness for the Forever Free substance abuse program at the California Institution for Women, Frontera, California. Sacramento: California Department of Corrections, Office of Substance Abuse Programs.

KAMRADT, B., & MEYERS, M. J. (1999). Curbing violence in juvenile offenders with serious emotional and mental health needs: The effective utilization of wraparound approaches in an American urban setting. *International Journal of Adolescent Medicine & Health, 11* (3–4), 381–399.

KAPLAN, M. S., & SASSER, J. E. (1996). Women behind bars: Trends and policy issues. *Journal of Sociology and Social Welfare, 23* (4), 43–56.

KASSEBAUM, G., & CHANDLER, S. M. (1994). Polydrug use and self-control among men and women in prisons. *Journal of Drug Education, 24* (4), 333–350.

KASSEBAUM, P. A. (1999). Substance abuse treatment for women offenders: Guide to promising practices. Rockville, MD: U.S. Department of Health and Human Services, Center for Substance Abuse Treatment.

KELLEY, M. S. (2001). Toward an understanding of responses to methadone maintenance treatment organizational style. In S. W. Hartwell & R. K. Schutt (Eds.), *The Organizational Response to Social Problems* (Vol. 8) (pp. 247–273). Amsterdam: JAI.

KELLEY, M. S., ROSENBAUM, M., KNIGHT, K., IRWIN, J., & WASHBURN, A. (1996). Violence: A barrier to methadone maintenance treatment for women injecting drug users. *International Journal of Sociology and Social Policy, 16* (5/6), 156–177.

KERR, D. (1998). Substance abuse among female offenders. *Corrections Today, 60,* 114–115.

KILMANN, P. R. (1974). Direct and nondirect marathon group therapy and internal–external control. *Journal of Counseling Psychology, 21* 380–384.

KOSKI-JANNES, A. (1997). Prevention and treatment of alcohol-related violence through prison programs: A Finnish perspective. *Contemporary Drug Problems, 24* (4), 765–785.

LIPTON, D. A. (1998). Principles of correctional therapeutic community treatment programming for drug abusers (Paper presented at the ONDCP Consensus Meeting on Treatment in the Criminal Justice System). Washington, DC: Office of National Drug Control Policy.

LIPTON, D. A., & JOHNSON, B. D. (1998). Smack, crack, and score: Two decades of NIDA-funded drugs and crime research at NDRI 1974–1994. *Substance Use & Misuse, 33* (9), 1779–1815.

LIPTON, D. S., PEARSON, F. S., & WEXLER, H. K. (1999). National evaluation of the residential substance abuse treatment for state prisoners program from onset to midpoint—final report. Rockville, MD: U.S. Department of Justice.

LO, C. C., & STEPHENS, R. C. (2000). Drugs and prisoners: Treatment needs on entering prison. *American Journal of Drug and Alcohol Abuse, 26* (2), 229–248.

LOCKWOOD, D., MCCORKEL, J., & INCIARDI, J. A. (1998). Developing comprehensive prison-based therapeutic community treatment for women. *Drugs and Society, 13* (1–2), 193–212.

LONG, C. A., LANGEVIN, C. M., & WEEKES, J. R. (1998). A cognitive-behavioral approach to substance abuse treatment: Canada embraces social learning concept in treatment of substance abuse. *Corrections Today, 60* (6), 102–104.

MADEN, A., SWINTON, M., & GUNN, J. (1994). A criminological and psychiatric survey of women serving a prison sentence. *British Journal of Criminology, 34* (2), 172–191.

MAGURA, S., ROSENBLUM, A., LEWIS, C., & JOSEPH, H. (1993). The effectiveness of in-jail methadone maintenance. *Journal of Drug Issues, 23* (1), 75–99.

MALYSIAK, R. (1997). Exploring the theory and paradigm base for wraparound. *Journal of Child & Family Studies, 6* (4), 399–408.

MARTIN, S. S., BUTZIN, C. A., & INCIARDI, J. A. (1995). Assessment of a multistage therapeutic community for drug-involved offenders. *Journal of Psychoactive Drugs, 27* (1), 109–115.

MARTIN, S. S., BUTZIN, C. A., SAUM, C. A., & INCIARDI, J. A. (1999). Three-year outcomes of therapeutic community treatment for drug-involved offenders in Delaware: From prison to work release to aftercare. *The Prison Journal, 79* (3), 294–320.

MARTIN, S. S., & INCIARDI, J. A. (1993). Case management approaches for criminal justice clients. In J. A. Inciardi (Ed.), *Drug treatment and criminal justice* (Vol. 27, pp. 81–96). Newbury Park, CA: Sage.

MASON, D., BIRMINGHAM, L., & GRUBIN, D. (1997). Substance use in remand prisoners: A consecutive study. *British Medical Journal, 314* (7099), 18(14).

MCCORKEL, J., HARRISON, L. D., & INCIARDI, J. A. (1998). How treatment is constructed among graduates and dropouts in a prison therapeutic community for women. *Journal of Offender Rehabilitation, 27* (3/4), 37–59.

MELNICK, G., DE LEON, G., HILLER, M. L., & KNIGHT, K. (2000). Therapeutic communities: Diversity in treatment elements. *Substance Use & Misuse, 35* (12–14), 1819–1847.

MONER, S. E. (1996). Acupuncture and addiction treatment. *Journal of Addictive Diseases, 15* (3), 79–100.

MOON, D. G., THOMPSON, R. J., & BENNET, R. (1993). Patterns of substance use among women in prison. In B. R. Fletcher, L. D. Shaver, & D. G. Moon (Eds.), *Women prisoners: A forgotten population* (pp. 45–54). Westport, CT: Praeger.

MOON, M. M., & LATESSA, E. J. (1994). Drug treatment in adult probation: An evaluation of an outpatient and acupuncture program. *Evaluation and Program Planning, 17* (2), 217–226.

MORASH, M., & BYNUM, T. (1995). *Findings from the national study of innovative and promising programs for women offenders* (NCJ 171667). Washington, DC: Michigan State University for the U.S. Department of Justice, National Institute of Justice.

MORASH, M., BYNUM, T. S., & KOONS, B. A. (1998). *Women offenders: Programming needs and promising approaches.* Rockville, MD: National Institute of Justice.

MORASH, M., HAARR, R. N., & RUCKER, L. (1994). A comparison of programming for women and men in U.S. prisons in the 1980s. *Crime & Delinquency, 40* (2), 197–221.

MORRISON-VELASCO, S. (2000). Wrapping around empathy: The role of empathy in the wraparound model. *Ethical Human Sciences & Services, 2* (2), 109–117.

MUMOLA, C. J. (1999). *Substance abuse and treatment, state and federal prisoners, 1997.* Washington, DC: U.S. Department of Justice.

NATIONAL CENTER ON ADDICTION AND SUBSTANCE ABUSE. (1998). *Behind bars: Substance abuse and America's prison population.* New York: Columbia University.

NATIONAL INSTITUTE OF JUSTICE. (1998). *The Women's Prison Association: Supporting women offenders and their families.* Washington, DC: U.S Department of Justice, Office of Justice Programs.

NATIONAL INSTITUTE ON DRUG ABUSE. (2001). *Treatment methods for women.* Bethesda, MD: U.S. Department of Health and Human Services, National Institute on Drug Abuse.

NATIONAL WOMEN'S LAW CENTER. (1995). *A vision beyond survival: A resource guide for incarcerated women.* Washington, DC: Women in Prison Project—National Women's Law Center.

NELSON-ZLUPKO, L., KAUFFMAN, E., & DORE, M. M. (1995). Gender differences in drug addiction and treatment: Implications for social work intervention with substance-abusing women. *Social Work, 40* (1), 45–54.

NEWBERN, D., DNASEREAU, D. F., & PITRE, U. (1999). Positive effects on life skills motivation and self-efficacy: Node-link maps in a modified therapeutic community. *American Journal of Drug and Alcohol Abuse, 25* (3), 407–423.

NICHOLS, M. (1997). Outside looking in. *Women's Review of Books, 14* (10–11), 8–10.

NIELSEN, A. L., SCARPITTI, F. R., & INCIARDI, J. A. (1996). Integrating the therapeutic community and work release for drug-involved offenders. *Journal of Substance Abuse Treatment, 13* (4), 349–358.

OFFICE OF JUSTICE PROGRAMS. (1999). *Conference proceedings: National Symposium on Women Offenders.* Washington, DC: Office of Justice Programs.

OFFICE OF NATIONAL DRUG CONTROL POLICY. (2001). *Drug treatment in the criminal justice system.* Washington, DC: Office of National Drug Control Policy.

OWEN, B. (1998). *In the mix: Struggle and survival in a women's prison.* New York: State University of New York Press.

———. (2001). Perspectives on women in prison. In C. Renzetti & L. Goodstein (Eds.), *Women, crime, and criminal justice* (pp. 243–254). Los Angeles, CA: Roxbury.

PAGE, R. C., & KUBIAK, L. (1978). Marathon groups: Facilitating the personal growth of imprisoned, black female heroin abusers. *Small Group Behavior, 9* (3), 409–416.

PAGE, R. C., RICHMOND, B. O., & DE LA SERNA, M. (1987). Marathon group counseling with illicit drug abusers: Effects on self-perceptions. *Small Group Behavior, 18* (4), 483–497.

PAN, H., SCARPITTI, F. R., INCIARDI, J. A., & LOCKWOOD, D. (1993). Some considerations on therapeutic communities in corrections. In J. A. Inciardi (Ed.), *Drug treatment and criminal justice* (Vol. 27, pp. 30–43). Newbury Park, CA: Sage.

PEASE, S. E., LOVE, C. T., HALL, F. B., & WHITE, K. L. (1996). *Evaluation of a prison-based therapeutic community for female substance abusers.* New Britain: Central Connecticut State University.

PETERS, R. H. (1993). Drug treatment in jails and detention settings. In J. A. Inciardi (Ed.), *Drug treatment and criminal justice* (Vol. 27, pp. 44–80). Newbury Park, CA: Sage.

PETERS, R. H., & SCHONFELD, L. (1993). Determinants of recent substance abuse among jail inmates referred for treatment. *Journal of Drug Issues, 23* (1), 101–117.

PETERS, R. H., STROZIER, A. L., MURRIN, M. R., & KEARNS, W. D. (1997). Treatment of substance-abusing jail inmates. *Journal of Substance Abuse Treatment,* 14 (4), 339–349.

PEUGH, J., & BELENKO, S. (1999). Substance-involved women inmates: Challenges to providing effective treatment. *The Prison Journal, 79* (1), 23–44.

PHILLIPS, S. D., & HARM, N. J. (1998). Women prisoners: A contextual framework. *Women and Therapy, 20* (4), 1–9.

POLLOCK, J. M. (1998). *Counseling women in prison.* Thousand Oaks, CA: Sage.

PRENDERGAST, M., WELLISCH, J., & BALDWIN, D. M. (2000). *Process evaluation of the Forever Free substance abuse treatment program.* Rockville, MD: National Institute of Justice.

PRENDERGAST, M. L., WELLISCH, J., & FALKIN, G. P. (1995). Assessment of and services for substance-abusing women offenders in community and correctional settings. *The Prison Journal, 75* (2), 240–256.

PRENDERGAST, M., WELLISCH, J., & WONG, M. M. (1996). Residential treatment for women parolees following prison-based drug treatment: Treatment experiences, needs and services, outcomes. *The Prison Journal, 76* (3), 253–274.

ROOM, J. A. (1998). Work and identity in substance abuse recovery. *Journal of Substance Abuse Treatment, 15* (1), 65–74.

ROSS, W. F., McREYNOLDS, W. T., & BERZINS, J. I. (1974). Effectiveness of marathon group psychotherapy with hospitalized female narcotic addicts. *Psychology Reports, 34* 611–616.

SACKS, S. (2000). Co-occurring mental and substance use disorders: Promising approaches and research issues. *Substance Use & Misuse, 35* (12–14), 2061–2093.

SARGENT, E., MARCUS-MENDOZA, S., & YU, C. H. (1993). Abuse and the woman prisoner. In B. R. Fletcher, L. D. Shaver, & D. G. Moon (Eds.), *Women prisoners: A forgotten population* (pp. 55–64). Westport, CT: Praeger.

SELDIN, S. F. (1995). A strategy for advocacy on behalf of women offenders. *Columbia Journal of Gender and Law, 5* (1), 1–32.

SHAPIRO, C. (1998). La Bodega de la Familia: Reaching out to the forgotten victims of substance abuse. Washington, DC: U.S. Department of Justice.

SIA, T. L., DANSEREAU, D. F., & CZUCHRY, M. L. (2000). Treatment readiness training and probationers' evaluation of substance abuse treatment in a criminal justice setting. *Journal of Substance Abuse Treatment, 19,* 459–467.

SIEGAL, H. A., WANG, J., CARLSON, R. G., FALCK, R. S., RAHMAN, A. M., & FINE, R. L. (1999). Ohio's prison-based therapeutic community treatment programs for substance abusers: Preliminary analysis of re-arrest data. *Journal of Offender Rehabilitation, 28* (3/4), 33–48.

SIMPSON, D. D. (1981). Treatment for drug abuse: Follow-up outcomes and length of time spent. *Archives of General Psychiatry, 38,* 875–880.

SIMPSON, D. D., JOE, G. W., & ROWAN-SZAL, G. A. (1997). Drug abuse treatment retention and process effects on follow-up outcomes. *Drug and Alcohol Dependence, 47* (3), 227–235.

SKIBA, R. J., & NICHOLS, S. D. (2000). What works in wraparound programming. In M. P. Kluger, G. Alexander, & P. A. Curtis (Eds.), *What works in child welfare* (pp. 23–32). Washington, DC: Child Welfare League of America.

SMITH, B. V., & DAILARD, C. (1994). Female prisoners and AIDS: On the margins of public health and social justice. *AIDS and Public Policy Journal, 9* (2), 78–85.

SNYDER-JOY, Z. K., & CARLO, T. A. (1998). Parenting through prison walls: Incarcerated mothers and children's visitation programs. In S. L. Miller (Ed.), *Crime control and women: Feminist implications of criminal justice policy* (pp. 130–150). Thousand Oaks, CA: Sage.

STRAUSS, S. M., & FALKIN, G. P. (2000). The relationship between the quality of drug user treatment and program completion: Understanding the perceptions of women in a prison-based program. *Substance Use & Misuse, 35* (12–14), 2127–2159.

THERAPEUTIC COMMUNITIES OF AMERICA. (1999). Therapeutic communities in correctional settings: The prison-based TC Standards Development Project (Final Report of Phase II). Washington, DC: Executive Office of the President, Office of National Drug Control Policy.

UNITED NATIONS. (1990). Basic principles for the treatment of prisoners (U.N. GAOR Supp. [No. 49A]). New York: United Nations. Available at http://www.umn.edu/humanrts/instree/g2bpt.htm.

U.S. DEPARTMENT OF HEALTH AND HUMAN SERVICES. (2000). Managed care carve-out programs more likely to provide specialized substance abuse services. CSAT, 5 (21).

U.S. DEPARTMENT OF JUSTICE. (1996a). *A corrections-based continuum of effective drug abuse treatment.* Washington, DC: National Institute of Justice.

———. (1996b). *OJP: Drugs and crime working group.* Rockville, MD: Office of Justice Programs.

————. (1996). *Treatment protocol effectiveness study.* Rockville, MD: Office of National Drug Control Policy.

————. (1998a). *Programs in correctional settings: Innovative state and local programs.* Rockville, MD: Office of Justice Programs.

————. (1998b). *State efforts to reduce substance abuse among offenders.* Washington, DC: Office of Justice Programs Corrections Program Office.

————. (2000a). *Promising strategies to reduce substance abuse.* Rockville, MD: Office of Justice Programs.

————. (2000b). Reducing offender drug use through prison-based treatment. *National Institute of Justice Journal, 20–23.*

WALLACE, B. C. (1992). Toward effective treatment models for special populations: Criminal, pregnant, adolescent, uninsured, HIV-positive, methadone-maintained, and homeless populations. In B. C. Wallace (Ed.), *The chemically dependent: Phases of treatment and recovery* (pp. 310–336). New York: Brunner/Mazel.

WEINMAN, B. A., & LOCKWOOD, D. (1993). Inmate drug treatment programming in the federal Bureau of Prisons. In J. A. Inciardi (Ed.), *Drug treatment and criminal justice* (Vol. 27, pp. 194–208). Newbury Park, CA: Sage.

WEISHEIT, R. A. (1985). Trends in programs for female offenders: The use of private agencies as service providers. *Comparative Criminology, 29* (1), 35–42.

WELLISCH, J., ANGLIN, M. D., & PRENDERGAST, M. L. (1993). Treatment strategies for drug-abusing women offenders. In J. A. Inciardi (Ed.), *Drug treatment and criminal justice* (Vol. 27, pp. 5–29). Newbury Park, CA: Sage.

WESSON, D. R. (1995). *Detoxification from alcohol and other drugs treatment improvement protocol (TIP), series 19.* Rockville, MD: U.S. Department of Health and Human Services, Center for Substance Abuse Treatment.

WEXLER, H. K. (1995). The success of therapeutic communities for substance abusers in American prisons. *Journal of Psychoactive Drugs, 27* (1), 57–66.

WEXLER, H. K., CUADRADO, M., & STEVENS, S. J. (1998). Residential treatment for women: Behavioral and psychological outcomes. In S. J. Stevens & H. K. Wexler (Eds.), *Women and substance abuse: Gender transparency* (pp. 213–233). New York: Haworth Press.

WEXLER, H. K., & LIPTON, D. S. (1993). From reform to recovery: Advances in prison drug treatment. In J. A. Inciardi (Ed.), *Drug treatment and criminal justice* (Vol. 27, pp. 209–227). Newbury Park, CA: Sage.

WEXLER, H. K., & LOVE, C. T. (1994). Therapeutic communities in prison. In F. R. Tims, G. DeLeon, & N. Jainchill (Eds.), *Therapeutic community: Advances in research and application.* Rockville, MD: National Institute on Drug Abuse.

WEXLER, H. K., & WILLIAMS, R. (1986). The Stay'n Out therapeutic community: Prison treatment for substance abusers. *Journal of Psychoactive Drugs, 18* (3), 221–230.

WINGFIELD, K., & KLEMPNER, T. (2000). What works in women-oriented treatment for substance-abusing mothers. In M. P. Kluger, G. Alexander, & P. A. Curtis (Eds.), *What works in child welfare* (pp. 113–124). Washington, DC: Child Welfare League of America.

WOLSTENHOLME, J., McHUGH, M., & JENNINGS, M. (1995). Alcohol and drugs groupwork. *Issues in Criminological and Legal Psychology, 23,* 56–59.

YOUNG, I. M. (1994). Punishment, treatment, empowerment: Three approaches to policy for pregnant addicts. *Feminist Studies, 20* (1), 33–57.

ZWEBEN, J. E. (1991). Counseling issues in methadone maintenance treatment. *Journal of Psychoactive Drugs, 23* (2), 177–190.

PART V

Family and Parenting Issues

One of the most compelling issues faced by women prisoners is the effect of their incarceration on their families. Unlike men in prison, a majority of women prisoners lived with their minor children immediately prior to incarceration. Additionally, these women were most often the sole caregivers for their children. Thus, when women are incarcerated, their children are severely traumatized.

In Chapter 10, Susan Sharp provides an overview of some of the child-related issues these women face, with particular attention paid to Oklahoma's women prisoners. Sharp begins by pointing out that current criminal justice policies are unduly punitive toward women of color and therefore their children. She then describes some of the problems that women in prison face as mothers. First and foremost, the placement of their children is problematic. With whom the children will live, whether siblings will be kept together or separated, how to handle economic pressures, and safety issues are all problems—often complex and interrelated—faced by the incarcerated mother. What might seem a good solution on the surface is often riddled with less visible problems.

The chapter then turns to other issues faced by mothers in prison, including the challenge of maintaining relationships with children during incarceration. Women prisoners often face obstacles in their attempts to parent from prison. Sharp points out that criminal justice policies for women prisoners often make visitation or telephone contact difficult. Thus, upon release the women and their children may have become virtual strangers, making successful reintegration into society harder.

Pregnancy and childbirth while incarcerated is another serious issue faced by some women prisoners, their physical discomforts exacerbated by the punitive stance taken by many jurisdictions. Sharp examines some of the existing policies surrounding labor, childbirth, infant–mother contact, and placement.

The final portion of the chapter examines a variety of prison programs for women prisoners and their children, ranging from compassionate policies, such as community alternatives to incarceration, to more restrictive policies, such as maintaining contact with children via e-mail. Strengths and weaknesses of individual programs are reviewed.

10

Mothers in Prison

Issues in Parent–Child Contact

Susan F. Sharp, Ph.D.

❖

The United States's love affair with incarceration has had a particularly deleterious effect on women offenders and their children. When prison populations exploded in the 1980s and 1990s, the female inmate population increased more than 500% (Ekstrand, Burton, & Erdman, 1999), and the growth of the female prisoner population has continued to outstrip that of males (Greenfeld & Snell 1999). At midyear 2000, 6.7% of all inmates were female, with 156,200 women incarcerated (Beck & Karberg, 2001). About two thirds of these women were mothers of children under the age of 18, and over 64% of these mothers reported living with their children prior to incarceration (Mumola, 2000). In 1999, this incarceration trend resulted in about 115,500 minor children whose mothers were incarcerated in state prisons and an additional 10,600 children whose mothers were incarcerated in federal prisons (Mumola, 2000).

MOTHERS IN PRISON: THE ISSUES

Although this chapter examines issues involving incarcerating mothers throughout the United States, particular attention is paid to the state of Oklahoma, noteworthy because it has the nation's highest female incarceration rate. Although the state population is only slightly more than 3 million, Oklahoma ranks eighth in the total number of female prisoners (Beck & Karberg, 2001). As of 1998, females accounted for more than 10% of the total inmate population (Oklahoma Department of Corrections, 1998) and were incarcerated at a rate of 122 per 100,000 female residents in the state (Greenfeld & Snell, 1999). In particular, Oklahoma incarcerates high numbers of female drug offenders, who made up nearly half of the new female inmates assigned to the Department of Corrections in 1998 (Oklahoma Department of Corrections, 1998).

Oklahoma's female prison-population numbers are troubling, as high incarceration rates have been linked in a recent report by the Oklahoma Department of Corrections to unhealthy environments for raising children. The authors used a number of indicators to rank the child-rearing environments, including the percentage of children allegedly abused or neglected, infant mortality, and juvenile arrests. They found that children fared worst in states with the highest incarceration rates, including Oklahoma (Ferrari et al., 2001). Although the report drew no causal conclusions about the relationship between child-raising environment and incarceration, there is nonetheless ample reason for concern about the effects on children when mothers are sent to prison.

Race and Incarceration: Women of Color and Their Children

Women of color and their children have been notably affected by current criminal justice practices, such as the high incarceration rates for drug possession. Indeed, Chesney-Lind has argued that the "War on Drugs" is more accurately a war on women, particularly women of color (1997). Other research supports her contention, demonstrating that minority women are far more likely to be incarcerated for drug offenses (Sharp, Braley, & Marcus-Mendoza, 2000; Greenfeld & Snell, 1999; Pollock, 1998; Culverson, 1998). Women who violate middle-class cultural standards of "appropriate" womanhood also are more likely to receive a prison sentence (Belknap, 2001; Culverson, 1998; Erez, 1992; Humphries et al., 1995; Kruttschnitt, 1981; Sharp, Braley, & Marcus-Mendoza, 2000).

Feinman (1986) has argued that women are often viewed through a Madonna/whore lens. Those conforming to the prescribed societal role are seen as "good girls"; those who do not are labeled "bad girls," perhaps deserving punishment for their norm violation as much as for their offense. This is particularly applicable to nonwhite female offenders, who are often seen as violating cultural standards of femininity in general. Indeed, it has been argued that for black women there is no "good girl" category (Young, 1986). Looking at the composition of the female offender population, there is reason for concern. Nonwhites account for nearly two thirds of the state female inmate population and over 70% of the women in federal prisons (Greenfeld & Snell, 1999). These disproportionate rates of imprisonment appear to be the result of discrimination. A study of drug offenders in Oklahoma found that black women were more likely than white women to receive sentences of 5 or more years, regardless of the offense or prior legal history, whereas white women typically received deferred adjudication (Sharp et al., 2000). It thus appears that women of color are more likely to be incarcerated for offenses, and to serve longer sentences.

The children of incarcerated women of color are thus being more severely affected. Indeed, children of color are nearly nine times more likely than white children, and Hispanic children are three times more likely than white children, to have a parent in prison (Mumola, 2000). This means that about 7% of children of color under age 18 have at least one parent incarcerated, resulting in nearly 800,000 black children and 300,000 Hispanic children with an incarcerated parent (Mumola, 2000). Although the majority of incarcerated parents are men, women of color are overrepresented in the incarcerated female population. Thus, programs for incarcerated mothers need to take the composition of the women prisoner population into account. Ideally, these programs must be culturally sensitive to be effective (Kurshan, 2001).

Placement of Children When Mother Goes to Prison

When a mother goes to prison, her children must be placed in someone else's care. Unlike the children of incarcerated fathers, children whose mothers are in prison rarely remain with the other parent (Mumola, 2000). Indeed, female offenders are about three times more likely than male offenders to have been the only parent living with the children immediately prior to arrest (Mumola, 2000), and their children are usually sent to live with family members (Sharp & Marcus-Mendoza, 2001; Mumola, 2000). Slightly more than half of the women in state prisons reported that their children were living with a grandparent, and another quarter with other relatives. An additional 10% said their children were being cared for by foster parents or by agencies (Mumola, 2000). Similarly, around 90% of federal women prisoners reported their family members were taking care of their children (Mumola, 2000). There also appear to be some differences in placement of children by race. White prisoners were more likely to report that their children were with the children's fathers or in foster care, whereas black and Hispanic women were more likely to report that grandparents or other relatives had the children (Enos, 2001).

More disturbing, many children are separated from siblings as well as from their mothers (Sharp & Marcus-Mendoza, 2001; Belknap, 1996). One in five incarcerated women has three or more children, increasing the likelihood that the children may be separated from each other during the mother's incarceration period (Mumola, 2000; Sharp & Marcus-Mendoza, 2001). Additionally, many placements do not last throughout the entire period of the mother's incarceration (McCarthy, 1980); children may be moved from one family member to another, further disrupting any sense of stability.

The most common placement is with the mother's own parents (Mumola, 2000; Enos, 2001; Sharp & Marcus-Mendoza, 2001). Most incarcerated mothers hope to resume their parental responsibilities upon release. Thus, they tend to resist nonfamily placement, fearing it might lead to permanent loss of custody (Gaudin & Sutphen, 1993; Enos, 2001). Indeed, loss of the relationship with their children is the greatest fear of many incarcerated mothers (Sharp & Marcus-Mendoza, 2000, 2001; Enos, 2001). Other research suggests

---

Box 10.1

PLACEMENT OF CHILDREN OF WOMEN PRISONERS

- 52.9% with grandparents
- 25.7% with other relatives
- 28% with child's other parent
- 9.6% with foster parents

Source: C. J. Mumola (2000), *Bureau of Justice Statistics bulletin: Incarcerated women and their children.* Washington, DC: U.S. Department of Justice.

that the maternal role is one of few positive ones open to women offenders. Loss of that role because of incarceration could thus have negative consequences on the woman's emotional stability (Correctional Service of Canada, 2001a; Correctional Service of Canada, 2001b).

Placement of children with family members may be preferable in some ways, but must be viewed with caution. First, many of these families are ill equipped, both financially and emotionally, to take on the added burden of caring for those children (Belknap, 1996; Enos, 2001; Sharp & Marcus-Mendoza, 2001). Additionally, many of the women come from families with histories of abuse. Indeed, over 60% of incarcerated women experience sexual or physical abuse before the age of 18 (Greenfeld & Snell, 1999). One study found that grandparents with a history of family violence were as likely as nonviolent grandparents to become primary caretakers for children of incarcerated mothers, and that at least 11% of these children were currently living with family members with a history of violence (Sharp & Marcus-Mendoza, 2001). Recent national data suggest that the percentage of female prisoners with abuse histories is rising, with almost half of the women prisoners in 1997 reporting histories of physical abuse and more than one third reporting sexual abuse (Ekstrand et al., 1999). In essence, children of incarcerated mothers may be placed in family settings that have been abusive in the past. When one considers the stress that supporting children may bring, the potential for the children's abuse is alarming.

To date, scant research has explored child placements, but information that has been gathered does not allay these concerns. One study compared the quality of care given to infants and preschool children by familial versus foster caregivers. Although the two types of placement were similar in the care of infants, significant differences were found in the care afforded to preschool children. Specifically, foster placements were associated with higher quality of care, both material/environmental and emotional. Family caregivers "offered significantly less verbal attention and positive social reinforcement to the children in their care" (Gaudin & Sutphen, 1993, p. 143). Further research certainly is needed in this area. Additionally, policies of terminating parental rights need to be reexamined and perhaps changed. Currently, women prisoners want their families to take care of their children because they fear that they will otherwise lose their parental rights. This may result in placement choices that are not safe for children. An alternative would be policies that work toward reunification of mother and children, regardless of where the children lived during the mother's imprisonment.

At times, custody issues are even more confusing. Consider the case of a young Native American mother in Oklahoma. This woman gave birth while incarcerated for a drug offense. To protect the mother's parental rights, a nurse-practitioner familiar with the case obtained temporary custody. However, this caregiver died, and her own young daughter then applied for custody, seeking to terminate the birth mother's rights. Meanwhile, the father and his family became aware that the young woman was seeking to terminate all rights of the natural parents. The natural father sued for custody as well. By the time this case was heard, there were a number of individuals seeking custody of the child, who had already lost her birth mother because of incarceration and one caregiver through death. The resulting agreement was that the young foster mother would retain temporary custody, but the birth mother could visit the child. Although she did not entirely lose her maternal rights, the experiences of this young woman demonstrate why so many women prisoners do not want their children placed in foster care. Inmates' fear of permanent loss of custody is justified.

Mother–Child Contact

For women prisoners who have been the primary caretakers of young children, incarceration not only has an impact on their current relationships but also can create problems upon release (Sobel, 1982). Thus, the level of contact maintained between imprisoned mothers and their children is of utmost concern.

There are three basic types of contact between incarcerated mothers and their children: mail, telephone calls, and visits. Approximately 60% of mothers in state prisons and 70% in federal prisons reported some sort of weekly contact with their children (Mumola, 2000). Mail contact appears to be the most common, with almost two thirds of the women in state prisons and three fourths of those in federal prisons reporting they received mail from their children at least once a month (Mumola, 2000).

Over half the federal and almost 40% of the state inmate mothers also reported telephone contact at least weekly. However, telephone contact can be financially devastating for families of inmates. For example, in Oklahoma, the first 5 minutes cost $5, and each additional minute costs 59 cents. Thus, a 15-minute telephone call can cost over $13 (Sharp & Marcus-Mendoza, 2000). Most of the inmates' families are from lower economic strata. Supporting the women's children during incarceration is a financial sacrifice, and telephone contact may place an additional strain on the families' budgets.

Oklahoma inmates face other restrictions on telephone contact. The Department of Corrections utilizes a level system, meaning privileges such as telephone contact must be earned. On Level 1, contact is restricted to legal counsel and clergy. Thus, mothers may not speak with their children at the time when their relationship has been disrupted suddenly. The inability to verbally reassure each other can lead to even more stress (Sharp & Marcus-Mendoza, 2000). Movement to Level II may take weeks or even months.

Visitation is perhaps the most problematic type of contact. Over half of the women in state prisons reported never receiving visits from their children (Ekstrand, et al., 1999). Because females compose a small percentage of total inmate populations, fewer correctional facilities exist for female prisoners. Thus, many inmates are housed at considerable distance from their families. Indeed, most women prisoners are housed over 100 miles from their residence immediately prior to incarceration (Beck & Karberg, 2001). Among federal prisoners, over half of the women are housed more than 250 miles from home, and nearly 30% are housed more than 500 miles from home (Ekstrand, et al., 1999). Again, economic issues may limit parent–child interaction. For families without privately owned automobiles, visitation may be virtually impossible. In Oklahoma, one state-run prison for women and the sole privately operated facility are located in rural areas that have limited public transportation. However, many of the state's female prisoners come from other areas in the state. Thus, the possibility of visitation is constrained by distance, access, and economics.

The use of privatized prisons to incarcerate women can also cause visitation problems. As states have turned to the private-sector prison industry to house their female inmate populations, many women find themselves transferred to private facilities in other states. Essentially, the private prisons are not constrained to service the states in which they are located. Instead, they often serve as warehouses, providing inmate beds to any willing payer. This can have effects on the inmates. For example, a research team was scheduled to visit Dr. Eddie Warrior Correctional Center in 1997 to administer a survey. On arrival, the research team discovered that over 80 women had been transferred suddenly without notice to a privately operated facility in Texas. The remaining women were in turmoil, and many expressed fear that they, too, would be moved out of Oklahoma and away from their children (Sharp et al., 1998; Sharp et al., 1999; Sharp & Marcus-Mendoza, 2001).

Oklahoma prisoners now have been returned to the state after the opening of a large private facility. However, that facility now houses out-of-state prisoners. Sixty-five women from Hawaii and fifty-four women from Wyoming were incarcerated there at the time of this writing. Given the distance from those states to Oklahoma, it is safe to assume that few of these women will have visits from their children.

The issue of limited visitation with children is particularly problematic given the positive benefits that have been reported from parent–child contact. Visits benefit both children and parents, allowing children to express their feelings about separation and parents to work through the grief surrounding separation. Furthermore, visitation can alleviate children's fears by allowing them to see the reality of their parents' incarceration. Finally, visitation is an important element of maintaining familial relationships and increasing the chances for successful family reunification (Gabel and Johnston, 1995; Henriques, 1996). Maintaining relationships with family while in prison is a strong predictor of reduced recidivism. A study of male inmates reported that the men were one sixth as likely to recidivate in the first postrelease year if they had three or more visitors in the year prior to their release. Furthermore, furloughs and overnight visits from family were also predictors of success (Hairston, 1991). Research is needed to explore the relationship between visitation by the women's children, including overnight visits, and women's postrelease success. Given the importance of their children to incarcerated mothers, it would seem that women should benefit from visits at least as much as men.

Pregnant Prisoners and Their Children

A final area of concern regarding parenting issues is corrections policies and pregnant inmates. In 1998, more than 1,400 children were born to incarcerated mothers. The conditions under which pregnant prisoners give birth are frequently appalling. A recent report by Amnesty International (1999) indicated that only one state had an outright ban on the shackling of pregnant women while moving them to the hospital to give birth. Furthermore, 29 states allowed the use of restraints during labor and sometimes even delivery. Women are often shackled to their hospital beds, and correctional officers maintain control of the keys. In one case, a woman reported that when the delivery began, the officer could not be found to unlock her shackles. Thus, she could not part her legs. Numerous instances were also reported of women unable to move about during labor because of shackles (Amnesty International, 1999).

Restraint policies for pregnant prisoners may compromise the health of both the mother and the infant. In birth situations that become critical, the loss of time to unshackle the mother may be a matter of life or death. It is important to remember that many of these pregnancies are far more likely than average to be high-risk. Women prisoners tend to come from low socioeconomic strata, and to have histories of drug use and domestic violence (Acoca, 1998; Amnesty International, 1999; Kitzinger, 2001). Thus, these women are also more likely to experience problems during childbirth. Yet, many correctional departments unnecessarily place the women and their babies at risk, in order to "protect" society from these primarily nonviolent offenders. Oklahoma, not surprisingly given their incarceration policies in general, is a state that does authorize shackling of inmates during labor (Sharp & Marcus-Mendoza, 2000).

Another issue faced by pregnant prisoners is that in many jurisdictions, mothers have little if any contact with their newborns. Thus, mothers and infants have little chance to develop a bond (Kitzinger, 2001; Owen, 1998). There are a few programs that allow prisoner mothers to keep their infants with them, and some of these will be examined later in this chapter. Oklahoma, like many states, allows minimal contact between mother and infant. The policy is not unlike what Owen (1998) described in California: Shortly before expected delivery, the prisoner is moved to Mabel Bassett Correctional Center, the largest female facility in the state. When the woman goes into labor, she is transported to a hospital nearby to deliver her baby. Custody arrangements for the infant, however, are nebulous. If the woman has opportunity to notify relatives who can come to the hospital, those relatives can take custody of the child. However, if the family cannot come, the baby is taken into state custody (Sharp & Marcus-Mendoza, 2000). One of the difficulties with this policy is that many of the families live some distance from the hospital. Their ability to gain custody of the newborn is thus contingent on both the prisoner's ability to notify them she has given birth and on their own ability to get to Oklahoma City within the time frame, often only 24 hours.

Historically in the United States, women prisoners and their newborn infants have not always been separated. Early reformatories, with their emphasis on traditional female roles, encouraged the bonding between mothers and newborns, allowing the infants to remain with the mothers for extended periods (Belknap, 2001). Other countries also tend to allow more time for bonding. For example, the Correctional Service of Canada (2001a; 2001b) allows pregnant prisoners to apply for compassionate release to community sentencing. Finally, in a limited number of jurisdictions in the United States, programs have been developed that keep infants with their mothers. We will examine those more closely in the latter part of the chapter.

However, there is not agreement about the best way to deal with women prisoners and their children. Some have advocated programs that allow children to remain with their mother; others have questioned whether the benefits of doing so truly outweigh potential harm to infants from being in a prison setting. The lack of normalcy and the lack of stimulation are cited as potential problems (Drummond, 2001). Indeed, some prisoners do not even want visits from their children, not wanting them to see their mother in the prison environment, and fearing their own emotional distress of seeing their families but not being able to leave with them (Owen, 1998).

The Effects of Incarcerating Mothers

Incarceration can disrupt the woman prisoner's family system in two ways: by threatening family cohesion and straining the parent–child relationship (Clear, 1996; Hagan, 1996; Hairston and Lockett, 1987, p. 162). According to Harris (1993), the degree to which parent–child separation is problematic is a "glaring difference between the male and female prison experience" (p. 53). Not only is separation an emotional strain, but it also results in a number of serious consequences for the mother as well as the children (Morris & Wilkinson, 1995).

First, considerable research links maternal incarceration with depression in both mothers and children (Koban, 1983; Henriques, 1996; Siegal, 1997; Sharp & Marcus-Mendoza, 2000, 2001). The women's relationships with children are often the only positive thing in their lives (AIM, Inc., 2001; Owen, 1998; Sharp & Marcus-Mendoza, 2000). Thus, loss of those relationships can be devastating. Hairston (1991) reported that contact with those outside the prison was an important aspect of prisoner mental health. However, the woman prisoner may deal with the loss by not allowing herself to think about her family "outside." Her detachment can then further harm the already tenuous relationships with her children (Owen, 1998). This in turn affects the prisoner's mental health even more, and so the cycle continues.

Children also are affected negatively. Depression is a very common response to the mother's incarceration (AIM, Inc. 2001; Moses, 1995; Sharp et al., 1999; Sharp & Marcus-Mendoza, 2001). Not only have children lost their caretaker, but they have lost their homes. They may fear for their mother, and they may be separated from their siblings (Belknap, 1996; Bloom & Steinhart, 1993; Markovic, 1995). School performance is also affected, often leading to dropping out (Hagan, 1996; Moses, 1995; Sharp et al., 1999; Sharp & Marcus-Mendoza, 2001). Finally, the children themselves may begin getting arrested (AIM, Inc., 2001; Bloom & Steinhart, 1993; Clear, 1996; Hagan, 1996; Owen, 1998; Siegal, 1997; Zaplin & Dougherty, 1998).

On the other hand, visitation has a number of benefits. First, children are able to express their feelings about the separation. Second, mothers are better able to deal with their grief surrounding separation and loss. Third, seeing the mother in prison allows the children to view the situation realistically, often assuaging fears. Fourth, it gives the mothers an opportunity to model appropriate interactions. Finally, it increases the chances of successful reunion after release (Gabel & Johnston, 1995).

The large numbers of mothers and children affected by current incarceration policies highlights the significance of addressing their problems through prison programming. To date, however, little has been done to acknowledge this pressing issue, much less to curtail the negative impact on incarcerated mothers and their children. In the following sections we will examine some of the programs currently existing in various places in the United States as well as suggesting other programs to help meet the needs of incarcerated mothers and their offspring.

Existing Programs and Suggestions for Future Programs

There are a number of current programs that work toward maintaining and improving relationships between incarcerated mothers and their children, including parent education, visitation programs, services for pregnant women, postrelease services, and alternatives to incarceration. The programs described below, although noteworthy, are by no means an exhaustive list. However, they do illustrate the nature of available programming for offender mothers.

Parent education. The Federal Bureau of Prisons reports that parent education is available at all federal institutions (Ekstrand et al., 1999). Most states also offer parenting classes to both male and female inmates. For example, California offers at least two programs. One, Friends Outside, is a 30-hour program provided by a private contractor. A more intensive 17-day program focusing on child-rearing skills is offered in many facilities as well. In many jurisdictions, parent education is one component of a larger program (Morash, Bynum, & Koons, 1998). For example, Hairston and Lockett (1987) describe a program in a men's prison that includes home study, classroom work, events, and projects.

Texas is a glaring exception. According to a 1999 report, the state does not fund any parent education program within its correctional system. However, a not-for-profit organization funded by churches and private donors does provide a 15-week parental training course for women prisoners (Ekstrand et al., 1999).

Facilitating contact. Programs to facilitate mother–child visitation exist at a number of facilities, and account for about half the parenting programs examined in a recent study (Morash, Bynum, & Koons, 1998). Contact between mother and child ranges from long-distance relationships to extensive visitation. One program in Florida, "Reading Family Ties," makes innovative use of computers to maintain contact between mothers and children (Bartlett, 2000; Drummond, 2001). In North Carolina, an attempt is made to help incarcerated mothers maintain contact with their children, offering occasional family retreats and home passes. Those women whose children are unable to visit regularly are given priority at the overnight retreats, which are sponsored in conjunction with a local church (Girshick, 1999).

An in-depth analysis of programs designed to help in women's prisons in three jurisdictions provides a good starting point. The report examined inmate needs as well as programs available in the Federal Bureau of Prisons, in California, and in Texas (Ekstrand et al., 1999). Other studies have examined programs in others states (Zaplin & Dougherty, 1998) that included regular visitation, overnight visitation, special programs for mothers and children, parental education, and residential mother–child programs. In the three jurisdictions covered by the Ekstrand (1999) report, only California offered overnight visitation.

Several states offer a more innovative program, "Girl Scouts Beyond Bars" (Moses, 1995), which began at the Maryland Correctional Institution for Women. Supporters of this program believe it is very beneficial in maintaining relationships between mothers and their daughters because it provides more than a simple visit. Participating prisoners attend two Girl Scout meetings per month on the prison grounds. The other 2 weeks each month the scout troop, including the inmates' daughters, meets in the community. In the biweekly prison meetings, mothers and daughters work on projects and crafts. To participate in the program, women prisoners must attend a 1-hour group meeting with a social worker each month. Although innovative and definitely a positive step in promoting family cohesion, the program does have several weaknesses. First, participating daughters and their caregivers do not receive any mental health support, unlike their mothers. Additionally, when a mother transfers to the Pre-Release unit, her participation ends. Finally, follow-up indicates that few mothers participate once released (Moses, 1995). It should also be noted that this program fosters relationships between mothers and daughters but there is no comparable program for mothers and their sons.

Pregnancy, birth, motherhood. Pregnant inmates need special services and programs. First, better prenatal care is essential (Markovic, 1998). Additionally, institutions must work toward ways to facilitate women prisoners obtaining adequate temporary child care, both for their existing children and those born in prison (Belknap, 2001). An interesting program developed in England might merit consideration in the United States: a volunteer group of London women assists women prisoners during labor and delivery. These women, known as *doulas,* help the incarcerated woman develop a birth plan, provide information and support prior to delivery, and support her through the birth process, acting as intermediaries with healthcare professionals (Parkinson, 2001).

A number of programs exist for incarcerated mothers and their children that are designed to help preserve the mother–child relationship. For example the MATCH (Mothers and Their Children) programs originated in a federal institution and have spread to other locations. Typical MATCH programs include Children's Centers where mothers and children work, learn, and play together, developing healthy bonds; support and referral services to help incarcerated mothers with child custody issues; parent education classes under the supervision of volunteer staff; programs to help inmates develop the skills to work with other inmates; and individual and family counseling services, transition/postrelease services, and referrals (Boudouris, 1996).

In Oklahoma, the Mabel Bassett Correctional Center offers CAMP (Children and Mothers Program) to foster stronger family relationships. The prison allows mother–child visitation at least twice each week in a child-centered setting with toys, books, and child-sized furniture. Occasional overnight visits may be approved, and children and mothers enjoy picnics and holiday celebrations.

Another program that has merit is the Mother–Offspring Life Development (MOLD) program, which uses a reward of 5 days visitation per month for good behavior (Zaplin & Dougherty, 1998). The Nebraska program is modeled in part on the renowned program for mothers and their children at the Bedford Hills Correctional Facility in New York.

The Bedford Hills program is important because it not only provides visitation opportunities, but also allows mothers to keep their infants with them, normally to the age of one, but if the mother is scheduled to be released within 18 months, some infants remain with the mother that long. The Bedford Hills program promotes parenting skills as well as regular visitation and a summer camp program. Here, children stay with host families while attending the on-site program during the day. An important component of the Bedford program is that inmates teach other inmates (Boudin, 1998; Morash, Bynum, & Koons, 1998).

Eleven states and the Federal Bureau of Prisons provide some type of program that keeps infants with their mothers. Seven of the states offer community-based incarceration that allows mothers to keep their newborn infants with them, while four states incorporate nurseries into prison facilities (Ekstrand, Burton, & Erdman, 1999). The Federal Bureau of Prisons has developed a program at eight locations that includes prenatal classes, social services, and life-skills training. Mothers are moved to a community facility location at least 2 months before their delivery due date. The infants and mothers remain for 3 months after birth, and then the mother is returned to prison (Ekstrand et al., 1999). The downside of this program, of course, is that after the brief initial period of bonding, the mother and infant are separated. California offers the Family Foundations Program for pregnant or parenting offenders. This program will be addressed in greater detail in the following section on alternatives.

One essential aspect of programs for prisoner mothers is the involvement of other prisoners as peer counselors and support (Morash et al., 1998). Programs for men in prison have demonstrated the impact of peer support on their potential success (Hairston & Lockett, 1985).

Postrelease services and alternatives to incarceration. Provision of post-release services is an important aspect of successful outcomes for women prisoners and their children. Some programs provide minimal transitional services. Oklahoma is beginning to acknowledge that women prisoners have different needs from men prisoners (Oklahoma Department of Corrections 1999; Oklahoma Department of Corrections, 2000). For example, the Mabel Bassett Correctional Center in Oklahoma has an 8-hour WIN program that consists of videos of former offenders who have adjusted successfully post-release. However, there are other, more proactive, programs that assist women prisoners and their children.

The Women's Prison Association (WPA) in New York City sponsors a promising innovative program. During 1996–1997, the WPA placed 99 women in permanent housing and aided 344 mothers and 286 minor children (Conly, 1998). Their programs are structured to help women work toward reunification with their children after incarceration. Acknowledging that regaining custody is often difficult, the WPA helps mothers with many practical steps, from supervised visitation to obtaining adequate housing. The program's first two stages deal with helping the women adjust to life outside of prison. In the third stage, offenders can be accepted into the Sarah Powell Huntington House, which has 28 apartments; 18 are for women and their children, and two women each share the other 10 apartments as they pursue reuniting with their children. In the roommate set-up, the children and mothers spend time together via supervised visits and eventually overnight stays. When a mother and children are deemed ready, they get their own apartment. The program has a number of important elements, including a Children's Center and on-site social services. Children are screened by a psychologist and referred for appropriate services. This is important, because both mother and children are assisted in dealing with the emotions and problems inherent in the reunification process. The Children's Center has a preschool, where others volunteer, and a school-age program that includes recreational activities, tutoring, arts and crafts, weekend programs, and afterschool activities (Conly, 1998).

The final phase of the WPA program is called "Steps to Independence." Here, mother and children prepare to establish themselves in the community again. The program provides assistance in obtaining permanent housing, suitable employment for the mother, financial and social services, peer support groups, life-skills training, parenting education, and extensive follow-up care and case management (Conly, 1998).

However, researchers and activists alike have argued that instead of after-the-fact attempts to undo the damage of maternal incarceration, finding alternatives to prison is a more fruitful direction (Acoca, 1998; Chesney-Lind, 1991; JusticeWorks Community, 2001). Acoca (1998) argues that maternal and infant health would require that women not be incarcerated during all or at least part of their pregnancies to ensure healthy outcomes. Thus, programs like California's Family Foundations Program and Community Prison Mother Program are suggested alternatives (Ekstrand et al., 1999). One innovative alternative program is a partnership between Kings County District Attorney's Office and the JusticeWorks Community. The program, PACT (Parents and Children Together), is dedicated to keeping nonviolent women offenders and their offspring together. It is not under the auspices of the state department of corrections, which is unusual. Part of the benefit of the program is that successful completion results in dismissal of the charges. Additionally, unlike many programs, there is no limit on the age or number of children allowed. The PACT program offers services for mothers and children including medical, child care, and counseling (JusticeWorks, 1999). Similarly, Brandon House in San Jose is an alternative sentencing program that is part of the California Mother-Infant Care Program, which allows mothers and infants to stay together in a community-based facility (Siegal, 1997). Mothers can eventually earn the right to have work furloughs, better preparing them for a return to the community (Ekstrand et al., 1999).

As seen above, there are some existing and pilot programs that have been developed for offender mothers and their children. In particular, programs that offer alternatives to incarceration or postrelease transition services have promise, although these programs are currently the exception rather than the rule. There is, however, a caveat to this. Many alternative programs require that the offender make restitution. Given the obligations to support the family and the low earning ability of most women offenders, this may simply set up the women for failure (O'Brien, 2001).

Further evaluation of what works for women offenders *and their children* is needed. It will be important to evaluate existing programs closely, along a number of dimensions. Not only should evaluations examine the effects of specific programs on recidivism, but perhaps more important, we need to begin examining the degree to which programs affect the life chances of mothers and children alike. Reunification is not an easy process in the best of circumstances. For many of these mothers and their children, successful relationships will need to be built on a foundation that includes life-skills preparation and transitional services. Thus, we need to begin assessing what works and for whom, keeping in mind the diversity of the target population.

DISCUSSION QUESTIONS

1. What are some of the negative effects of incarceration on mothers? What are some of the effects on their children? How can prison programs address these issues? Why is it important to address these issues?

2. Is placement of children with family members always a good option? What are some of the issues that need to be considered in placement?

3. Why do women prisoners want their children to be placed with family rather than with agencies, even when such a placement is not a good option? What could be done to address this problem?

4. Why is contact between women prisoners and their children important? What are some of the obstacles to maintaining contact?

5. What program components do you think are important in prison programs for incarcerated mothers?

WEBNOTES

Go to the Family and Corrections network web site (http://www.fcnetwork.org/) and select an article to read. Be prepared to discuss your article in class.

REFERENCES

Acoca, L. (1998). Defusing the time bomb: Understanding and meeting the growing health care needs of incarcerated women in America. *Crime & Delinquency, 44,* 32–48.

AIM, Inc. (2001). *Facts about mothers in prison.* Aid to Inmate Mothers, Inc. Available at: http://www.inmatemoms.org/facts.htm.

Amnesty International. (1999). *United States of America: "Not part of my sentence"—Violations of the human rights of women in custody.* Amnesty International. Available at: http://www.amnesty.org.

Bartlett, R. (2000). Helping inmate moms keep in touch—Prison programs encourage ties with children. *Corrections Today.* Available at: http://www.corrections.com/aca/cortoday/december00/bartlett.html.

Beck, A. J., & Karberg, J. C. (2001). *Bureau of Justice Statistics bulletin: Prisoners at midyear 2000.* Washington, DC: U.S. Department of Justice.

Belknap, J. (1996). Access to programs and healthcare. *Federal Probation, 60,* 34–39.

———. (2001). *The invisible woman: Gender, crime and justice.* Belmont, CA: Wadsworth.

Bloom, B., & Steinhart, D. (1993). *Why punish the children?* San Francisco: National Council on Crime and Delinquency.

Boudin, K. (1998). Lessons from a mother's program in prison: A psychosocial approach supports women and their children. *Women & Therapy, 21,* 103–125.

Boudouris, J. (1996). *Parents in prison: Addressing the needs of families.* Lanham, MD: American Correctional Association.

Chesney-Lind, M. (1997). *The female offender: Girls, women and the criminal justice system.* Thousand Oaks, CA: Sage.

———. (1991). Patriarchy, prisons and jail: A critical look at trends in women's incarceration. *The Prison Journal, 71,* 51–67.

Clear, T. (1996). *Backfire: When incarceration increases crime.* Paper presented at conference organized by Vera Institute of Justice, January 1996.

Conly, C. (1998). *The Women's Prison Association: Supporting women offenders and their families.* Washington, DC: National Institute of Justice.

Correctional Service of Canada. (2001a). Creating choices: The report of the task force on federally sentenced women. Correctional Service of Canada. Available at: http://www.csc–scc.gc.ca/text/prgrm/fsw/choices/toce.shtml.

———. (2001b). Mothers in prison: Perspectives on the mother's role during incarceration and upon reintegration. Available at: http://www.csc–scc.gc.ca/text/rsrch/regional/outline-r68.html.

Culverson, D. (1998). The welfare queen and Willie Horton. In C. R. Mann & M. S. Zatz (Eds.), *Images of color, images of crime* (pp. 97–107). Los Angeles: Roxbury Press.

Dowden C., & Andrews, D. A. (1999). What works for female offenders: A meta-analytic review. *Crime & Delinquency, 45,* 438–452.

Drummond, T. (2001). Mothers in prison. Available at: Time.com: http://www.time.com/time/magazine/printout/0,8816,58996,00.html.

Ekstrand, L., Burton, D., & Erdman, E. (1999). *Women in prison: Issues and challenges confronting U.S. correctional systems.* Washington, DC: General Accounting Office.

Enos, S. (2001). Mothering from the inside: Parenting in a women's prison. Albany: State University of New York Press.

Erez, E. (1992). Dangerous men, evil women: Gender and parole decision-making. *Justice Quarterly, 9,* 105–126.

Feinman, C. (1986). *Women in the criminal justice system,* (2nd ed.). New York: Praeger.

Ferrari, F., Spivak, A., Dyer, L., & Chown, B. (2001). Comparing rankings of the U.S. States for child-raising quality and incarceration rate. Available at: http://www.doc.state.ok.us/docs/childrearing.htm.

GABEL, K., & JOHNSTON, K. (1995). *Children of incarcerated parents.* Lexington, MA: Lexington Books.

GAT, I. (2000). *Incarcerated mothers: Effects of the mother/offspring life development program.* Poster Presentation, American Psychological Association Meetings, Psychologists in Public Service Session, August, 2000.

GAUDIN, J. M., JR., & SUTPHEN, R. (1993). Foster care vs. extended family care for children of incarcerated mothers. *Journal of Offender Rehabilitation, 19,* 129–147.

GIRSHICK, L. (1999). *No safe haven.* Boston: Northeastern University Press.

GREENFELD, L. A., & SNELL, T. L. (1999). *Bureau of Justice Statistics bulletin: Women offenders.* Washington, DC: U.S. Department of Justice.

HAGAN, J. (1996). *The next generation: Children of prisoners.* Paper presented at conference organized by Vera Institute of Justice, January, 1996.

HAIRSTON, C. F. (1991). Family ties during imprisonment: Important to whom and for what? *Journal of Sociology & Social Welfare, 18,* 87–104.

HAIRSTON, C. F., & LOCKETT, P. (1985). Parents in prison: A child abuse and neglect prevention strategy. *Child Abuse & Neglect, 9,* 471–477.

———. (1987). Parents in prison: New directions for social services. *Social Work, 32,* 162–164.

HARRIS, J. W. (1993). Comparison of stressors among female vs. male inmates. *Journal of Offender Rehabilitation, 19,* 43–56.

HENRIQUES, Z. (1996). Imprisoned mothers and their children: Separation–reunion syndrome dual impact. *Women & Criminal Justice, 8,* 77–96.

HUMPHRIES, D., DAWSON, J., CRONIN, V., KEATING, P., WISNIEWSKI, C., & EICHFELD, J. (1995). Mothers and children, drugs and crack: Reactions to maternal drug dependency. In C. Feinman (Ed.), *The criminalization of a woman's body* (pp. 203–211). New York: Harrington Press.

JUSTICEWORKS COMMUNITY. (2001). Mothers in prison, children in crisis campaign. Available at: http://www.justiceworks.org/html/mothers.html-ssi.

KITZINGER, S. (2001). Mothers and babies in prison. Available at: http://www.sheilakitzinger.com/Prisons.htm.

KOBAN, L. A. (1983). Parents in prison: A comparative analysis of the effects of incarceration on the families of men and women. *Research in Law, Deviance & Social Control, 5,* 171–183.

KRUTTSCHNITT, C. (1981). Social status and sentences of female offenders. *Law & Society Review, 15,* 247–265.

KURSHAN, NANCY. (2001). Women and imprisonment in the U.S. Available at: http://www.prisonactivist.org/women/women-and-imprisonment.html.

MARKOVIC, V. (1995). Pregnant women in prison: A correctional dilemma? *The Keeper's Voice, 16* (3).

MCCARTHY, BELINDA R. (1980). Inmate mothers: The problems of separation and reintegration. *Journal of Offender Counseling, Services and Rehabilitation, 4,* 199–212.

MORASH, M., BYNUM, T. S., and KOONS, B. A. (1998). *Women offenders: Programming needs and promising approaches.* Washington, DC: U.S. Department of Justice.

MORRIS, A., & WILKINSON, C. (1995). Responding to female prisoners' needs. *The Prison Journal, 75,* 295–305.

MOSES, M. (1995). *Keeping incarcerated mothers and their daughters together: Girl Scouts beyond bars.* Washington, DC: National Institute of Justice.

MUMOLA, C. (2000). *Bureau of Justice Statistics bulletin: Incarcerated women and their children.* Washington, DC: U.S. Department of Justice.

O'BRIEN, P. (2001). *Making it in the free world.* Albany: State University of New York Press.

OKLAHOMA DEPARTMENT OF CORRECTIONS. (1998). *Oklahoma Department of Corrections 1998 annual report.* Oklahoma City: Oklahoma Department of Corrections.

———. (1999). *Female Offender Task Force work summary.* Oklahoma City: Oklahoma Department of Corrections.

———. (2000). *Female Offender Task Force 2000 work summary.* Oklahoma City: Oklahoma Department of Corrections.

OWEN, B. (1998). *In the mix: Struggle and survival in a women's prison.* Albany: State University of New York Press.

PARKINSON, D. (2001). Doulas for women prisoners. Available at: http://www.sheilakitzinger.com/Prisons.htm.

POLLOCK, J. M. (1998). *Counseling women in prison.* Thousand Oaks, CA: Sage.

RAFTER, N. (1990). *Partial justice: Women, prisons, and social control.* New Brunswick, NJ: Transaction Books.

SHARP, S. F., BRALEY, A., AND MARCUS-MENDOZA, S. (2000). Focal concerns, race and sentencing of female drug offenders. *Free Inquiry, 28,* 3–16.

SHARP, S. F., & MARCUS-MENDOZA, S. (2000). *Female inmates in Oklahoma: Issues in sentencing, transfers and parenting.* Paper presented at the American Society of Criminology Meetings, November 2000.

———. (2001). It's a family affair: Incarcerated women and their families. *Women & Criminal Justice, 12.*

SHARP, S. F., MARCUS-MENDOZA, S. T., BENTLEY, R. G., SIMPSON, D. B., AND LOVE, S. R. (1998). Gender differences in the impact of incarceration on the children and families of drug offenders. *Journal of the Oklahoma Criminal Justice Research Consortium, 4,* 1–14.

———. (1999). Gender differences in the impact of incarceration on the children and families of drug offenders. In M. Corsianos & K. Train (Eds.), *Interrogating social justice* (pp. 217–246). Toronto: Canadian Scholars' Press.

SIEGAL, N. (1997). Mother's day in prison: Why 10,000 Californians need family-oriented alternatives to incarceration. Available at: News. Http://www.sfbg.com/News/31/32/Features/prison.html.

SOBEL, S. (1982). Difficulties experienced by women in prison. *Psychology of Women Quarterly, 72,* 107–118.

YOUNG, V. (1986). Gender expectations and their impact on black female offenders and victims. *Justice Quarterly, 3,* 305–328.

ZAPLIN, RUTH T., AND DOUGHERTY, JOYCE. (1998). Programs that work: Mothers. In *Female offenders: Critical perspectives and effective interventions* (pp. 331–347). Gaithersburg, MD: Aspen.

PART VI

Preparing for Return to Society

In the final section of the book, the focus turns toward the future, as women prisoners return to society. In Chapter 11, Lori Girshick asserts that successful reintegration planning should begin at the time of arrest. Incarceration itself is counterproductive, and she suggests that the most successful rehabilitation of women prisoners would probably occur in nonprison settings. However, because of the current criminal justice climate favoring high incarceration rates, she addresses the issues, given this situation.

She stresses that no program will be very successful with unmotivated participants. Drawing from her previous research, Girshick lets the women themselves tell the reader of their own resistance to prison programs. She then moves on to a second important consideration—the prison environment itself. As previously discussed in Chapter 8, it is difficult to administer therapeutic programs in the hostile environment of the prison. Finally, she focuses on the situations to which women return after completing their sentences, and how these often difficult conditions may hamper their success.

Girshick then examines the elements of "successful" prison programs for women, followed by an in-depth evaluation of several extant programs that encompass one or more elements identified as essential to success.

Finally, the chapter ends with her perspectives about what programs are likely to enhance successful reintegration into society upon release. Alternatives to incarceration should be a primary focus in intervention efforts. These programs would not sever the women prisoners' bonds to their families and communities. However, she does recognize that we must begin where we are today, with high levels of female incarceration for nonviolent offenses. Thus, her second suggestion is that we focus on supplying effective aftercare to facilitate movement back into society. Third, Girshick stresses the need to modify existing programs in light of the special requirements of women prisoners and the nontherapeutic environment of U.S. prisons.

The final chapter of the book reflects on the needs and types of programs identified throughout earlier chapters and provides thoughtful commentary on issues needing to be addressed in programming for women prisoners.

11

Leaving Stronger

Programming for Release

Lori B. Girshick, Ph.D.

❖

Writing about programs that lead to successful release appears to be a straightforward task. We already have identified the many specific needs of female inmates, we can develop effective programs to address them, and we can recommend that only respectful, caring people facilitate those programs. And voilà, success. But it is not as simple as that. In fact, there are at least three major problems outside of the content of the programs that affect their viability: the desire to change on the part of the individual inmate, the environment of the prison in which the programs operate, and the challenges the woman is confronted with on release. I will address these issues, discuss programs that meet the chronic needs of so many of the women who are incarcerated today, and explore whether most of the women in prison today could be better treated and helped outside of the prison complex. My participation in this discussion of prison programs does not imply my approval of the incarceration approach.

IS SHE WILLING?

The individual inmate has to be receptive, ready to change the behaviors that brought about her incarceration. Some effort is required on her part. But many women are not open, and for different reasons. Some women I have spoken with felt their early and brief periods of incarceration were easy to take, like, as Tammy put it, being at "kiddie camp." But longer stretches of time, going in and out one too many times, getting emotionally worn out, or realizing their kids are growing up without them can force a change in attitude. Before that point, however, here are some of the types of women who may not be ready for change:

- The woman filled with fear. She is intimidated by prison and the other women around her. She cannot act on her own behalf. She tries to protect herself by keeping to herself. She does not feel she is worthy, and change is not what is on her mind. Evanne, who was afraid and insecure during her first incarceration, told me,

    I didn't understand that I needed to better myself or I'd go back to the same ways. . . . Plus I felt bad about myself, what I had done, and the sadness of my kids, and the losses in my life, you know, thinking there was no life after prison, there was no life after drugs. There was no hope, and for me, without hope, there's nothing.

- The woman consumed with anger. She strikes out at every opportunity. Being tough is how she survives. "Needs" are not her concern. She stays in trouble and wouldn't waste her time on programs or meetings. Tammy, in and out of prison six times, has stated, "Nothin' could help me in there. I wasn't tryin' for you to help me, I was makin' it hard for myself." She relates this story:

    I was so violent, they say, we bringin' a woman in from the outside to help you, to separate you from the others. They brung that woman in, that lady said somethin' to me. You know what I did to that lady? Took the desk and beat that lady. Stayed in the hole two years. Just 'cause that lady said somethin' loud to me. She wanted me to read or somethin'. And I couldn't stand for you to say "read." I was just so angry inside. Just angry. And I beat that lady and I beat her. I couldn't sit down with nobody back then and try to teach me nothin' or help me. I didn't want to.

- The woman who cares externally, says the right things, and attends programs. But she does not feel worthy. She has been treated like garbage so often throughout her life that she expects to be used. Going along with whatever is happening is how she makes it. Programs do not really affect her. Tracy, for example, tells me "I did get a lot out of the programs. I think, though there's something there, some part of me wanted to get high more than I wanted to stay clean."

All of these women have deep self-esteem problems. They do not feel worthwhile as human beings. They have experienced serious trauma, and are not in a condition to receive, to hear, to reveal, or to be open. While they are in this state of mind, prison programming will not be beneficial to them. Internally they are too frightened, angry, or shut down.

Having said this, all of these women may still benefit from programs at a later time, as in fact the women quoted above all did. But while in these mental states, we cannot expect them to be receptive just because the programs are provided. Their hostility or noncompliance may have nothing to do with not needing help, deficient programming, or poor quality of providers. Reframing our focus leads to issues not directly related to the groups and sessions of regular programming: an examination of the prison environment and how management of inmates affects their anger, sense of safety, and self-esteem.

The Prison Environment

Although punishment takes precedence over rehabilitation as the goal of incarceration in prisons today, there are still prison programs that can help the inmate (Pollock, 1998). But it is questionable whether the environment inherent in a prison setting lends itself to promoting personal growth and change. Rather, powerlessness, dependency, retraumatization, stress, fear, lack of autonomy, monotony, and arbitrary rule enforcement—and its accompanying degradation—promote retreat (repressing their anger and pain) or hostility (acting out or speaking up) as inmates' primary coping mechanisms.

The contradiction of treating these women like children, but demanding that they act as adults is obvious. The prison becomes like the punitive parent with total control over the inmates (Girshick, 1999; Watterson, 1996), with its forced dependency and isolation that heightens the powerlessness of the inmates. As Watterson (1996) points out, "Forced dependency also is illogical, especially when we expect people to come out of prison as independent, law-abiding, responsible citizens. Our prison system strips people of responsibility, independence, human contact and dignity" (p. 79). Because inmates lack control over behavior or decisions in their daily lives, they experience an acute lack of autonomy that hinders their development of responsibility. There is no dignity without autonomy (Pollock, 1998; Watterson, 1996). It defies reason that prison authorities expect inmates to respond positively in an emotionally abusive environment.

Their high rates of previous traumas, such as incest, rape, and battering, mean that women inmates risk experiencing post-traumatic stress symptoms while in prison. Strip searches, pat searches, lack of privacy, sexual harassment by guards, fear of other inmates, loud noises (such as frequent clanging of gates), cell searches, and restraints can trigger hyperarousal, nightmares, flashbacks, and fear in an abuse survivor (Bill, 1998). These negative issues are complicated by the fact that for some survivors of abuse, prison is a respite from the craziness of the streets or their home life (Girshick, 1999; McQuaide & Ehrenreich, 1998).

Surviving the stress of incarceration—the separation from families, worry about their children, loss of control over their lives, arbitrary rule enforcement, and loss of self-respect—takes enormous energy (Fogel, 1993; Pollock, 1998). Fogel reports that depression, weight gain, and physical symptoms such as headaches, backaches, and fatigue are common responses to prison stress. In addition, Pollock found more destructive reactions to stress: high rates of self-mutilation, drug use, and either retreat or threatening behavior. Pollock states, "Because of the stress induced by entry into and adaptation to prison, many women have little energy or inclination to deal with personal issues. Just surviving in prison, without succumbing to depression or serious mental distress, is sometimes a triumph" (p. 29).

Negotiating the prison world successfully requires skills that may be contrary to positive adaptation upon release. As Owen (1998) discusses, fitting in to the prison subculture requires becoming prison-smart. Learning the system and being "in the mix" means being part of a pseudo-family or perhaps in a homosexual relationship, interacting in the yard, and gaining respect. An inmate can build a new personal world with all the intricate negotiations of how things are done on the inside. Status is usually gained from successfully resisting the official rules—such as engaging in loan-sharking, drug dealing, fighting, covering for others, getting things done, as well as from treating others fairly. These inmates are less likely to benefit from programming than those inmates who choose to stay outside of the potentially harmful prison subcultures.

Release Issues

Do inmates carry insights and skills gleaned from programs in prison with them into the community upon release? While surely many times we can answer that question in the affirmative, the challenges women face are often so complex and overwhelming that gains made in the prison may not be of much use *without aftercare programming* or other assistance.

Women released from prison are confronted with many demands. They may face parole or probation conditions, immediate housing needs—especially for safe housing away from violence or drugs—problems finding an employer willing to hire an ex-convict at a job that will support them and their children, expectations from children about their reunited family, or struggles to regain custody of lost children, coping with sobriety or other addictions, and meeting their mental and physical health care needs. Top needs (listed in order) in a study of jail inmates by Singer and Bussey (1995) were: housing, drug counseling, mental health counseling, financial assistance, alcohol counseling, education and training, medical care, family support, items such as clothing and food, and help getting children back. Women also mentioned that they needed to achieve some stability in their lives and make a fresh start. Several said relocating was essential if they wanted to avoid pressures from pimps and drug dealers.

Programs cannot help with low wages, child care needs, or availability of housing. Evanne said, "If I didn't have a place to go, what would I do? The shelters are full." Tracy's situation summed up many of the challenges. She got a job fairly quickly but she didn't have a driver's license or transportation. She was trying to readjust to being a parent after being away from her children for 16 months. Tracy relapsed under all the pressures.

Box 11.1

NEEDS OF JAIL INMATES

- Housing
- Drug counseling
- Mental health counseling
- Financial assistance
- Alcohol counseling
- Education and training
- Medical care
- Family support
- Clothing and food
- Help getting children back

I wasn't doing the footwork after I got out. And it was really overwhelming. I didn't know how to act. I really didn't. That's how I felt. I felt like I had a lot of expectations from other people on me. Like I wasn't gonna meet up to them. Fear and stress, and everybody looking at you like you're under a magnifying glass, [wondering] what she gonna do now?

When Caretha was released according to her parole conditions she had 14 days to find a job. She was lucky to find an employer who understood her circumstances. The hardest part for her was "coming home, being home. And my children, they were small, but I had lost that tie. And I couldn't get it back."

Smith (1999) suggests that plans for "re-entry must begin as soon as someone is arrested" (p. 2). Programs in jails and prisons should be considered part of a larger process of recovery and rehabilitation. Even relapse is part of recovery, as the next attempt at recovery can build on a foundation "further along the road" (p. 1). We never know when a particular program at a particular time will have a profound influence on a woman. We develop and offer these programs in hope that this transformation will happen, that they will make a difference. With this in mind, we turn now to the special needs of women inmates and how we might facilitate successful transition after prison.

GENERAL FRAMEWORK FOR SUCCESSFUL PROGRAMS

A survey by the National Institute of Justice (NIJ) of state correctional, prison, jail, and program administrators revealed that successful programming was hampered at the front end of the inmates' incarceration. They admitted that classification and screening procedures did not give them the information they needed to effectively match women's needs with programs (Morash, Bynum, & Koons, 1998). In most cases, administrators used the same classification instrument for women and men, despite women's different needs and risk profiles. Screening missed histories of domestic violence or child abuse, and needs related to children. Despite the fact that housing relates to program access, assessment was unrelated to housing assignment. Crowding and high movement of inmates also hindered matching needs with programs (Morash et al., 1998).

Seven in ten state-level prison administrators also agreed that women worked best with a management style that differed from that traditionally used with men. The preferred style recognized women's greater concern with interpersonal relationships and expression of emotions by including skills such as "active listening, patience in explaining rules and expectations, awareness of emotional dynamics, and the capacity to respond firmly, fairly, and consistently" (Morash et al., 1998, p. 4). To achieve this style, administrators recommended being fair but strict, training staff to increase sensitivity to female inmate needs, hiring more female staff, and involving inmates in decision making and carrying out some responsibilities (p. 5).

Carp and Schade (1993) suggest that, ideally, programming should "proceed through a series of phases that take [inmates] logically from one skill level to the next, building on the skills gained in each previous phase. These phases span an inmate's entire incarceration period, from assessment and diagnosis through work release and parole" (p. 39). Koons and Burrow (1997) stress that although the intersecting needs of women benefit from a holistic approach, programs should be sensitive to subgroups of women, such as those with children or who have been battered, and I would add, to race and ethnicity, including language, values and beliefs, and customs.

The NIJ survey identified program elements related to success:

- Staff is dedicated, caring, and qualified. They are often ex-addicts or ex-offenders and serve as strong role models for the inmates.
- Programs are comprehensive and address basic needs. There is a continuum of care.
- Voluntary participation is most desirable. Inmates like and help run the program.
- Program participants support each other. There is positive peer influence.
- Treatment plans are individualized through appropriate screening and assessment.
- Marketable job skills, parenting and life skills, education, and anger management are offered.
- The program environment is "homey." Communication is open. Confidentiality is maintained. Programs are small with good rapport between participants. It feels safe.
- Programs are available to address victimization. Self-esteem, domestic violence, empowerment and self-sufficiency are addressed. Women are treated like human beings.
- Management style is nonaggressive. Security staff is supportive.
- Some staff are from outside the DOC. Private–public partnerships exist (Morash et al., 1998, p. 7).

Specific Needs, Specific Responses

Women in prison frequently have multifaceted, interacting needs resulting from abuse (childhood and adult), addiction, low education levels, poor work histories, family disorganization, and poor health care (Girshick, 1999). To assess what works in prison programs by looking only at recidivism rates minimizes the complexity of these inmates' lives. It overlooks factors outside the control of the individual woman as she leaves the prison walls. Is she living in a housing project surrounded by dope dealers? Do potential employers dismiss her out of hand because of her criminal record? Is her ex-boyfriend stalking and harassing her? Is she fighting the odds in regaining custody of her kids? Does her parole officer work with her or play strictly by the book? Is she having problems handling her multiple responsibilities after release from a system that made every decision for her? Realistically, what are her resources and what are her options? Without an aftercare program in place, recidivism rates seem a measure of program "success"; what is needed is individualized assistance during the adjustment period after release.

What I have heard from countless women inmates is a craving for self-respect, for self-worth. They respond to people and programs that help them feel like worthwhile human beings. A frequent turning point in their lives comes when they decide they will no longer be treated like garbage. They will no longer be abused or accept anything less than they deserve. Program staff who believe in the women they work with and who care about them help reinforce a sense of self-worth. Many women recognize their self-worth and will to live when they realize they would have been killed—by their abuser, by their drug use, by living on the streets. Prison time might be hard on them; they just can't live the old way anymore. They are tired. It may be at this point, when a woman is ready to help herself, that a program can provide the content and context for her change. Tammy, quoted earlier, felt "Programs don't help you, you help yourself." She changed after her husband was murdered while she was incarcerated. She realized it could have been her if she'd been out with him. She had spent so much time in prison she finally got tired of her anger and realized, "It's time to go home. I learned to control [my anger]."

I believe this sense-of-self issue is so fundamental that I am concerned above all with dealing with inmates' trauma from childhood sexual and physical abuse, often compounded by adult rape and battering. For females, interpersonal abuse occurs throughout their lives, whereas for males, most abuse ends in childhood. I see this trauma as most significant because of its impact on the sense of self, particularly problems with maintaining boundaries, low self-esteem, depression, post-traumatic stress symptoms, mental illness, sexual dysfunction, distrust and fear of others (especially men), and suicidal ideation.

Widom (1989) found that abused girls were more likely to be involved in criminal activity than nonabused girls were. Child abuse has been shown to be one of the leading causes of juvenile delinquency and adult criminality (Straus, 1991). According to the Bureau of Justice Statistics (1999) nearly 6 in 10 women in state prisons had experienced physical or sexual abuse in the past. In my study of women in a minimum security prison in North Carolina, 68% reported abuse as a child, 85% had been battered as an adult, 83% had been emotionally abused as an adult, and 43% had been raped as an adult (Girshick, 1999). In a study of battered women inmates in California, Leonard (2000) found that 55% had been sexually abused and 48% had been sexually assaulted as children. Many other studies of female inmates across the country have found high rates of childhood and adult abuse (see, for example, Fletcher, Shaver, & Moon, 1993; Gilfus, 1988). These rates compare with national average estimates that 25% of female children have been sexually abused by the age of 18 (Finkelhor, Hotaling, Lewis, & Smith, 1990) and that nearly one in three adult women experience at least one physical assault by a partner (American Psychological Association, 1996).

Post-traumatic stress disorder (PTSD) symptoms thus become the foundation for many of the women in terms of how they live their lives in prison. Traumatic sexualization, conditions of childhood abuse that shape sexuality in inappropriate and dysfunctional ways, is replicated in prison when women are institutionally assaulted in the name of security

---

Box 11.2

ABUSE HISTORIES OF WOMEN IN A NORTH CAROLINA PRISON

Abused as a child	68%
Battered as an adult	85%
Emotional abuse as an adult	83%
Raped as an adult	43%

Source: Adapted from L. B. Girshick (1999), *No safe haven: Stories of women in prison.* Boston: Northeastern University Press.

through pat searches, strip searches, handcuffing, and shackling. Powerlessness and help-lessness are reinforced through daily prison life (Bill, 1998; Heney & Kristiansen, 1998).

Abuse victimization combines powerfully with economic marginalization and drug and alcohol addiction. It is easy to see how these feed on one another. Escape through addiction from the pain of abuse and/or poverty leads to a need for more resources to pro-cure drugs. Psychiatric disorders based on PTSD, mental breakdown, chronic depression, or chemical imbalances are interconnected with chronic abuse, addiction, and poverty. Studies have found high rates of mental disorders among women in prison, with over 40% having been diagnosed with a DSM-III psychiatric disorder (Washington & Diamond, 1985). The American Correctional Association (1990) has found that one to two thirds of women admitted to jails require mental health services.

Elsewhere in this book specific needs and programs on abuse, drug treatment, parent-ing, educational and vocational needs, and health care are dealt with. I would like to com-ment on how these programs can assist a woman to leave stronger than when she came in to prison. The one reservation I have about singing praises of any program is that the prison setting itself is contrary to the trust and safety needed to do the intimate work of recon-structing the self, and women face tremendous odds in doing programming work there.

Abuse treatment groups.   Trauma symptoms preclude healthy functioning and adjust-ment to a world of family, work, and recovery demands. To leave prison in better shape than when they entered, women coping with the trauma of incest, rape, or battering can benefit from abuse counseling in the form of one-on-one therapy, psychosocial group coun-seling, or peer group support. In many prisons one-on-one meetings with psychologists or psychiatrists are scarce, often limited to occasional assessments or crisis situations. Abuse groups can examine the circumstance of abuse itself as well as the coping mechanisms survivors develop that might have been effective once but now are maladaptive. These strategies include dissociation, alcohol, drugs, compulsive behaviors, self-mutilation, and inappropriate risk taking.

Pollock (1998) suggests that trauma survivors have dysfunctional cognitive patterns such as all-or-nothing thinking, overreaction, personalization, and magical thinking. Mem-ories long blocked may come out in nightmares or flashbacks. Impulsive and compulsive behavior are also characteristic. Identifying and treating these behaviors in a way that empowers the abuse survivor to feel competent in her life can help her cope with release.

The New Pathways Program at the Federal Correctional Institution for Women in Dublin, California, was designed to treat the trauma symptoms of women inmates. Inmates are frequently treated through medication, which might help with their depression but does not teach new skills or uncover their underlying problems. New Pathways is a 9-month program, divided into three parts, that enrolls about 20 women. The overall goals of the program are

> to help female offenders become more effective problem-solvers, protect themselves and their children from abuse, and heal from past injuries of abuse. The program focuses on teach-ing women practical skills to face life's problems and to bolster self-esteem to reduce their chances of being victimized again or victimizing others. Women are taught to accept respon-sibility for their criminal actions, regardless of their personal circumstances. (Kotulski & Allison, 2000)

The first stage of the program is effective coping skills, which includes anger and stress management. Participants focus on reducing arousal levels, learning muscle relaxation and deep-breathing techniques, as well as the role of diet and exercise for their well-being. These skills help women reduce symptoms of nightmares, hypervigilence, criminal thinking, perceived mistrust, and violent feelings such as wanting to punch walls. The next phase is trauma and recovery. Here, women talk about what happened to them, and the boundary issues they have. They engage in psychodrama and trust-building exercises. The last stage is self-esteem and empowerment. Participants bring it all together and build a new identity of self. An optional aftercare phase is open to those who graduate from the program.

The most common trauma symptoms measured before the program began included worrying and obsessive thinking, paranoia, lower back pain, loneliness, trouble falling asleep, repeated unpleasant thoughts that won't stop, depression, and sensitivity to having feelings easily hurt by others. After the program, most of these symptoms disappeared or were significantly decreased, with the exceptions of feeling that most people cannot be trusted, awakening early in the morning, feelings easily hurt by others, and having ideas or beliefs that others do not share (Kotulski & Allison, 2000).

Programs such as New Pathways are especially promising because they are comprehensive, long in duration, multifaceted, skills-building, and process-oriented. They involve more than talk therapy and medication, drawing on expressive arts and various workbooks. Each stage builds on the previous step to optimize the individual woman's goal of developing a new sense of self. Fundamental changes in attitude and new coping skills can be extremely useful on release. She can "leave stronger."

Drug/alcohol treatment. Women are primarily arrested for drug and property offenses. Seventy percent of the women in my study (Girshick, 1999) were in prison for either committing a drug offense or a crime (such as theft or prostitution) in order to buy drugs, or they were high at the time of their crime. Female inmates are more likely to test positive for drug use at the time of their arrest (Mann, 1995; Merlo, 1995) and to use more drugs regularly than male inmates are (Snell, 1994). Over 60% of women report alcohol-related problems at the time of their arrest as well (Fogel, 1991).

By the time women enter prison they may have attempted drug treatment on the outside one or more times. Treatment may have been a condition of probation or previous parole. Their efforts may have been thwarted by the paucity of in-patient programs that accept children or admit those with a dual diagnosis of substance abuse and mental illness. Problems affording programs and lack of family support hinder many attempts. The reasons women use are more complicated than those of men. Histories of family physical and sexual abuse, adult victimization, eating disorders, anxiety, and depression all contribute to many women's substance abuse (Bloom, Brown, & Chesney-Lind, 1996; McClellan, Farabee, & Crouch, 1997).

It is fruitless to attempt drug or alcohol treatment without addressing the underlying reasons someone uses drugs, as well as current issues that might be exacerbating their addiction. Female addicts might have health problems ranging from mental illness or PTSD to pregnancy, may be under- or unemployed, may be in a battering relationship, and may be coping with single parenthood, poor support networks, or losing their children to social services. Inmates' individual circumstances vary, and treatment that will succeed for one inmate may not work for another.

Prendergast, Wellisch, and Falkin (1995) discovered serious gaps in drug treatment for women offenders. Their study of treatment programs found a shortage of slots, inadequate case management, lack of adequate support services based on the women's needs and transitional components for prison-based programs, and programs that were not gender-sensitive.

Many women I have worked with in North Carolina have been through the DART program at the Correctional Institute for Women, the only one in the state for women. Inmates at every custody level are involved. Counselors have created a gender-sensitive program. They recognize that the women may have children and are likely to be single parents. They know that inmates may have childhood abuse backgrounds and may have been in battering relationships as adults. Consequently, group therapy focuses on issues of codependency, intimate relationships, and parenting. There is an emphasis on family participation (Frazee, Hevener, Freeman, Jones, & Katzenelson, 2000). The other women's prisons have DART Aftercare programs, which many inmates attend along with Narcotics Anonymous and Alcoholics Anonymous 12-step programs.

In addition to these prison programs, some inmates are able to go to off-site drug rehabilitation programs. For example, inmates at Black Mountain Correctional Center for Women in North Carolina attend the Blue Ridge Center program. This 12-week psychosocial program covers issues such as HIV, cravings, women's health, domestic violence, and stress management, along with meditation, daily journals, and exercise. Group therapy is held once weekly and inmates attend two 12-step meetings each week. The co-therapists view substance abuse as one of a multitude of interrelated problems the inmates face, and they hope that the program helps the women change their maladaptive beliefs that prevent healthier lifestyles. The co-therapists work on the women's needs and wants, and try to build a healthy self-esteem. This program is very popular with the inmates, who feel that the co-therapists really listen and genuinely care about them (Girshick, 1999).

Parenting.   Programming on parenting roles and the developmental needs of children is a priority for incarcerated mothers as most of them want to reunify with their children when they are released (Koons & Burrow, 1997). In 1997, 65% of women in state prisons and 59% of women in federal prisons had children under 18 (Bureau of Justice Statistics, 2000). Only one fourth of them had their children living with their fathers (Morash et al., 1998); about 10% were in state care and the rest were with other family members (Snell, 1994). Separation from their children and worries about their children's welfare is probably the most difficult aspect of incarceration for mothers (Bloom & Steinhart, 1993; Clark, 1995; Lord, 1995). The separation strikes at their self-definition as women (Zalba, 1964). Whatever else was happening in her life before incarceration, the mother had her children. Imprisonment is a huge loss (Baunach, 1985). Although education about children's developmental needs is important, it is perhaps more crucial to work with these women on their sense of what it means to be a mother, and how this role affects their self-esteem.

Mothers in prison suffer not only from the physical separation but also from restrictive prison visiting and contact policies and from problems with child-welfare agencies (Johnston, 1997). They are not involved in their children's lives and must struggle later to regain custody. There are very few visitation programs where there is meaningful contact.

Family and Corrections Network (FCN) Report (1995, p. 6) listed eight crucial components for a successful parenting program based on a survey of 30 agencies providing programs. They include: conducting an evaluation and needs assessment, involving inmates in program development, having outside community-based advocates, offering a children's visiting program or games and activities, teaching parent education to learn skills, providing social services such as transportation and housing for visits, special events, and developing support services for caregivers to maintain family stability.

There are a few programs in prisons that allow children on extended visits or that even allow infants to live with their mothers at the prison. For example, at Bedford Hills, New York, mothers and children visit in a Children's Center, which has a homelike atmosphere. One program allows children to visit for a week, though they stay in the outside community at night. The Parenting Center allows women to keep their newborns for 1 year, while parents take a class called Choices and Changes that focuses on their parenting skills, how to work with the child-welfare system, and how to successfully reunify their family (Kaplan & Sasser, 1996).

The MATCH program in San Antonio, Texas, helps inmates keep in close contact with their children. It offers advocacy, counseling, information and referral, support groups, and workshops. Issues that are covered include parenting skills, self-esteem, child development, drug abuse and domestic violence prevention, health care, and a GED program. MATCH also supports the women on release through advocacy and networking, as well as support groups for children (Bloom & Steinhart, 1993).

A different option is found at Summit House in North Carolina. This community-based corrections program allows children to live with their incarcerated mothers. The goal is to strengthen the family and to support the women through this highly structured therapeutic program. The children attend play therapy while the mothers choose from an array of programming—parenting classes, substance abuse counseling, group and individual counseling, financial management assistance, GED classes or college or job training, and learning other skills to enhance their chances of being successful, independent families upon release (Girshick, 1999).

I believe these programs' value lies in the sense the mother may feel about her worth as a parent. That she can mother and mother well, that she is vitally important to her family, gives a sense of accomplishment and a sense of self that children need to feel from parents. Most likely the mother did not feel this from her own parents. Most women in prison were raised in families with high rates of dysfunction, disorganization, substance abuse, domestic violence, child abuse, and criminal activity (Girshick, 1999). This hinders their sense of efficacy in parenting their own children. Prison programs can help restore or even create a new sense of self. In this way, an inmate can leave stronger for her children and the well-being of her family. Again, she needs support, especially if she fights to regain custody, and most likely, faces the multiple problems of locating housing, finding a job, and staying clean and sober.

Education and job training.   Most women in prison have poor work histories and low education levels, two strikes that feed one another. It is difficult to find a job without a high school education, and it is impossible to support yourself and a family on a minimum-wage job. A woman may quit high school (or junior high school) because her family needs her to work; she does not realize the value of an education; poor performance in school and falling through the cracks; teen pregnancy; delinquency; running away (very likely due to abuse at home); and a general reinforced sense of failure. On the positive side, education and job skills can be very valuable to the inmate when combined with other programming that helps build a sense of self. Completing certificate programs, obtaining a GED, and taking college courses can help instill a sense of accomplishment as well as provide entry into a new job. What this does not account for, of course, are factors such as how the inmate will be received by prospective employers or if the inmate with a low level of ability will be able to successfully accomplish programs in prison or out.

Additionally, vocational and technical training for women in prison lags behind that provided for men. Women in prison are at risk of leaving prison older but without job skills. Most training for women falls into stereotypical gender-based jobs with low pay and no benefits such as cosmetology, sewing, food service, housekeeping, and clerical. Most education is remedial rather than training for new skills that would provide better jobs on the outside such as computer technology or nontraditional female jobs such as auto mechanic or electrician. It is the rare prison budget that provides for the type of equipment, technology, or instructors needed for these improved opportunities, and prison programs fall back to the lesser goal of providing minimal skills for job entry on the outside (Winifred, 1996).

Women in prison are trapped by the same problem faced by women outside of prison—the traditional role of women is seen as a homemaker and mother. However, most women and mothers work, and for single parents, as most mothers in prison are, the need for jobs that pay enough to support their families is crucial if we want them not only to stay out of poverty, but also away from criminal activity. The need for marketable skills is acute. Prison is a setting that could provide new skills given the failure of our schools to provide educational success for these women when they were younger (Carp and Schade, 1993; Girshick, 1999; Moyer, 1984).

CONCLUSION

If I were asked, "What is the most useful programming approach to prepare women in prison for release?" my first response would be "Don't incarcerate them in the first place." Given that most of these women are not violent offenders or a danger to society, I feel programs could more effectively be offered outside of prison. That way, these women would not have to be separated from their children, and they could continue to be part of their communities. However, to meet their other needs, we as a society would have to provide resources for intervention in child abuse, services for battered women, drop-out prevention programs, programs for pregnant teens, accessible drug and alcohol treatment, job training opportunities, jobs paying a livable wage, parenting programs, and most important for women, decriminalization of drugs. Prevention is the number-one solution to the incarceration of women, not programs for women in prison.

If, however, we accept our current situation where women are in fact incarcerated, we need aftercare programs. Programs in prison can only do so much. As discussed above, there are factors that enhance how programming can address effectively the needs of women. But once a woman walks out the prison gates she faces a maelstrom of demands that could lead her right back into the clutches of criminal behavior and therefore to prison. Support services are needed to assist women in finding their way through the multiple parole conditions, job search, housing quest, filling child care needs or fighting custody battles, and struggles to remain off drugs. It is essential to acknowledge ex-offenders' need for support, and find new ways to distribute our criminal justice and social services resources.

Finally, we need to reprioritize what we do in prison. It is near impossible to claim that a system focused on security can be a system simultaneously working toward rehabilitation. A system based on control cannot be a system encouraging empowerment. These are contradictory goals. Decarceration is the only way to alter this. The best we can do within the present constraints is to make prison and aftercare programs the best possible. Programs that reinforce hopelessness and dependency are worse than no programs at all, and so they should focus on helping women develop sources of inner strength, a new sense of self, and a determination to beat the odds. Others of us, not in prison, have an obligation to change the societal context of poverty, of racism, of sexism. Is it possible to "leave stronger?" Yes, I think it is. But to leave stronger to live in a system of injustice is not enough. Programs in prison are one small part of the whole notion of leaving in better shape than when you came in. When we see the whole, we must admit that programming is a Band-Aid. We must simultaneously provide the Band-Aid while we work to alter the conditions that led the women into prison in the first place.

DISCUSSION QUESTIONS

1. What are some of the types of women prisoners described in this chapter? How well can existing programs help them succeed?

2. In what ways can the prison environment work against building skills necessary for success upon release? How do women prisoners respond to stressors in the prison environment?

3. With what types of problems faced by women prisons can programs help? With what types of problems can programs *not* help?

4. What is meant by "reentry must begin as soon as someone is arrested"?

5. What are the elements and skills of a management style that is recommended for use with women prisoners?

6. Why might recidivism rates not be the best measure of effectiveness of programs?

WEBNOTES

The state of Delaware has instituted a model mentoring program to assist women prisoners adjust to their release. Go to their web site (http://www.delawarementorprogram.org/) and read some of the materials. What programs have they instituted? How effective do you think these programs are?

REFERENCES

AMERICAN CORRECTIONAL ASSOCIATION. (1990). *The female offender.* Washington, DC: St. Mary's Press.

AMERICAN PSYCHOLOGICAL ASSOCIATION. (1996). *Violence and the family.* Presidential Task Force on Violence and the Family. Washington, DC: American Psychological Association.

BAUNACH, P. (1985). *Mothers in prison.* New Brunswick, NJ: Transaction Books.

BILL, L. (1998, December). The victimization and revictimization of female offenders. *Corrections Today,* 106–112.

BLOOM, B., BROWN, M., & Chesney-Lind, M. (1996). Women on probation and parole. In A. J. Lurigio (Ed.), *Community corrections in America: New directions and sounder investments for persons with mental illness and disorders.* Seattle, WA: National Coalition for Mental and Substance Abuse Health Care in the Justice System.

BLOOM, B., & STEINHART, D. (1993). *Why punish the children? A reappraisal of the children of incarcerated mothers in America.* San Francisco: National Council on Crime and Delinquency.

BUREAU OF JUSTICE STATISTICS. (1999). *Women offenders.* Washington, DC: U.S. Department of Justice, Office of Justice Programs.

———. (2000). *Incarcerated parents and their children.* Washington DC: U.S. Department of Justice, Office of Justice Programs.

CARP, S. V., & SCHADE, L. S. (1993). Tailoring facility programming to suit female offenders' needs. In American Correctional Association (Ed.), *Female offenders: Meeting needs of a neglected population* (pp. 37–42). Laurel, MD: American Correctional Association.

CLARK, J. (1995, September). The impact of the prison environment on mothers. *The Prison Journal, 75* (3), 306–329.

FCN REPORT. (1995, June). Eight crucial components for a successful parenting program. *FCN Report, 5,* 6.

FINKELHOR, D., HOTALING, G., LEWIS, I. A., & SMITH, C. (1990). Sexual abuse in a national survey on adult men and women. *Child Abuse and Neglect, 14,* 19–28.

FLETCHER, B., SHAVER, L., & MOON, D. (Eds.). (1993). *Women prisoners: A forgotten population.* Westport, CT: Praeger.

FOGEL, C. I. (1991). Health problems and needs of incarcerated women. *Journal of Health & Jail Issues, 10,* 43–57.

———. (1993). Hard time: The stressful nature of incarceration for women. *Issues in Mental Health Nursing, 14,* 367–377.

FRAZEE, S., HEVENER, G., Freeman, L., JONES, K., & KATZENELSON, S. (2000, April 15). *Program monographs.* Raleigh: North Carolina Sentencing and Policy Advisory Commission.

GILFUS, M. (1988). *Seasoned by violence/tempered by law: A qualitative study of women and crime.* Unpublished doctoral dissertation, Florence Heller School for Advanced Studies in Social Welfare, Brandeis University.

GIRSHICK, L. B. (1999). *No safe haven: Stories of women in prison.* Boston: Northeastern University Press.

HENEY, J., & KRISTIANSEN, C. M. (1998). An analysis of the impact of prison on women survivors of childhood sexual abuse. *Women & Therapy, 20* (4), 29–44.

JOHNSTON, D. (1997). Developing services for incarcerated mothers. In C. Blinn (Ed.), *Maternal ties: A selection of programs for female offenders* (pp. 1–9). Lanham, MD: American Correctional Association.

KAPLAN, M. S., & SASSER, J. E. (1996, December). Women behind bars: Trends and policy issues. *Journal of Sociology and Social Welfare, 23* (4), 43–56.

KOONS, B. A., & BURROW, J. D. (1997, October). Expert and offender perceptions of program elements linked to successful outcomes for incarcerated women. *Crime & Delinquency, 43* (4), 512–533.

KOTULSKI, D., & ALLISON, S. (2000, November). Treating trauma in women: A first look at the new pathways program. Paper presented at the annual meeting of the American Society of Criminology, San Francisco, CA.

LEONARD, E. D. (2000, November). *Convicted survivors: Comparing and describing California's battered women inmates.* Paper presented at the annual meeting of the American Society of Criminology, San Francisco, CA.

LORD, E. (1995, June). A prison superintendent's perspective on women in prison. *The Prison Journal, 75* (2), 257–269.

MANN, C. (1995). Women of color and the criminal justice system. In B. Price and N. Sokoloff (Eds.), *The criminal justice system and women: Offenders, victims, and workers* (2nd ed.) (pp. 118–135). New York: McGraw–Hill.

McCLENNAN, D. S., FARABEE, D., & CROUCH, B. M. (1997, December). Early victimization, drug use, and criminality: A comparison of male and female prisoners. *Criminal Justice and Behavior, 24* (4), 455–476.

McQUAIDE, S., & EHRENREICH, J. H. (1998, Summer). Women in prison: Approaches to understanding the lives of a forgotten population. *Affilia: Journal of Women & Social Work, 13* (2), 233–247.

MERLO, A. (1995). Female criminality in the 1990s. In A. Merlo and J. Pollock (Eds.), *Women, law, and social control* (pp. 119–133). Boston: Allyn and Bacon.

MORASH, M., BYNUM, T. S., & KOONS, B. A. (1998). *Women offenders: Programming needs and promising approaches.* National Institute of Justice Research in Brief. Washington, DC: U.S. Department of Justice, Office of Justice Programs.

MOYER, I. (1984). Deceptions and realities of life in women's prisons. *The Prison Journal, 64,* 45–56.

OWEN, B. (1998). *"In the mix": Struggle and survival in a women's prison.* New York: State University of New York Press.

POLLOCK, J. M. (1998). *Counseling women in prison.* Thousand Oaks, CA: Sage.

PRENDERGAST, M. L., WELLISCH, J., & FALKIN, G. P. (1995, June). Assessment of and services for substance-abusing women offenders in community and correctional settings. *The Prison Journal, 75* (2), 240–256.

SINGER, M. I., & BUSSEY, J. (1995, January). The psychosocial issues of women serving time in jail. *Social Work, 40* (1), 103–114.

SMITH, G. (1999, August). Thoughts on re-entry, relapse and recovery. *FCN Report, 21,* 1–3.

SNELL, T. L. (1994). *Women in prison* (Report No. NCJ-145321). Washington, DC: U.S. Government Printing Office.

STRAUS, M. A. (1991). Discipline and deviance: Physical punishment of children and violence and other crime in adulthood. *Social Problems, 38* (20), 131–154.

WASHINGTON, P., & DIAMOND, R. J. (1985). Prevalence of mental illness among women incarcerated in five California county jails. *Research in Community and Mental Health, 5,* 33–41.

WATTERSON, K. (1996). *Women in prison: Inside the concrete womb.* (Rev. ed.). Boston: Northeastern University Press.

WIDOM, C. S. (1989). The cycle of violence. *Science, 244,* 160–166.

WINIFRED, SISTER M. (1996, August). Vocational and technical training programs for women in prison. *Corrections Today,* 168–170.

ZALBA, S. (1964). *Women prisoners and their families.* Sacramento: California Department of Social Welfare and Department of Corrections.

12

Where Do We Go from Here?

Susan F. Sharp, Ph.D.

❖

The purpose of this book is to give the reader an overview of the needs of women prisoners, the availability and efficacy of programs to meet their needs. We have examined programs for women prisoners from several dimensions: educational/vocational needs, health needs, mental health needs, family needs, and release needs. Encouragingly, we have seen that there are a number of programs around the country that do a fairly good job of meeting some, if not all, of the needs of women prisoners. However, we have also seen that these programs reach only a small percentage of women in prison. Additionally, we have identified issues that must be taken into account when designing and implementing programs for this population. Several themes have emerged.

First, the authors of this book clearly suggest that greater emphasis be placed on the *assessment* of women prisoners. All too often, women are assessed using instruments that were designed for male prisoners, and placed in programs geared toward male prisoners. Thus, many of their urgent needs are overlooked. The path to prison for women is qualitatively different than that for men, as Chesney-Lind has shown us. Women are overwhelming incarcerated for drug-related offenses and offenses related to their poverty status. Additionally, women prisoners have a high incidence of abuse in their histories—childhood sexual and physical abuse as well as domestic violence as adults. For programs to be effective, this must be considered (Morash, Bynum, & Koons, 1998). However, the smaller number of women prisoners has frequently meant that women's needs are overlooked in the assessment process (Morash, Bynum, & Koons, 1998).

Second, the needs of women prisoners are frequently interrelated and should not be treated as separate issues. For example, Marcus-Mendoza and Wright explored how women's histories of victimization affect their mental health needs. They emphasize how abuse can result in feelings of helplessness and distrust. Thus, the researchers conclude that any therapeutic interventions must treat abuse issues of women prisoners if they are to succeed on release. They go on to examine how certain types of therapeutic programs, such as boot camps, may actually exacerbate women's mental health problems. Kelley, in her examination of substance abuse programming for women prisoners, points out that in many women prisoners, addiction and mental illness coexist. The chapter on motherhood in prison focuses on an additional problem stemming from the abuse histories of these women: Many children are being cared for by family members who have been abusive in the past. Indeed, virtually every author touches on the issue of abuse.

Likewise, it is impossible to disentangle women's depression from their separation from children and resultant feelings of loss. Additionally, their roles as single mothers have often precluded their ability to obtain drug treatment or education. This in turn leads to an inability to provide for their families, depression, and more substance abuse. Clearly, the problems of women need to be approached in a more holistic manner. If programs are to benefit women, they must be designed to address the complex interrelated problems of women offenders.

Third, many of the readings stress the importance of providing healthy female role models for women prisoners through the increased use of female staff, volunteers, and offenders who have successfully completed programs. We have seen some examples of this in the programs described by Schram and Kelley. However, at present the need is still largely unmet.

Fourth, one of the most important elements in reduction of recidivism is transitional care. All too often, women are released back into the community with little or no assistance and follow-up. Essentially, the women are thrown back into the same situation that they left. Imagine being an unskilled single mother, with few if any resources available to you. After months or years in prison, you now find yourself back in your community. You are expected to find work, housing, and child care, and yet you have more problems now than you did prior to prison. You now must also pay fines, restitution, and parole or other legal fees, and you may have difficulty finding work because you are a convicted felon. What would you do? If you are like many of the women discussed in this book, you will likely feel overwhelmed, give up on "going straight," and return to your preincarceration lifestyle.

Fifth, care must be used in seeking parity. As Chesney-Lind points out, becoming more equal with male prisoners is not always a good thing. Men prisoners are often subject to deplorable conditions and situations. Instead, the focus should be on a higher standard of care for women prisoners. "Equity with a vengeance" is a potential outcome of seeking equal treatment. What we seek is equal treatment for women prisoners, not equal mistreatment.

Finally, alternatives to incarceration must be explored. Most women prisoners are nonviolent drug offenders. Incarceration of these women is a harsh response to what is more of a mental health issue than a criminal one. In the chapter on leaving prison, Girshick stresses that she does not believe that incarceration is the appropriate response for many women offenders. However, alternatives to incarceration have their own pitfalls. Many alternative programs require restitution and payment of fines. For the unskilled woman offender, meeting these types of financial obligations while also supporting herself and her children may be out of her reach. Other programs, such as house arrest, may unwittingly force the woman offender to remain in a setting with an abusive or addicted male partner. Clearly, the flaws in these programs increase her likelihood of failure. For alternatives to incarceration to succeed for women offenders, the problems and needs of this population must be recognized.

So, where do we go from here? Clearly, current policies are creating more problems than they are redressing. However, as O'Brien (2001) suggests, "It could be otherwise." Many changes are needed, and in the following paragraphs I offer a few suggestions. Although certainly not an exhaustive list, it is hopefully a beginning.

To be successful, women must have access to appropriate programs. However, making more programs available is not a complete solution; careful and thoughtful examination of women's needs is imperative as well. Some feminist approaches have focused on equal rights and equal treatment for women prisoners. Prison programming, from that perspective, should be gender-neutral, and parity in programs becomes the goal. But, is this approach in the best interest of women prisoners? Kelly Hannah-Moffat warns us that we may have "failed to recognize that the standard by which equality is measured is based on a male norm" (1994, p. 2). Rather than trying to make a woman prisoner "more like a man," we should instead champion the needs of women. This approach would empower women by being more woman-centered. By restructuring correctional policies and practices to better reflect the lives of women, we may develop more successful programs. Indeed, by redefining punishment, the focus may shift to alternatives to incarceration that would better benefit women offenders (Hannah-Moffat, 1994).

Development of alternatives to incarceration and transitional programs are both worthy goals, but the imperative to focus on the needs of women remains. For example, alternatives such as shock incarceration programs and boot camps have experienced high female drop-out rates. This is not, however, because women are less motivated than men, but because women offenders have different health and mental health issues (Clark & Kellam, 2001). We cannot expect women offenders to do exactly the same types of things in these programs that men can do. Programs must be developed that acknowledge women offender's high rates of hypertension, diabetes, tuberculosis, and even HIV/AIDS. Poor health is no reason to exclude women from the opportunity to reduce their sentences or receive deferred adjudication.

Other aspects of alternative programs demand attention. The economic marginalization of women offenders means that they often cannot meet the financial burdens of probation and community programs. This suggests at least two needed changes: first, reexamination of policies requiring offenders to pay high court and second, supervision costs and programs that increase their access to community resources. One critical issue for many women offenders is safe and affordable housing for themselves and their children. This in turn necessitates supplying the tools to be self-sufficient. Additionally, women may need temporary income maintenance during periods of training and reestablishing their households (O'Brien, 2001). In Chapter 10, we examined the New York Women's Prison Association's four-stage program (Conly, 1998). Other jurisdictions would do well to model future programs on the WPA program, which has many of the necessary elements to empower women to become contributing members of their communities. The WPA prepares women at each stage for more responsibility at the next level, while providing substantive and emotional support. As the women move through each level, they earn both more free-dom and more responsibility. At the final stage, the woman and her children are on their own in the community, but each woman has a caseworker to help her make the final transi-tion to complete independence (Conly, 1998). Although the cost of this type of program is high, the potential for future savings is even higher. By allowing women offenders to become self-sufficient gradually, we could reduce the incidence of incarceration, not only for women today but also for their children in the future.

We must also recognize that, in some cases, prison may be the best alternative. In Chapter 11, Girshick points out that for prison programs to be effective, the women must be willing to receive some benefit from them, something many inmates are not ready to accept. Indeed, for some women, "prison as a correctional intervention seems to work" (O'Brien, 2001, p. 147). For them, women-centered programs must be developed. As we have seen in the previous chapters, these programs should have certain elements.

Programs should be designed for women prisoners' abuse issues, parenting issues, substance abuse treatment, education, and health care needs. Interrelated programs that consider the nature of the woman offender are the ideal. To be successful, programs should be designed to empower women offenders. There are many aspects to empowerment, including a sense of self, an understanding of healthy relationships and healthy sexuality, and a sense of connection to the community (Covington, 2001). Additionally, empower-ment occurs by helping the woman to realistically assess her own behavior and to deter-mine her need for change (Hale, 2001) through the use of positive role models, such as community volunteers and women who have successfully transitioned into the community (Hale, 2001; O'Brien, 2001), and by encouraging the women to give to other women. Sev-eral of the women interviewed by Patricia O'Brien talked about the self-esteem that came from helping other women once they achieved stability in their own lives (2001). Finally, building a healthy support system can enable the women to feel strong and capable (Hale, 2001; O'Brien, 2001).

The corrections system also needs to take a more proactive role in the placement of children. Currently, women sent to prison often must decide between dysfunctional family settings or foster-care placement. They frequently opt for the former, fearing the latter will lead to permanent loss of custody. While the mother is incarcerated, programs must be in place to facilitate interaction between the mothers and their children (Bartlett, 2000), and therapy for the inmates' children should be a part of the correctional process, including the transition period. By taking steps to preserve the mother–child bond and to help the children deal with *their* loss, more successful reunification can occur upon release. The dilemma of whether or not to allow infants to remain with their mothers needs further research (Markovic, 1995). Currently, a few model programs allow mothers to keep new-born infants with them. Most prisons, however, permit little if any time for mother–infant bonding, despite significant research indicating that failure to bond in infancy leads to adjustment problems later in life, and that maintenance of family bonds can help tie the woman offender to society, providing motivation for change.

The problems involved in treating the woman offender are not easy and defy simplis-tic solutions. However, programs are beginning to emerge around the country that focus on the special problems and needs of female inmates. Evaluation of these programs is impera-tive, so that we can more clearly understand what works for female offenders. As we learn more, better and more effective programs for women can thus be developed.

DISCUSSION QUESTIONS

1. What factors should be considered in developing programs for women?

2. Are alternatives to incarceration always preferable? If alternatives are used, what issues must be addressed?

W E B N O T E S

Search the World Wide Web for alternatives to incarceration for women. Find a web site on this topic and summarize the suggestions made.

R E F E R E N C E S

BARTLETT, R. (2000, December). Helping inmate moms keep in touch—prison programs encourage ties with children. *Corrections Today.* Available at: http://www.corrections.com/aca/cortoday/ archives.html.

CLARK, C., & KELLAM, L. (2001, February). These boots are made for women. *Corrections Today.* Available at: http://www.corrections.com/aca/cortoday/archives.html.

CONLY, C. (1998). *The Women's Prison Association: Supporting women offenders and their families.* Washington, DC: National Institute of Justice. Available at: http://www.corrections.com/aca/ cortoday/archives.html.

COVINGTON, S. S. (2001, February). Creating gender-responsive programs: The next step for women's services. *Corrections Today.* Available at: http://www.corrections.com/aca/cortoday/ archives.html.

HALE, T. (2001, February). Creating visions and achieving goals: The women in community service's lifeskills program. *Corrections Today.* Available at: http://www.corrections.com/aca/ cortoday/archives.html.

HANNAH-MOFFAT, K. (1994). Unintended consequences of feminism and prison reform. *The Forum, 6* (1). Available at: http://www.csc-scc.gc.ca/text/pblct/forum/e06/e061b.shtml.

MARKOVIC, V. (1995). Pregnant women in prison: A correctional dilemma? *The Keeper's Voice, 16* (3).

MORASH, M., BYNUM, T. S., & KOONS, B. A. (1998). *Women offenders: Programming needs and promising approaches.* Washington, DC: Office of Justice Programs/National Institute of Justice.

O'BRIEN, P. (2001). *Making it in the "free world."* Albany: State University of New York Press.